Degen, Marie Louise.
    The history of the Woman's Peace Party. With a new introd. for the Garland ed. by Blanche Wiesen Cook. New York, Garland Pub., 1972 [c1939]

    17, 266, xiv p. 22 cm. (The Garland library of war and peace)

    Original ed. issued as ser. 57, no. 3 of the Johns Hopkins University studies in historical and political science.
    Bibliography: p. 253–256.

    1. Woman's Peace Party.   I. Title. II. Series. III. Series:
Johns Hopkins University. Studies in historical and policital
science. ser. 57, no. 3.

JX1965.D4 1972   327′.172′0621   76-147442
IS N 0-8240-0232-6   MARC

Library of Congress   72 [4]

The
Garland Library
of
War and Peace

The
Garland Library
of
War and Peace

Under the General Editorship of
Blanche Wiesen Cook, *John Jay College,* C.U.N.Y.
Sandi E. Cooper, *Richmond College,* C.U.N.Y.
Charles Chatfield, *Wittenberg University*

The History
of the
Woman's Peace Party

by

Marie Louise Degen

with a new introduction
for the Garland Edition by

Blanche Wiesen Cook

Garland Publishing, Inc., New York & London
1972

Library of Congress Cataloging in Publication Data

Degen, Marie Louise.
    The history of the Woman's Peace Party.

    (The Garland library of war and peace)
    Original ed. issued as ser. 57, no. 3 of the Johns
Hopkins University studies in historical and political
science.
    Bibliography: p.
    1. Woman's Peace Party. I. Title. II. Series.
III. Series: Johns Hopkins University. Studies in
historical and political science, ser. 57, no. 3.
JX1965.D4 1972   327'.172'0621   76-147442
ISBN 0-8240-0232-6

Introduction

The Women's International League for Peace and Freedom (W.I.L.P.F.) is the oldest continually active peace organization in the United States. Established by women who spent their lives working for political justice, equal economic opportunity, and women's rights, it has remained a large and dedicated group working to establish peace and freedom. Like the women of 1915, the W.I.L.P.F. of 1970 remains convinced that the only guarantee for permanent peace is the "positive social amelioration" of oppressive economic and social conditions.

Marie Louise Degen's History of the Woman's Peace Party, *here reproduced for the first time, is the only in-depth study of the first years of the W.I.L.P.F. Written as a doctoral dissertation for the Johns Hopkins University, Miss Degen's work referred to many of the archival sources and pamphlets which the Woman's Peace Party deposited with the Swarthmore College Peace Collection. Today there are many additional manuscripts available which increase our knowledge of the women who founded the W.I.L.P.F. It is likely that a new history of the Woman's Peace Party will some day be written. But Degen's work, published in 1939, will not be entirely replaced because it is as important for her insights in the*

5

period immediately preceding the Second World War as it is for her account of the period 1915-1919.

Most of the founding members of the Woman's Peace Party saw a connection between violent imperialism abroad and social violence at home. As early as 1912 Lucia Ames Mead, one of the most prominent members of the Woman's Peace Party wrote in Swords Into Plowshares *that it was "no mere coincidence that race hatred and civic corruption have had such a recrudescence among us since we have become imperialistic in our foreign policy." The members of the Woman's Peace Party also were among the first Americans to claim that the existence of an industrial-military complex promoted war. In cooperation with the American Union Against Militarism (both groups were led by many of the same people, including Jane Addams, Lillian Wald, Crystal Eastman, and Emily Greene Balch), the Woman's Peace Party organized a campaign to nationalize the arms industry so as to minimize military profits and to discourage congressional appropriations for military spending.*

Few of the founders of the Woman's Peace Party were active in the pre-war peace movement. Committed to positive action, they considered the traditional peace societies stuffy and lethargic. Their work as social reformers and militant suffragists made the injustices experienced by victimized minorities a personal reality. When English suffragist Emmeline Pethick-Lawrence spoke in New York City in Novem-

6

INTRODUCTION

ber 1914, she called for a world-wide "Women's war against war." She declared that there was "no life worth living, but a fighting life." Imprisoned in England's Holloway jail for her militant suffragism, she had been on a hunger strike and had been brutally force fed. Now Mrs. Pethick-Lawrence announced, it was time for the peace movement to learn from the women's movement. The established peace societies were "passive and negative" and it was time for women to be angry, "active and militant."[1]

After Emmeline Pethick-Lawrence's speech, Crystal Eastman, a radical attorney famous for her work in fair labor practices and workman's compensation, established a committee called the Woman's Peace Party of New York. Several weeks later, a Chicago audience which heard Pethick-Lawrence and Rosika Schwimmer, an Austrian suffragist, responded by calling a national conference of women's organizations in January 1915. The national Woman's Peace Party emerged out of this convention, which was attended by over 3000 women. In February an international congress of women was held at the Hague and the International Committee of Women for Permanent Peace was established, with the Woman's Peace Party its American section.

Anticipating today's woman's liberation movement which continues to wonder at the results of a male-dominated foreign policy, the founders of the

---

[1] *Emmeline Pethick-Lawrence quoted in* The Washington Herald, *19 November 1914, copy in Wald Papers, Box 8, Columbia University.*

7

INTRODUCTION

Woman's Peace Party insisted that the equality of women was essential to peace because "the bed-rock of humanity is motherhood." They announced that it was time "for men to stand down and for the women whom they have belittled to take the seat of judgment." The women of 1915 believed that there was a connection between militarist policies and the oppression of women. They believed that "the military state is the state in which a woman has no place; the military mind is the mind that sees in women only a drudge or a toy, and gives her the one right only to existence — the possibility of bearing sons who will in time become soldiers. . . ." It is, they concluded, the "spirit of militarism," and "the glorification of brute force" which has "kept women in political, legal, and economic bondage throughout the ages. . . ." [2]

The preamble and platform of the Woman's Peace Party reflected the connection its founders made between the struggle for women's rights and the fight against war:

> *As women, we feel a peculiar moral passion of revolt against both the cruelty and waste of war. . . .*
>
> *As women, we have builded by the patient drudgery of the past the basic foundation of the home and peaceful industry. We will not longer endure without a protest that must be heard and heeded by men, that hoary evil which in an hour destroys the social structure that centuries of toil have reared. . . .*

---

[2] Grace I. Colbron, The Woman Voter, *V (November 1914), p. 9.*

8

INTRODUCTION

> *Therefore, as human beings and the mother half of
> humanity, we demand that . . . women be given a share
> in deciding between war and peace in all the courts of
> high debate — within the home, the school, the church,
> the industrial order, and the state. . .*

*In its program, the Woman's Peace Party called
upon "all civilized nations" to reenforce democracy
by "admitting the mother half of the human race to
articulate citizenship" and to insure the democratic
control of foreign policy. The Party also demanded
an organized opposition to militarism, the nationalization of all manufacturing of armaments, "a veto
upon the export of armaments from one country to
another," the removal of the economic causes of war,
and the principle of the "concert of nations" to
replace the "balance of power."[3]*

*Crystal Eastman perhaps best expressed the atti-
tude of many of the members of the WPP towards the
new woman's movement:*

> *The value of making this a woman's movement lies . . .
> in the fact that it is an international movement and the
> internationalism of women . . . at the beginning of the
> war did not wholly break down. The fact that women of
> the warring nations met and discussed the war problems
> . . . in friendship while all their male relatives were out
> shooting each other is to my mind a great and significant*

[3]*The Preamble and Platform of the W.P.P. was adopted 10 January
1915, see Degen pp. 40-41.*

9

*event in history. . . This international character of the
Woman's peace movement. . . is the unique and priceless
thing about it . . .*[4]

Because so many of the leaders of the Woman's
Peace Party were also on the executive committee of
the American Union Against Militarism, many domestic activities, such as opposition to compulsory
military education and conscription, were pursued
jointly by both committees. But gradually the two
groups focused on different issues. After the United
States entered the war, the American Union
organized the National Civil Liberties Bureau, which
later became the American Civil Liberties Union, to
protect civil liberties in wartime and to provide legal
counsel for conscientious objectors. The Woman's
Peace Party remained conscious of the profound
importance of keeping peace ideals before the
American people. The Party believed that their work
for peace was as important to internationalism in
wartime "as a similar body of public opinion was to
the abolition of slavery."[5] On the other hand, the
national board agreed that it would avoid "all
criticism" of the government by avoiding any activity
which might be considered obstructive to the war
effort. Consequently, much of the Party's wartime
work was to assist the civilian relief effort of more

[4]*Alice Lewisohn to Crystal Eastman, 16 February 1916, Woman's
Peace Party-New York Papers, Box 16, S.C.P.C.*

[5]*Harriet P. Thomas to Elizabeth Glendower Evans, 14 November
1916 Woman's Peace Party Papers, Box 4.*

*conservative groups. Jane Addams herself appealed to
the members of the Woman's Peace Party to volunteer
in service to America to relieve the suffering caused by
war and she herself volunteered to work with Herbert
Hoover's Food Administration programs.*

*Most of the branches of the WPP agreed with Jane
Addams' decision and some branches spent the entire
war knitting socks. Nevertheless, some of the Party's
founders believed that any wartime interest in peace
was dangerous, if not treasonous, and quit despite the
conservative orientation of the national board.
Florence Kelley, for example, resigned after she
accepted an appointment as Secretary of the Board of
Control of army contracts for soldiers' clothing. She
also chaired the committee on industrial mobilization
of the Woman's Committee of the Council of National
Defense, while Lillian Wald, who did not quit, chaired
the committee on Public Health and child welfare.*[6]

*The wartime programs of both Lillian Wald's
Henry Street Settlement and Jane Addams' Hull
House reveal that while both ladies opposed
conscription in principle, they maintained active
registration programs. Indeed, Jane Addams received
a military citation for her assistance to the selective
service people. Moreover, the Henry Street Settlement
program for 1918, included an active campaign for
"Americanization." This program consisted of*

[6] *Woman's Peace Party Papers, 25 October 1917, Box 4; Florence
Kelley to Margaret Lane, 27 August 1917, WPP-NY, Box 16; and
Frances Perkins to Lillian Wald, 9 February 1918, Wald Papers, Box
8, Columbia University.*

INTRODUCTION

house to house canvassing for "Americanization" purposes, meetings and classes on "Americanization and citizenship," and "patriotic services" to enlist committees of volunteers for the Red Cross, Liberty Loans, Four Minute Men, the Food Administration, the state military census, the Enemy Alien Registration, draft registration and the entertainment of men in uniform.[7]

The one notable exception to these good works for peace was the New York City branch of the Woman's Peace Party. Crystal Eastman was credited with having "built the peace party up from a polite society affair into an active democratic decisive organization."[8] *Because the New York branch was considered too radical, many people joined the national Woman's Peace Party instead. One letter from a New York resident requesting national membership was very specific about it all: "I cannot join the party in New York as the sentiments expressed at their meetings are very extreme and dangerous."*[9] *Many members opposed the spirited manner in which the*

[7]*Jane Addams spoke both for Herbert Hoover's Food Administration and the Committee on Public Information on food conservation, education, and other topics.*
See Herbert Hoover to Jane Addams, 2 March 1918, Jane Addams Papers, Box 6; Ernest Poole for the C.P.I., Foreign Press Brueau to Jane Addams, 12 July 1918, Ibid. For the Henry Street program for 1918 see Lillian Wald Papers, Box 37, Columbia University.

[8]*Margaret Lane to Crystal Eastman, 28 April 1915, WPP-NY, Box 15.*

[9]*Miss Georgie Day to Lucia Ames Mead, 5 July 1916, WPP Papers Box 4.*

New York branch did business. Mabel Hyde Kittredge, for example, resigned from the Woman's Peace Party because she objected to the fact that the NYC branch used "ridicule" and "made fun" of munitions makers in a War against War Exhibit, which featured a huge dragon representing the war machine.[10]

The single most abrasive source of antagonism between New York and the national office of the Woman's Peace Party was Four Lights, *New York's fortnightly newsletter. In the first issue of* Four Lights, *the editors announced that it sought to become the voice of the "young, uncompromising woman's peace movement in America, whose aims are daring and immediate: To stop the war in Europe, to federate the nations for organized peace at the close of the war, and meanwhile to guard democracy from the subtle dangers of militarism." The editors declared that they had become fighters for peace because America had been "deceived into establishing an enormous military machine which must not only destroy her own liberties but endanger the liberties of other peoples. . .;" and because America was "busily forging weapons to menace the spirit of freedom struggling to life in exhausted Europe at the close of the war. . ."*

Four Lights *harbored no illusions about war relief work and devoted an entire issue to ladies of mercy, entitled the "Sister Susie Number." Without men-*

[10]*Mabel H. Kittredge to WPP-NY, 3 April 1916, Box 16.*

tioning Jane Addams' association with Hoover's commission it published an article, "Hoover How Can You?"

> *Evidently the women of the country are of two minds on the subject of food economy. For lack of more dignified designation they might be called the "Hoover Helpers" and the "Hoover Hooters"—the first being those who accept their position beside the garbage cans as they have always accepted what God and man has put upon them to endure;—the second, those who fail to see the crux of the food situation in the gospel of the clean plate, while bushels of peas and rows of lettuce are being plowed under because their price is too low to satisfy the food speculators. . . .*

Attacking Hoover specifically for his reaction to a woman who doubted that housewives alone were responsible "for the wholesale waste of food manipulators," the article declared that the Quaker head of the Food Administration had revealed "the cloven hoof of the military dictator" when he insisted that " 'this woman's attitude is one that we simply cannot stand for. . . .' " While the New York branch acknowledged that Hoover showed "his broadmindedness" by admitting that the woman was not "in the employ of the German government," his entire position revealed "a naughty little temper, which is bound to be encountered by any of his co-operators except the most docile plate-lickers and unremitting garbage-guarders."[11]

[11] *"Hoover How Can You?"* Four Lights, *14 July 1917*, SCPC.

14

INTRODUCTION

On 24 March 1917, Four Lights *announced in blacker and bolder ink that it hailed "The Russian Revolution with mad glad joy. It pledges itself uncompromisingly to the cause of democracy. It recognizes that nations must be deomcratized before a federated world can be achieved." Editorials such as these moved the national Peace Party to attempt to dissociate itself from the New York group. The national even considered changing its name to the Woman's League for International Law and Order.*[12]

Members of the New York branch considered a change of name "silly and cowardly and short-sighted." Anne Herenden, one of the editors of Four Lights *wrote: "The main point of the organization to my mind is that it voiced the spontaneous objection of WOMEN TO WAR at the very beginning of the mess and it will have justified its existence and brought credit upon our sex IF it appears to remain unchanged in its principles. . . . If the National is going to change. . ., so much the worse for it. Wait till you read the chortling of the* Times *over Jane Addams and her ilk having seen the light, for the change will be interpreted only in that way. . . ."* [13] *The change was never made.*

Despite the caution exercised by Jane Addams and the national Woman's Peace Party, she and most of

[12] *Lucia Ames Mead to Jane Addams, 28 September 1917, WPP Papers Box 4.*

[13] *Anne Herenden to Margaret Lane, 2 December 1917, WPP-NY Papers, Box 15.*

15

the members of the national board were vilified after the war. Their names were added to lists of "those who did not help us win the war" and during the Red Scare of A. Mitchell Palmer they were associated with Bolsheviks and other "traitors."

At the second international meeting of the Woman's Peace Paris in Zurich in 1919, when it was renamed the Women's International League for Peace and Freedom, the organization became the first body to protest the punitive Treaty of Versailles. Ethel Snowden of England and Jeannette Rankin of the United States introduced the resolution:

> *This International Congress of women expresses its deep regret that the terms of peace proposed at Versailles should so seriously violate the principles upon which alone a just and lasting peace can be secured, and which the Democracies of the world had come to accept. By guaranteeing the fruits of the secret treaties to the conquerors the terms tacitly sanction secret diplomacy. They deny the principle of self-determination, recognize the right of the victors to the spoils of war, and create all over Europe discords and animosities, which can lead only to future wars.*

From 1919 to 1971, the Women's International League has continued to search, as all peace organizations in America must, for the viable means by which to actualize its precepts. But it has continued to be in the vanguard of all issues relating to peace and freedom. W.I.L. was among the first to protest the Truman Doctrine, the key statement of America's

16

INTRODUCTION

Cold War policies. The League maintained that it threatened peace far more that it bolstered freedom. The same was true for the establishment of N.A.T.O. which the League also opposed. W.I.L.P.F. has also been among the pioneers in the civil rights movement, from its vigorous support of the Wagner-Gavagan anti-lynching bill to its demand in 1971 for the release of Angela Davis and all political prisoners. In sum, the Women's International League has remained committed to its basic assumption that peace and freedom are inseparable and that permanent peace will not be achieved until economic equality, political freedom and social justice are insured. Marie Louise Degen's study reveals the cruel fact that none of the issues raised by the women of World War I has ever been successfully answered, because none of their alternatives has ever been tried.

Blanche Wiesen Cook
Department of History
John Jay College, CUNY

SERIES LVII   NUMBER 3

THE JOHNS HOPKINS UNIVERSITY STUDIES IN
HISTORICAL AND POLITICAL SCIENCE
Under the Direction of the Departments of History,
Political Economy, and Political Science

THE HISTORY OF THE WOMAN'S PEACE PARTY

By

MARIE LOUISE DEGEN
Maryland College for Women

BALTIMORE
THE JOHNS HOPKINS PRESS
1939

The Johns Hopkins Press of Baltimore

Albert Shaw Lectures on Diplomatic History. Under the direction of the Walter Hines Page School of International Relations. 12mo. Twenty-three volumes have been issued. (*See* page v.)

American Journal of Mathematics. Edited by E. T. BELL, A. COHEN, T. H. HILDEBRANDT, F. D. MURNAGHAN, and J. F. RITT. Quarterly. 8vo. Volume LXI in progress. $7.50 per volume. (Foreign postage, 50 cents.)

American Journal of Philology. Edited by TENNEY FRANK, with the cooperation of H. CHERNISS, K. MALONE, B. D. MERITT, and D. M. ROBINSON. Quarterly. 8vo. Volume LX in progress. $5.00 per volume. (Foreign postage, 25 cents.)

Biologia Generalis (International Journal of General Biology). Edited by L. ADAMETZ, K. EHRENBERG, O. PORSCH, C. SCHWARTZ, and J. VERSLUYS of Vienna. 8vo. Volume XIV in progress.

Bulletin of the History of Medicine. Edited by HENRY E. SIGERIST. Monthly except August and September. 8vo. Volume VII in progress. $5.00 per year. (Foreign postage, 50 cents.)

Bulletin of the Johns Hopkins Hospital. Edited by JAMES BORDLEY III. Monthly. 8vo. Volume LXV in progress. $6.00 per year. (Foreign postage, 50 cents.)

Comparative Psychology Monographs. Edited by R. M. DORCUS. 8vo. Volume XV in progress. $5.00 per volume.

E L H, a Journal of English Literary History. Edited by RAY HEFFNER, EDWARD N. HOOKER, CLIFFORD P. LYONS, EDWARD T. NORRIS, and LOUIS TEETER. Quarterly. 8vo. Volume VI in progress. Subscription $2.50 per volume.

Hesperia. Edited by WILLIAM KURRELMEYER and KEMP MALONE. 8vo. Thirty volumes have appeared.

Human Biology. Edited by RAYMOND PEARL. Quarterly. 8vo. Volume XI in progress. $5.00 per volume. (Foreign postage, 35 cents.)

Johns Hopkins Historical Publications. Under the direction of the Department of History. 8vo. Six volumes have been issued. (See fourth cover.)

Johns Hopkins Monographs in Literary History. Founded by EDWIN GREENLAW. 12mo. Three volumes have been issued.

Johns Hopkins Studies in International Thought. Edited by GILBERT CHINARD. 4to. Two volumes have been issued.

Johns Hopkins Studies in Romance Literatures and Languages. Edited by GILBERT CHINARD and H. C. LANCASTER. 8vo. Forty-nine volumes have been published.

Johns Hopkins University Studies in Archaeology. Edited by DAVID M. ROBINSON. 8vo. Twenty-nine volumes have been published.

Johns Hopkins University Studies in Education. Edited by FLORENCE E. BAMBERGER. 8vo. Twenty-eight numbers have appeared.

Johns Hopkins University Studies in Geology. Edited by E. B. MATHEWS. 8vo. Thirteen numbers have been published.

Johns Hopkins University Studies in Historical and Political Science. Under the direction of the Departments of History, Political Economy, and Political Science. 8vo. Series LVII in progress. $5.00 per volume. (See pages vii to xii.)

Modern Language Notes. Edited by H. C. LANCASTER, W. KURRELMEYER, KEMP MALONE, HAZELTON SPENCER, R. D. HAVENS, and C. S. SINGLETON. Eight times yearly. 8vo. Volume LIII in progress. $5.00 per volume. (Foreign postage, 50 cents.)

Reprint of Economic Tracts. Edited by JACOB H. HOLLANDER. 8vo. A fifth series is in progress. (*See* page vi.)

Terrestrial Magnetism and Atmospheric Electricity. Edited by J. A. FLEMING. Quarterly. 8vo. Volume LXIV in progress. $3.50 per volume.

Walter Hines Page School of International Relations Publications. 8vo. Eight volumes have been issued. (*See* third cover.)

Wilmer Ophthalmological Institute Monographs. 8vo. Two volumes have been issued.

THE JOHNS HOPKINS UNIVERSITY STUDIES IN HISTORICAL AND POLITICAL SCIENCE

Under the Direction of the Departments of History,
Political Economy, and Political Science

VOLUME LVII

BALTIMORE
THE JOHNS HOPKINS PRESS
1939

PRINTED IN THE UNITED STATES OF AMERICA
BY J. H. FURST COMPANY, BALTIMORE, MARYLAND

CONTENTS

THE HISTORY OF THE WOMAN'S PEACE PARTY

SERIES LVII

NUMBER 3

THE JOHNS HOPKINS UNIVERSITY STUDIES IN HISTORICAL AND POLITICAL SCIENCE

Under the Direction of the Departments of History, Political Economy, and Political Science

THE HISTORY OF THE WOMAN'S PEACE PARTY

BY

MARIE LOUISE DEGEN

Maryland College for Women

BALTIMORE

THE JOHNS HOPKINS PRESS

1939

PRINTED IN THE UNITED STATES OF AMERICA
BY J. H. FURST COMPANY, BALTIMORE, MARYLAND

To

ELIZABETH MATHEWS VAN HORN

AND

MARY MATHEWS VAN HORN

ACKNOWLEDGMENTS

The author gratefully acknowledges the assistance of many persons who made possible the writing of this book. Dr. Albert K. Weinberg, formerly Lecturer in Political Science at The Johns Hopkins University, directed the project and gave aid and encouragement. Dr. Johannes Mattern of the same department served as an advisor throughout the period in which the study was in progress. Mrs. Elizabeth Mathews Van Horn assisted in the collecting of the material and gave of her time at every stage of the work. Valuable library assistance was received from Miss Ellen Starr Brinton, Curator of the Jane Addams Peace Collection, Miss E. Virginia Walker of the Friends Historical Library of Swarthmore College, and Miss Eleanor W. Falley, Head Librarian of the Goucher College Library, and her staff. Miss Emily Greene Balch and Mrs. Louis F. Post, leading figures in the peace movement, offered corrections and valuable suggestions with reference to the manuscript. Professor Carl Brent Swisher of the Department of Political Science corrected errors in form and substance. The manuscript was read by Professor Gertrude Carman Bussey, Professor of Philosophy at Goucher College and President of the United States Section of the Women's International League for Peace and Freedom, by Miss Dorothy Detzer, Executive Secretary of the United States Section of the Women's International League for Peace and Freedom, and by Professor Annette B. Hopkins, Professor of English and Chairman of the Committee on Fellowships of Goucher College. Miss D. Lucille Haven, secretary of the Departments of History and Political Science, also read the manuscript and corrected the proof. The author wishes to express her appreciation to the teachers, other than those mentioned above, under whom she studied at Johns Hopkins: Mr. Leon Sachs of the Department of Political Science; Mr. Wallace McClure of the United States Department of State,

Lecturer in the Department of Political Science in 1936-1937; and Professors Arthur O. Lovejoy and George Boas of the Department of Philosophy.

For the financial support which made possible the preparation and publication of the study, the author is indebted to the Goucher College Committee on Fellowships. The Committee twice awarded her funds from the Elizabeth King Ellicott Fellowship for the Political Education of Women.

It is obvious from the concluding pages of this work that it went to press before the outbreak of the European War. This world tragedy may influence in one way or another the opinion of the readers with regard to the present value of the philosophy of which the book treats. But the recurrence of a general war such as brought the Woman's Peace Party into being may well add to the significance and interest of this historical account. It places before the present peace movement of America the same problem as that faced by Jane Addams and her associates, and it is a question of the greatest interest whether the contemporary women pacifists will follow or depart from the policies and ideas which guided the Woman's Peace Party twenty-five years ago.

CONTENTS

THE HISTORY OF THE WOMAN'S PEACE PARTY

CHAPTER I

WAR AND DISILLUSIONMENT

In January 1915 a large group of American women, among whom were such distinguished figures as Jane Addams, Carrie Chapman Catt and Fannie Fern Andrews, formed in Washington an organization which struck public opinion as a curious novelty. It was called the Woman's Peace Party—a name which used the word "party" in a non-political sense. If not the first women's peace society in the United States, it was at least the first in this country, and one of the first in the world, to command widespread attention. It was destined in the course of the momentous events with which its dramatic history became intertwined to exert rather considerable influence upon many Americans, men as well as women, to receive the commendation of President Wilson and other statesmen for its plans of international reconstruction, and ultimately, rechristened as the Women's International League for Peace and Freedom, to figure powerfully among the public pressures shaping the present foreign policy of the United States. At the outset, however, the Woman's Peace Party attracted notice chiefly because a separate women's movement for peace not only was a deviation from tradition but also seemed inherently an odd if not a pointless thing.

The impulse which prompted the women to their unusual undertaking can be understood only with some study of its background, both immediate and distant. The immediate background of the Woman's Peace Party was formed by the first six months of the European War. To a considerable degree the organization was the result of the harassing impact of the World War upon sensitive American women. But some of the forces which led to the organization are to be found, as are the ultimate causes of historical events generally, in the rather distant past. The course of the women was to some extent determined, consciously or unconsciously, by the previous history of the American peace movement, especially by the part played by women in this history. In some respects the women of 1915 were inspired by the traditions of the American peace movement and in other respects they reacted against it, feeling that they were blazing a new and more hopeful trail.

Pacifism, if by this one means merely an appreciation of peace and a disposition ordinarily to adhere to it, has been an old and basic American attitude. This attitude, which gradually became converted into a national tradition, is the product on the one hand of American humanitarianism and on the other hand of more selfish factors such as the policies of non-intervention and neutrality. An abstract hope for world peace, together with recognition of the duty to guide national conduct in this direction, is generally manifested in official expositions of America's international policies and for the most part—four wars are exceptions—in the actual conduct of American foreign relations. But in the terminology of social philosophies pacifism means something more than this mere preference for peace. It comprises the doctrines of those who " refuse to sanction war for any purpose, defensive or otherwise," [1] and who feel that the elimination of war is the most pressing need of international life, worthy of the best efforts of nations and individuals. In this thoroughgoing form pacifism is expressed chiefly in the ideas and activities of individuals, especially of those who became the founders of peace societies.

There are many American names which are memorable in the history of pacifism: David Low Dodge, the well-to-do New York merchant whose customers found peace tracts in his shipments, the founder of the American pacifist organization, the New York Peace Society; Noah Worcester, the Congre-

---

[1] Article " Pacifism " by Norman Angell, *Encyclopædia of the Social Sciences*, XI, 527. The word " pacifism " did not enter into general use until a few years before the World War, when it came to be applied to the views of members of peace societies and of others who were engaged in organized effort to eliminate war. *Ibid.*

gationalist minister from New Hampshire, who prepared the first really efficacious call to American peace workers—" A Solemn Review of the Custom of War "; William Ladd, sea captain and prosperous Maine farmer, who in 1828 founded the American Peace Society, a federation of thirty local groups; Arthur Love, the Philadelphia woolen merchant, who after the Civil War launched his Universal Peace Union with methods and a program deviating from those of the more utopian pre-war organizations; Andrew Carnegie, of still more recent times, whose works for peace are too well known to need mention. Recalling such persons and such organizations, only a fraction of the noteworthy, the women pacifists could well feel encouraged by a national history of great individual and organizational aspiration for peace.

However, in certain respects the previous American peace movement did not set encouraging precedents for women pacifists of the twentieth century. In the first place, with few exceptions, the history of American pacifism had for long been a record of the efforts of men and not of women. To some extent this fact was, of course, due to the prejudices entertained even by relatively enlightened men at a time when women were virtually excluded from public life. In 1838 even the radical New England Non-Resistance Society lost a number of charter members when it adopted William Lloyd Garrison's suggestion that women be allowed to serve on committees. To a considerable degree, however, the women themselves had no great desire for such services or considered them beyond their powers. Furthermore, even after women did become workers in the peace movement, they for some time worked chiefly within the framework of established peace societies, which as late as the twentieth century gave relatively few offices to women. Finally, even after organizations of women began to devote themselves to the cause of peace, they were such as had the promotion of peace only as one objective among many. It did not seem that peace required the undivided effort of organized women, much less that it was a cause which it was appropriate to promote by separate action.

In other respects, however, the previous rôle of women in

the American peace movement was one which not merely encouraged the women pacifists of 1915 but, through the force of social heritage, largely contributed to their emergence. While the women's peace movement was relatively late in starting, it grew apace once the seeds had been sown. The woman whose activity marks the birth of the women's peace movement was Julia Ward Howe, who, after she had blessed musically the Civil War with her "Battle Hymn of the Republic," was intensely disturbed and prompted to pacifism by the Franco-Prussian War. In 1872 she went to Europe for the purpose of organizing a women's international peace congress—an enterprise similar to one of the Woman's Peace Party in 1915—but met failure because too many women, like the Duchess of Argyll, took literally the words of St. Paul, "I suffer not a woman to teach." [2] But within her own country the pacifist poetess had more success, for peace meetings of women were held in eighteen cities. Julia Ward Howe was the first of a series of earnest women who, increasing in number as women became more conscious of public issues and entered more into professional and public life, achieved a prominence in the peace movement equal to that of male leaders. Another such was Belva Lockwood, a woman lawyer, the first to practice before the Supreme Court, who for almost forty years lobbied for the Universal Peace Union and other pacifist organizations, and drafted Senator John Sherman's resolution of 1890 favoring permanent treaties of arbitration. Other women who demonstrated the capacity of their sex in both the organizational and the educational activities of the peace movement were Lucia Ames Mead of the American Peace Society, Fannie Fern Andrews of the American School Peace League, and Anna B. Eckstein, who single-handed collected petitions for the first and third Hague conferences in behalf of specific positive objectives. Spurred by such examples as well as by their own impulses, women affiliated themselves with the peace societies in increasing numbers,

---

[2] Edwin D. Mead, "Julia Ward Howe's Peace Crusade," *World Peace Foundation Pamphlet Series*, IV, 7.

and by 1914 formed a substantial proportion of their membership.

The increasing activity of women in the peace movement did not manifest itself merely in their entrance into peace organizations inclusive of both sexes. Another phase of the history of American women as pacifists is the contribution made to the cause of peace by women's organizations of the most varied character. The first large women's organization in this country to emphasize peace as one of its aims was the American National Council of the International Council of Women, which was formed in 1888 for general purposes of women's international cooperation. In 1896 it adopted a resolution committing its members to peace and arbitration. When, in 1899, the International Council also resolved to make the promotion of peace and arbitration a primary aim, the American National Council set up a Standing Council to function in regard to these ends. The Women's Christian Temperance Union and the Daughters of the American Revolution were also early in their adoption of peace and arbitration as ends to be promoted through their organizational activities. The number of women's organizations promoting pacifist endeavors increased in the twentieth century as the Hague Court and the professions of governments and public leaders made the ideal of peace more and more popular and promising. A cynic might say that to women's organizations pacifism was an added feather in their respectability. However, pacifism did command the sincere moral devotion of women, particularly because of its apparent appropriateness to their humane sentiment. Mrs. May Wright Sewall, president of the International Council of Women, exemplified this sense of women that peace was particularly their concern when she said at the Third American Peace Congress: "I wish only to increase sentiment. . . . To a large degree this seems to be the woman's part of the work. . . ."[3] Whatever the reasons, the number of American women committed to peace by their organizational affiliations just before the outbreak of the World War was

---

[3] *Proceedings of the Third American Peace Congress*, 1911, p. 416.

staggeringly large. Mrs. Lucia Ames Mead, speaking in 1912 at the Seventh Annual Conference on Arbitration, undertook to give some idea of this number by instancing only a few of the largest women's organizations that had professed pacifism: the Federation of Women's Clubs with 800,000 members, the Council of Mothers with 100,000, the Women's Christian Temperance Union with 325,000, the Woman's Relief Corps with 161,000, and the National Council of Women with about fifteen national organizations comprising hundreds of thousands of members.[4]

The previous growth of pacifism among American women, however, is less important in accounting for the Woman's Peace Party than the imaginative enterprise of a few women. Of these the most noteworthy is Jane Addams, who not only played the central rôle in the birth and life of the organization but gave it prestige in the eyes of the world through lending to it the luster of her own dignity and reputation. Had Miss Addams not shared in their point of view, it is doubtful whether the group of women forming the Party could have entered with any hope of success upon a venture which, indeed, was not just another pacifist society, but something which in both ideology and tactics struck a new note in American pacifism. To this venture she contributed not merely her undisputed repute as leader of progressive movements among American women but the rare personal qualities which underlay that repute. These qualities comprised not merely a deep human sensitiveness, an indefatigable and courageous social idealism, and an irresistible charm but also a really commanding intellect the full stature of which was perhaps concealed from many by the extent to which it was made instrumental to causes of emotional and moral aspect.[5]

Pacifism, at least in its nuclear logical and psychological elements, was doubtless a part of Miss Addams' social outlook from the beginning. The emergence in her of a conscious pacifist philosophy did not, however, come about until later,

---

[4] Julius Moritzen, *The Peace Movement in America*, p. 325.
[5] For my interpretation of Jane Addams and the sources of her pacifism, I am largely indebted to Miss Emily G. Balch, one of Miss Addams' closest associates in the peace movement.

and according to her own account through the influence of two phases of her experience. One was her reading of Tolstoy, who erected a philosophy of non-resistance upon Christian ethics and the doctrine that the sentiments of direct human relationships provide the pattern after which even political relations should be modeled. The other source of her pacifism was identified by Miss Addams with that pioneering experience in social settlement work which caused the name of Hull House to become a household term in the national vocabulary. Her contacts with the immigrants of many nations developed in Miss Addams a friendly understanding of many nationalities which is at the heart of genuine internationalism. The same experience, involving as it did a constant observation of the cooperativeness of persons of different nationalities in slum areas, also engendered in her a faith that the same cooperativeness could be carried over from individuals to nations. Such a confidence she expressed in the following words:

When a South Italian Catholic is forced by the very exigencies of the situation to make friends with an Austrian Jew, representing another nationality and another religion, both of which cut into all his most cherished prejudices, he finds it harder to utilize them a second time, and gradually loses them. . . . If an old enemy working by his side turned into a friend, almost anything may happen.[6]

Would not the increasing interdependence of nations, Miss Addams asked as early as 1896, bring about the same cooperativeness as resulted from the forced internationalism of American cities?

The actual manifestations of Miss Addams' pacifism are still later than the crystallization of the philosophy, and the early part of her career gives no foreshadowing of the important rôle which she was to play in the peace movement. The first time she centered educational activity upon the ideal of peace was at the age of thirty-five, when she tried to get boys in the gymnasium of Hull House to substitute sewer spades for the wooden bayonets with which they had been drilling. The effort was more felicitous as a symbol of her philosophy of pacifism than as an exercise in education; for, as Miss Addams humorously confessed, the boys kept the

---

[6] James W. Linn, *Jane Addams, a Biography*, p. 292.

2

spades only as long as she was watching. Her first public participation in the peace movement was in 1899, when she added her voice to the widespread agitation of anti-imperialists against the annexation of the Philippines. Her stand in this issue was prophetic of her later association of peace with anti-imperialism. Also significant was the fact that, beginning in 1904, when a convention of National Peace Societies was held in Boston, Miss Addams identified herself more and more with the organized peace movement. She was a principal speaker at the convention of 1904 and also at the National Peace Congress of 1907, the first such congress to be held in the United States. In 1906 Miss Addams delivered a course of lectures at the University of Wisconsin summer school on the subject of the " Newer Ideals of Peace." In the next year she published a book bearing that title. The work was received with an enthusiasm that contrasts with the opprobrium which not much later was to attach to Miss Addams for her pacifism. The belligerent Theodore Roosevelt, it is true, was not prevented even by his general admiration for the social reformer from telling a friend of Miss Addams that " she has just written a bad book, a very bad book ! " [7] But the general view was quite different, and even a Hearst editor praised " the reach of this woman's sympathy and understanding." [8] The reception of the book, which established Miss Addams as a spokesman of the American peace movement, reflected a climate of opinion in which, since there were no strong gusts of nationalist emotion, peace was one of the most conventional of values.

However, the enthusiasm over *Newer Ideals of Peace* reflected also the originality of the work. It not only justified the implication of its title that pacifism was being presented from a new point of view, but it gave the pacifist movement an ideology which accorded much better than the old with the general philosophy of modern social reformism. As contrasted with the older " dovelike " ideal of peace, Miss Addams declared, the newer ideals were " active and dynamic." These

---

[7] *Ibid.*, p. 294.   [8] *Ibid.*

newer ideals were also different from the old in that, whereas
the latter " required fostering and recruiting, and have been
held and promulgated on the basis of a creed," the newer
ideals would, if their forces were made really operative upon
society, " in the end, quite as a natural process, do away with
war." More specifically, the older pacifist ideology was said
to proceed along two great lines: " the appeal to the higher,
imaginative pity," as represented in the moral philosophy of
Tolstoy; and " the appeal to the sense of prudence," that is,
to the sense of the economic wastefulness and futility of war—
an appeal represented in the work of another Russian, Jean
de Bloch. The difficulty with the first seemed to Miss Addams
its suggestion of " passivity, the goody-goody attitude of in-
effectiveness." The inadequacy of the second lay in its ignoring of the moral factor altogether. While the moral approach
was the more correct, it needed to rely upon a more positive
impulse than merely " the desire for a conscience at rest, for
a sense of justice no longer outraged." In fact, pacifism, like
morality in general, needed to rely not upon moral theorems
but rather upon inherent social impulses, which, later becoming habits of action, would ultimately flower into moral codes
and institutions. In behalf of peace there were " strenuous
forces at work reaching down to impulses and experiences as
primitive and profound as are those of struggle itself." What
were these impulses and experiences? They partook of that
" ancient kindliness which sat beside the cradle of the race,"
but they had been developed particularly by the socializing
forces of the era of industrialism. The entire book was
devoted to describing the specific manifestations of the new
" cosmopolitan interest in human affairs with the resultant
social sympathy." [9] These manifestations were many and
diverse—the cooperativeness of immigrants in slums, movements of municipal reform, social legislation, the protection
of children, and the growth of public-spiritedness in women.

A chapter on " The Passing of the War Virtues " was the
only consideration of the pacifist ideal in the ordinary sense.

---

[9] Jane Addams, *Newer Ideals of Peace*, pp. 3-9.

This chapter was built about the main idea of the book—that pacifism was less the mere avoidance of war than the replacement of the war virtues by virtues which sublimate the heroic but anachronistic energies of the soldier into aspirations toward harmony and justice in society. In other words, Miss Addams envisaged " the moral equivalent for war "— an idea of William James to whom she acknowledged indebtedness. The virtue which in particular would bring about this sublimation was characterized by Miss Addams as a " new internationalism " and also as a " cosmic patriotism." [10] However named, it was an emotion impelling toward the widest possible fellowship, both with people throughout the world and with a power for righteousness that expressed itself in human relationships. And this emotion, developing not only through its own vitality, but also through the necessities of cooperation imposed by modern industrialism, seemed to Miss Addams to have become " a rising tide of moral enthusiasm slowly engulfing all pride of conquest and making war impossible." [11]

Would not this pacifist philosophy, partaking as does Marxism of an element of determinism, lead logically to the conclusion that the peace movement was unnecessary? Certainly the entire point of Miss Addams' book was that there are stronger forces making for peace than the efforts of peace societies and congresses which decried the evils of war. Yet, like the Marxian in the sphere of economic reconstruction, she did not advocate passivity. She believed in organized activity in behalf of peace, a manifestation of the impulse toward wider fellowship, and objected only to that misinterpretation by pacifists of their own motivation which led them to stress the negative aspect of pacifism. For the present, it is true, she was disposed less towards leadership in the so-called peace movement than towards participation in the movements of positive social amelioration which seemed to her to be the best guarantee against war.

In the years following the publication of her book Miss Addams became, like pacifists in general, increasingly opti-

---

[10] *Ibid.*, p. 237.   [11] *Ibid.*, p. 238.

mistic about the elimination of war through natural processes
of evolution. Never was this optimism greater than in the
year 1913, when a great palace had been opened at The Hague
to give center to the efforts throughout the world in behalf of
substituting arbitration for war. It is difficult in these disil-
lusioned days to recall the time when the mere existence of the
Hague Court seemed to many a powerful antidote to the nationalist passions that would resort to the arbitrament of the
sword. But in 1913 there was held in Carnegie Hall a great
peace meeting which celebrated with pathetic exuberance the
tangible completion of Carnegie's effort and its implications
for peace. Miss Addams was one of the speakers and expressed her participation in the general hopefulness. "There,
was rising in the cosmopolitan centers of America," she declared, "a sturdy and unprecedented international understanding which in time would be too profound to lend itself to
war." [12] It is true that nothing in these words committed
Miss Addams to the prophecy that permanent peace was just
around the corner. And in her reminiscences she expressly dis-
claims entertaining at the time the foolish belief that because
a World Court of Conciliation and Arbitration had been established at The Hague in 1899 war had been abolished. Yet
she confesses that she and other pacifists had believed that
"war would become less and less frequent as all the nations
in the world formed the habit of taking their difficulties to
an international court." [13] Certainly, in the year when David
Starr Jordan wrote that a European war was impossible,[14] she
did not foresee that Armageddon lay but a year ahead.

"For many reasons," Miss Addams later wrote, "it was
hard to believe in August, 1914, that war had broken out between Germany and France and later to receive the incredible
news that England had also declared war." The fact that was
at first incredible was shortly to be made realistic to Miss
Addams by a spectacle that was visible from her summer home
on Mount Desert—near Bar Harbor. Two days after the

---

[12] Linn, p. 296.
[13] Jane Addams, *The Second Twenty Years at Hull-House* . . . ,
pp. 116-117.
[14] Quoted by Walter Millis, *The Road to War*, p. 19.

declaration of war, on a beautiful August morning, a huge German liner, an amazing sight for Frenchman's Bay, loomed up in the waters adjacent to the house. Later Miss Addams learned that the captain of the ship, which was carrying a cargo of gold bullion, had been informed of Germany's declaration of war while at sea and at once had turned towards shore lest the vessel be captured. "The huge boat in her incongruous setting," she recorded, "was the first fantastic impression of that fantastic summer when we were so incredibly required to adjust our minds to a changed world." [15]

A difficult adjustment, indeed, it was. "It is impossible now," wrote Jane Addams in retrospect, "to reproduce that basic sense of desolation, of suicide, of anachronism, which that first news of the war brought to thousands of men and women who had come to consider war as a throwback in the scientific sense." [16] Adjustment to this throwback meant abandonment of the too hastily adopted theories about the quick tempo of the evolution of natural impulses toward the elimination of war. It meant the framing of new or changed plans of action to assist this evolution. It did not for a moment, however, mean to the pacifists acquiescence in the catastrophe.

The pacifists were encouraged at the outset by the fact that, as Miss Addams has recorded, the reaction in the United States against war was "almost instantaneous throughout the country." [17] She noted as the most striking manifestations of this reaction the newspaper cartoons and comments which expressed astonishment that Europe had reverted to the archaism of war. There were also more sensational demonstrations of protest such as the procession through the streets of New York of a group of women led by the daughter of the American pacifist, William Lloyd Garrison. But there were other men and women who, though stirred just as deeply, preferred to postpone open protest until they had clarified their own minds by quiet discussion with those of similar interests.

---

[15] *The Second Twenty Years*, pp. 117-118.
[16] *Ibid.*, p. 119.
[17] Jane Addams, *Peace and Bread in Time of War*, p. 1.

Thus in the fall of 1914 Jane Addams, Lillian D. Wald and
Paul Kellogg, editor of the *Survey*, national organ of social
workers, invited a small group of community leaders and
social workers to a round table at the Henry Street Settlement
to discuss the war and a possible plan for concerted action.[18]
Because of their work among immigrants from many countries, the group had come to believe that, to quote Miss
Addams, "the endeavor to nurture human life even in its
most humble and least promising forms had crossed national
boundaries; that those who had given years to its service had
become convinced that nothing of social value can be obtained
save through widespread public opinion and the cooperation
of all civilized nations." In their eyes, war "not only interrupted but fatally reversed this process of cooperating good
will which, if it had a chance, would eventually include the
human family itself." [19]   The *Survey* later published in a
special number the analyses of war and plans for peace which
had been developed by this conference at the Henry Street
Settlement. The number contained an appeal from Miss
Addams "not to put aside, as if it had never existed, the long
intellectual and moral effort toward securing better international relations—the work of such men as Grotius and Im-
manuel Kant, continued through hundreds of years." Miss
Addams also quoted the appeal made by Romain Rolland in
the first days of the war:

Come, Friends, let us make a stand! Can we not resist this conta-
gion—whatever its nature and virulence be—whether moral epidemic
or cosmic force? Do we not fight against the plague and strive even
to repair the disaster caused by the earthquake? [20]

Determined to fight against the spreading plague of militarism and to seek to repair the damage of the war by a lasting peace, the social workers who had met at Henry Street
formed the Union Against Militarism and elected Miss Wald
as its first president.

In joining this organization—it was the first of several

---

[18] Lillian D. Wald, *Windows on Henry Street*, p. 289.
[19] *Peace and Bread*, p. 3.
[20] "War and Social Reconstruction," *Survey* (1915), XXXIII, 603.

peace societies which she helped to form in the months following the outbreak of war—Miss Addams evidenced a change from the days when she wrote of the elimination of war through the natural process of moral evolution.[21] The realization had evidently grown upon her that the evolution toward peace was not spontaneous but was largely contingent upon the organization of pacifists to fight for their ideal. However, though the Union Against Militarism was led by a woman, Miss Addams seems to have had at first no thought of a peace society composed solely of women. The influences which led directly to her interest in such a society came into play only subsequently. And yet before we turn to these we must revert briefly to certain experiences and attitudes of Miss Addams in the pre-war years which at least made her receptive to the idea of a separate women's peace movement.

One element in her many-sided reformism prior to the World War was her interest in woman suffrage, which dated from her graduation from college. It had never, indeed, been a dominating interest in this woman who was as little capable of dividing her humanitarianism on the basis of sex as on the basis of nations. But, while not dominant as with so-called feminists, woman suffrage was an important part of the program which Miss Addams conceived essential to social amelioration. If for a long time she refrained from active participation in the political suffrage movement it was merely because, as one suffrage leader expressed it, she "had too much else on her hands." However, the years directly preceding the war saw her entrance into the very center of the political fight for women's votes. Her campaigning for Theodore Roosevelt was partly in the interest of woman suffrage. In the following year she attended the Budapest convention of the International Woman Suffrage Alliance, members of which were later, through their combination of feminism and pacifism, to furnish her the immediate stimulus to the creation of the Woman's Peace Party.

---

[21] In a letter to the author Miss Emily G. Balch disagrees with this interpretation: " I think you exaggerate the passivity and determinism of her earlier belief. I think it was rather that the effort which she had always believed in suddenly became an ' emergent ' necessity in all haste."

But what is of greater interest to us for the present is the likelihood that for Miss Addams, as for many other American women, the woman suffrage movement had psychological and ideological connections with the later women's peace movement. Exclusion from the suffrage produced in some women a bitter sense of common injustice which, in turn, could scarcely but have led to a kind of sex clannishness. Moreover, the practical exigencies of the woman suffrage movement developed a policy of separate action by women. Finally, the ideology of the struggle for woman suffrage contained elements which were preeminently preparatory for feminist pacifism. Miss Addams' principal justification of woman suffrage appears in the following words written in 1911:

Life is full of hidden remedial powers which society has not yet utilized, but perhaps nowhere is the waste more flagrant than in the matured deductions and judgments of the women, who are constantly forced to share the social injustices which they have no recognized power to alter.[22]

This idea of the maturity of women's judgments, remedial and yet unutilized, led logically not merely to woman suffrage but also to a program of direct attack by women upon social problems in general, foremost of which was war.

It must also be noted that in the woman suffrage movement there were some whose proud feminism went far beyond asserting the intellectual maturity of women. An example is offered by the popularity just before the World War of the book *The Man-Made World,* the authoress of which, Charlotte Perkins Gilman, was to be one of the charter members of the Woman's Peace Party. Mrs. Gilman, perhaps the leading theorist of the extreme American feminist movement, took as her premise Lester F. Ward's gynocratic theory—the hypothesis that in racial evolution woman had originally been dominant and had been displaced from the dominance merely by a historical accident. She interpreted this theory to mean that man was congenitally inferior to woman in the characteristics making for social progress, and that consequently a man-made world was a regrettable deviation from the natural

[22] Jane Addams, *A New Conscience and an Ancient Evil,* p. 192.

course of evolution. Looking out upon the stupidities and evils of the world, she blamed virtually all of them upon an " androcentric culture." One of the evils which could only be interpreted in terms of masculine causation was warfare, to which she devoted a chapter of incisive feminist criticism. The criticism was directed not only against war but also against males:

> In warfare, *per se*, we find maleness in its absurdest extremes. Here is to be studied the whole gamut of basic masculinity, from the initial instinct of combat, through every form of glorious ostentation, with the loudest possible accompaniment of noise.[23]

That women occasionally use nails upon each other and regularly vie with each other in invidious even if peaceful ostentation was not mentioned by Mrs. Gilman, although doubtless she did not mean that women were without faults. In any event, it was the clear implication of her discussion that only through women, somehow free from the combative instinct, could our man-made militarism be eliminated.

It should be said that Miss Addams' feminism contained nothing suggestive of sex-antagonism or of depreciation of the male sex. Her demand for woman suffrage was based upon the usefulness to society of feminine potentialities as of all politically dormant human energies. It is equally true, however, that the necessity of arguing for woman's rights led Miss Addams as well as other suffragists to give much thought and stress to those specially developed feminine traits of intellect and moral sentiment which, even if they did not make women superior to men, at least gave them opportunity for a distinctive contribution to social reform. What is even more important, it was natural that the outbreak of the World War, the apparent result of the accumulating stupidities and sins of men as rulers, should bring the disillusionment of feminists with a man-run world to a climax. Would not the hope of eliminating war seem now to depend upon bringing into action, politically and otherwise, the special repugnance to war which since the days of Lysistrata had been the merit of the gentler sex?

---

[23] Charlotte Perkins Gilman, *The Man-Made World* . . . , p. 211.

Even in Miss Addams, certainly no man-hater, there is distinct evidence of this psychological development. Reviewing her lecture on peace in the fall of 1914 under the auspices of the Carnegie Endowment, Miss Addams herself underlines the feminist ideas which she used in her addresses. In referring to an address in September before a Boston woman's club, in which she compared warfare to human sacrifice, she writes:

We instanced the fact that at least once in the history of the world in response to their own sensitiveness, women had called a halt to the sacrifice of human life, although it then implied the abolition of a religious observance long believed to be right and necessary. In the history of one nation after another it was the mothers who first protested that their children should no longer be slain as living sacrifices upon the altars of the tribal gods, although priests and patriarchs contended that human sacrifice was bound up with all the traditions of religion and patriotism and could not be abolished without destroying both. The women led a revolt against the hideous practice which had dogged the human race for centuries, not because they were founding a new religion but because they rebelled against the destruction of their own children, the waste of the life they had nurtured. The patriarch who here and there gave heed to the pleading of the mother whose child had been set aside for sacrifice was the forerunner of the multitude who later discovered that national courage and religious zeal were on the side of those who urged the abolition of human sacrifice. There is no record that Sarah protested against the sacrifice of Isaac. Probably she knew nothing about it until the danger was safely past, but certainly Cly[te]mnestra did not tamely accept the sacrificial offering of her child, and the fate of Iphigenia disturbed Greece from one end to the other.[24]

From the idea that women tend to revolt against the sacrifice of human life it is not a far cry to that of the necessity of their separate action in pacifism. Yet neither in the foregoing address nor others of that fall did Miss Addams give any indication of contemplating a woman's peace movement. In all probability the device would not have occurred to her independently, for her policies in matters of social action did not tend towards any exclusiveness on the basis of sex. The impulse for the women's organization, Miss Addams herself attests, " came from Europe when, in the early winter of 1914, the great war was discussed from the public platform in the United States by two women, well-known suffragists and

---

[24] *The Second Twenty Years*, pp. 120-121.

publicists, who nationally represented opposing sides of the conflict." She further says:

> Mrs. Pethick-Lawrence of England first brought to American audiences a series of "War Aims" as defined by the League of Democratic Control,[25] in London, and Mde. Rosika Schwimmer, coming from Budapest, hoped to arouse American women to join their European sisters in a general protest against war. Occasionally they spoke from the same platform in a stirring indictment of "the common enemy of mankind." They were unwilling to leave the United States until they had organized at least a small group pledged to the advocacy of both objects; the discussion of reasonable terms of peace, and a protest against war as a method of settling international difficulties.[26]

The foregoing account requires amplification. Rosika Schwimmer (prominent in recent years for being denied American citizenship on the ground of her unwillingness to bear arms) was a Hungarian journalist, author, and social worker who had come into prominent relation with the international women's movement about 1904 when she addressed in Berlin the International Woman's Congress, which resulted in the formation of the International Woman Suffrage Alliance. Here she came into contact with Mrs. Carrie Chapman Catt, President of the Alliance, who was later to support the endeavor to form a women's peace movement in the United States. For some time after 1904 Mme. Schwimmer did her chief work in the woman suffrage movement, organizing this movement in her own country and in 1913 helping to organize the International Woman Suffrage Congress in Budapest, which Miss Addams attended. In 1914 Mme. Schwimmer was living in London, where she served as International Press Secretary of the International Woman Suffrage Alliance and as correspondent of several important European newspapers. A frequently noted episode in her dramatic career is her giving Lloyd George warning, at a breakfast with him on July 9, 1914, that the Sarajevo incident, " unless something were done immediately to satisfy and appease resentment . . . would certainly result in war with Serbia, with the incalculable consequence which such an operation might precipitate in

---

[25] The Union of Democratic Control.
[26] *Peace and Bread*, p. 6.

Europe." [27]   The words quoted are those of Lloyd George in
his *War Memoirs,* who indicates that Mme. Schwimmer was
the only person he met at that time who realized the imminence of a world war.

Upon the outbreak of war a few weeks following her warning, Mme. Schwimmer began to devote to the cause of peace
the same imaginativeness, energy, and emotionalism which she
had given to the suffrage movement. She was bestirred to
action by the conviction that " a war ended by militarists
meant a peace dictated by militarism, with new causes for
future conflict." [28]   She took a leading part in organizing
among European women's groups, especially of the International Woman Suffrage Alliance, a peace movement aiming to
bring pressure upon the neutral governments to induce action
in behalf of an early and enlightened peace. The main element in the plan of the women was the offer of mediation to
the belligerent governments by the United States and other
neutrals—Switzerland, The Netherlands, Sweden, Denmark,
Norway, and Spain. Other points in the program related to
the prevention of new wars and included the establishment of
a world parliament, a world court, and international non-military sanctions.[29]   By the latter part of August, women of
Great Britain, Germany, France, Russia, Austria-Hungary,
Italy, Switzerland, Denmark, Sweden, Norway, and Holland
had signed a petition in behalf of these objectives. One resolution in the petition provided:

That we urge the President of the United States to invite the neutral countries of Europe to send envoys to meet the delegates he will
appoint to carry the message of our nation, and that these envoys
shall unite in a demand upon the nations now at war that they
declare a cessation of hostilities until this message shall have been
delivered, being confident that this armistice would be the first step
toward permanent peace.[30]

The appeal of the women, reflecting such wishful confidence,
was immediately translated into a number of languages, circu-

---

[27] David Lloyd George, *War Memoirs,* I, 50.
[28] International Committee for World Peace Prize Award to Rosika
Schwimmer, *Rosika Schwimmer—World Patriot,* p. 2.
[29] *New York Times,* September 19, 1914.
[30] " Women and War," *Outlook* (1915), CIX, 676.

lated internationally, and endorsed by prominent women's organizations and individuals all over the world.

Mme. Schwimmer was appointed to take the petition to President Wilson, as well as to enlist the support of American women in the international women's pacifist movement. Arriving in this country on September 6, Mme. Schwimmer immediately attracted wide attention by announcement of her intention of asking the President to take more active steps for mediation.[31]   In company with Mrs. Carrie Chapman Catt, she first interviewed Secretary Bryan.   On September 18, again in the company of Mrs. Catt, she was presented by Senator Thomas to President Wilson.   On the following day, the *New York Times* carried an interview with Mme. Schwimmer, who was presented dramatically as the bearer to the President of an appeal from a million women of thirteen countries.   Mme. Schwimmer said of her visit to Wilson:

The President told me he was thinking day and night about the possibility of peace in Europe.   He seemed to be deeply interested in the movement and said that he would lose no opportunity of taking practical steps to end the war.[32]

The first part of her mission dispatched, Mme. Schwimmer turned to the second—the enlistment of American women in a world-wide protest of women against war and a demand for international institutions which would not permit the catastrophe to recur.   She went about the country speaking before women's clubs or groups called together for the occasion.   The dramatic quality in her mission, the apparent blessing given it by President Wilson, and the general revulsion of American women from the European mass slaughter all set the stage in her favor.   Personally Mme. Schwimmer had the qualities to take advantage of her opportunity—a dynamic personality, forcefulness as a speaker, and a sense for the emotional appeals most effective with women audiences.   That her ideas were often extremely quixotic was apparently overlooked in view of the worthiness of her purpose.   Indeed, when these ideas were most venturesome they succeeded best

---

[31] *New York Times*, September 6, 1914.
[32] *New York Times*, September 19, 1914.

in gaining for her the press attention that was essential to her venture. On one occasion this prophetess of the World War made a conditional prophesy that was featured in the *New York Times*. It was the statement, made on December 7 before a meeting of rabbis and Jewish women in New York, that if the belligerent governments were given only a week to " get sober " and think, they would stop fighting. In accordance with the usual function of the sex in relation to men, women were to make the governments sober. In Europe, Mme. Schwimmer declared, the women were already " united to resist the command to fight." Explaining this firm union of women, the Hungarian used an idea which was fast becoming a cliché of contemporary feminist pacifism: " We are united by the motherhood instinct and by the knowledge that the terrible waste of life is unnecessary." [33]

The statement that European women were united against war was a very bold generalization, but American women were the more disposed to believe it since not Mme. Schwimmer alone but a second European visitor as well was telling them the same thing. Mrs. Emmeline Pethick-Lawrence, the other European woman mentioned by Miss Addams in relating the origin of the Woman's Peace Party, was in general talking along the same lines as Mme. Schwimmer and no less effectively. Her background was as dramatic as the Hungarian visitor's, though not in all respects as pacific. Mrs. Pethick-Lawrence, the wife of a well-known British scholar, had worked with Mrs. Emmeline Pankhurst as one of the leaders of the militant group of English suffragists. Together with Mrs. Pankhurst, she had incurred imprisonment for the use of violence, but in the summer of 1914 she announced her split with Mrs. Pankhurst and the methods of the latter. This split was convenient for her later career, although American critics were to point to her past in arguing that her disclaimer of violence was insincere. After the outbreak of the war Mrs. Pethick-Lawrence took up the cause of peace with as much vehemence, even if not violence, as she had formerly devoted to woman suffrage. The latter ideal, how-

---

[33] *New York Times*, December 8, 1917.

ever, was by no means dropped, but it was presented as one
of the major prerequisites of world peace and as always
having implied peace in its principle of "the solidarity of
women." [34] Mrs. Pethick-Lawrence's pacifism, however, was
influenced not merely by the ideology of the woman suffrage
movement but also by the platform of the Union of Democratic Control, an organization formed by English liberals
and socialists "to ensure a permanent peace at the close of
war." [35] Its principles included the self-determination of
peoples, parliamentary control over foreign relations, an international council with machinery for securing international
agreements in the interest of peace, reduction of armaments,
and international control of their manufacture and export.
To these objectives Mrs. Pethick-Lawrence added some of her
own, including not only woman suffrage but also direct participation of women in international adjustments.   Her
amalgamation of feminism and internationalist pacifism resulted in the project of a world movement of women similar
to Mme. Schwimmer's save that the greater emphasis was not
upon early termination of the war but rather upon a program
for a constructive peace.   In October 1914 she received an
opportunity to further such a movement in the United States,
which she conceived as the land of promise for both feminists
and pacifists, by virtue of an invitation to inaugurate a new
suffrage campaign in this country. "It seemed," Mrs. Pethick-Lawrence writes, "to offer an opportunity for enlisting
the support of the suffrage movement in the neutral country
of America for the idea of a world peace secured by negotiation, and therefore just to all." [36]

While at a disadvantage beside Mme. Schwimmer in not
bearing a petition attesting the support of millions of women,
Mrs. Pethick-Lawrence had distinct qualifications for her
proselytizing task. She was good-looking, high-spirited, and
eloquent; furthermore, she had a name which was better

---

[34] Emmeline Pethick-Lawrence, *My Part in a Changing World*,
p. 307.

[35] *The International Peace Year-Book, 1915*, ed. Carl Heath, pp.
82-83.

[36] Pethick-Lawrence, p. 308.

known to American women than Mme. Schwimmer's and a
nationality which was more impressive to them. Immediately
upon her arrival in New York on October 27, the suffrage
leader was taken under the wing of such prominent American
women as Lillian D. Wald and Alice Lewisohn. The day
after her arrival she declared in an interview that "if we are
going to accept war as inevitable women might just as well
give up living at once, for under those circumstances it is not
worth while to continue the race." She had come to the
United States, she said, because in this country there existed
freedom from tradition, a mingling of nationalities, and consideration for woman's point of view—all of them things
which gave one hope even in the present terrible crisis.[37] In
her first address in this country, which was at a mass-meeting
of the Women's Political Union of New York on October 31,
she introduced the idea of rallying the suffrage movement to
the cause of peace. After the New York address Mrs.
Pethick-Lawrence entered upon a lecture tour—at times she
and Mme. Schwimmer spoke from the same platform.

The Englishwoman had a single but very broad theme,
"Woman and War"—the effects of war upon women and the
effects which women might have upon war. Upon this theme
she not merely talked but wrote. In the fall of 1914 one of
her articles was published in the *Survey* and another in a
more popular magazine, *Harper's Weekly*. Both articles were
good examples of the mixture of feminism and pacifism with
which numerous American women were being indoctrinated.
The article in *Harper's* stressed the former element, arguing
for woman suffrage as essential to peace:

It is vital to the deepest interests of the human race that the mother
half of humanity should now be admitted into the ranks of the articulate democracies of the world, in order to strengthen them and enable
them to combine the more effectively in their own defense against
the deadly machinery of organized destruction that threatens in the
future to crush the white races and to overwhelm civilization.

Woman suffrage was said to be essential to peace because "the
bed-rock of humanity is motherhood." In contrast with men,
creatures of conflicting interests, women all over the world

---

[37] Newark *Evening News*, October 29, 1914.

3

had but one passion—the creation and expression of life. It was this common passion which produced in women a solidarity against the destruction of the blossoming manhood of the race.[38]

The article in the *Survey* was primarily a plea for a general program for a constructive peace. It emphasized, however, the special duty of women to peace which arose from their peculiar revulsion from war. Women, it was said, might well stand aghast at the contemporary spectacle of ruin in Europe, for they had no responsibility for the cataclysm. It was solely the doing of male government, which had disregarded the warnings of women and had arrogantly denied them the vote. "Today," the feminist proclaimed, "it is for men to stand down and for the women whom they have belittled to take the seat of judgment." Women were to demand "a new peace, expressing the birth of a new spirit." The elements of this new peace, as conceived by Mrs. Pethick-Lawrence, included first of all the bestowal of representation in the government of nations upon the "mother-half" of the human race. The rest of the program was in most respects similar to that of the Union of Democratic Control—adequate international machinery for ensuring democratic control of foreign policy, legislative ratification of all treaties and alliances, nationalization of the manufacture of armaments and prohibition of the export of ammunition, insistence that the present war should end war, the principle of self-determination and plebiscites in the peace settlement, an international agreement to apply sanctions to aggressors, and the formation of a European Senate for the discussion of international concerns. As a feminist, Mrs. Pethick-Lawrence called for two additional objectives—the sharing of women in any plebiscites to determine the disposition of territories, and the sending of women as well as men to the Hague Conference.

The most striking words in the article were those which set forth the immediate task of the women in striving for the above aims:

---

[38] Pethick-Lawrence, "Motherhood and War," *Harper's Weekly* (1914), LIX, 542.

I believe a great campaign for organizing public opinion and bringing its pressure to bear upon the governments of the world, could be initiated now by the woman's movement in America and carried through the length and breadth of the United States. Women of the neutral European states, women of England and Ireland, to say nothing of women of the other belligerent nations, would fall into line. A world-wide movement for constructive and creative peace such as the world has never yet seen might even now come into being—a movement which would influence the immediate development of humanity.[39]

The previous successes of her own addresses and contacts gave the Englishwoman some justification for her belief that such a movement could be launched among American women. In the article quoted she pointed out that the campaign in its behalf had already been started in Boston and Philadelphia. The movement, though it had no formal character with a national center, was referred to sometimes as the " Women's Movement for Constructive Peace." [40]   Largely as a result of Mrs. Pethick-Lawrence's efforts in New York City, Crystal Eastman, sister of the radical Max Eastman, formed a committee that called itself the Woman's Peace Party of New York.[41] But Mrs. Pethick-Lawrence's greatest organizational success was in Chicago in December. After she spoke in that city a small committee was organized to see what could be done with her program, and this committee called together leaders of various peace, civic, and professional organizations of the local area. The result was the formation of the Chicago Emergency Federation of Peace Forces, with Jane Addams as its chairman. The Federation adopted a tentative program which on the whole was in line with the ideas that Mrs. Pethick-Lawrence was espousing. Its general object was said to be the organization of all peace forces and the bringing of their pressure to bear upon public opinion and the governments of the world. Its specific ends included an effort to secure a cessation of hostilities through action by neutral powers, the establishment of a concert of nations (the immediate nucleus of which would be a league of neutral nations),

---

[39] Ibid, " Union of Women for Constructive Peace," Survey (1914), XXXIII, 230.

[40] George W. Nasmyth, " Constructive Mediation . . . ," ibid., p. 617.

[41] Pethick-Lawrence, p. 309.

principles of justice and democracy in the peace settlement and international relations generally, and woman suffrage.[42]

By the end of 1914 the ground had been laid for an endeavor to give peace groups, new and old, cohesion in a national movement. Only the prestige and organizational talent of leaders of American women were still needed.

Mrs. Carrie Chapman Catt, who had associated herself with Mme. Schwimmer's early visit to President Wilson, was the American woman who now took the initiative. She was the leader of the American woman suffrage movement. Hitherto she had not been particularly active in the peace movement, but perhaps for the same reason that Miss Addams had long been somewhat inactive in relation to the suffrage movement —that there had been too much else to do. The messages of the two European visitors had impressed upon the American leader that the doctrines of pacifism and of feminism were organically related. Probably, too, she was aware of the possibility of gaining new adherents to woman suffrage by sponsoring a program which linked equal suffrage with the then dominant interest of pacifism. Thus Mrs. Catt decided in December to promote a national conference of women's organizations to give organizational embodiment to the ideals and program that Mme. Schwimmer and Mrs. Pethick-Lawrence had been advocating.[43] She needed, however, an ally— some woman who had been particularly prominent in the peace movement but who at the same time commanded recognition in the women's movement generally, and even more important, in the nation as a whole. There was one woman who answered preeminently to these qualifications. This was Jane Addams, who was already associated with Mrs. Catt in the suffrage movement. Mrs. Catt invited Miss Addams to join her in sending informal invitations to all the national women's organizations which had standing peace committees to send delegates to a congress of women at Washington on January 10 and 11.

---

[42] "National Efforts Crystallizing for Peace," *Survey* (1915), XXXIII, 393-394.

[43] Mrs. Catt's place in the Woman's Peace Party became secondary to that of Miss Addams after the formation of the organization. Eventually she left the movement. See below, pp. 188-189.

Miss Addams, apart from her inveterate reluctance to decline assistance to any movement for peace, was particularly receptive at this time to such an undertaking. As was evident from an editorial which she had just written for the *Ladies' Home Journal*,[44] she was concerned then to show her belief that the peace movement did not need to confess to failure but rather to become more active. Greater activity in the peace movement had, in her recent thinking, identified itself particularly with the idea of greater participation in pacifist effort by women, the traditional humanitarians. She was doubtless familiar with the assertion of John Ruskin that women could stop all wars if they were only determined to do so.[45] It was probably with high hopes that Miss Addams viewed the venture of bringing about this determination. She could not have foreseen all the trials that lay ahead on this path—trials which included even the temporary loss of her own high place in national esteem. Joining in the summons to the leaders of American women, she took the first step on a new road to peace.

---

[44] Jane Addams, "Is the Peace Movement a Failure?" *Ladies' Home Journal* (November, 1914), p. 5.

[45] "I tell you . . . that at whatever moment you choose to put a period to war, you could do it with less trouble than you take any day to go out to dinner." "War," in *The Crown of Olives*.

CHAPTER II

An Offspring of Women's Ideals

On the afternoon of January 10, 1915, the Grand Ballroom of the New Willard Hotel at Washington, D. C., generally the scene of elegant frivolity, presented an unusual spectacle. About three thousand women, far from frivolous in either dress or countenance, crowded into it while hundreds were turned away. Their purpose was not enjoyment, but the earnest consideration of a great tragedy—the World War. Some eighty-six were delegates, representatives of many thousands, who had come in response to the invitation of Miss Addams and Mrs. Catt to form a woman's peace party. The size of both the official and unofficial attendance at the conference signalized the success of the first step in the venture.

The Washington Peace Association, a society which had been formed in the fall of 1914, had made the detailed arrangements for the meeting and acted as hostess to the assembly. The opening of the conference had been preceded by meetings of a platform committee, consisting, in addition to Miss Addams and Mrs. Catt, of Mrs. Fannie Fern Andrews, Mrs. Lucia Ames Mead, Mrs. Louis F. Post, and Mrs. Anna Garlin Spencer.[1] Mrs. Andrews, a veteran worker in the American peace movement, as already noted, was at the time secretary of the American School Peace League and a director of the American Peace Society; Mrs. Mead was a lecturer and writer on peace and internationalism; Mrs. Post was a vice-president of the American Anti-Imperialist League and former managing editor of the *Public*; and Mrs. Anna Garlin Spencer was professor of ethics and sociology at Meadville Theological College. The platform committee framed a brief statement of eleven principles which were to be presented to the conference for its approval. Unfortunately there are available no records of the discussions which led to the framing of this platform for the proposed society. The platform itself indicates,

---

[1] *Year Book of the Woman's Peace Party, 1916*, p. 41.

however, that the committee drew upon the ideas not merely of Mrs. Pethick-Lawrence and Mme. Schwimmer, but also of a number of contemporary peace societies and pacifist thinkers.

At any rate there had been considerable eclecticism in the choice of the members of the proposed organization. While all the delegates were women and nearly all were suffragists, they displayed the greatest heterogeneity in respect to the organizations represented. Most of the groups, indeed, were established peace societies—the American Peace Society, the American Peace and Arbitration League, the American School Peace League, the American Association for International Conciliation, the World Peace Foundation, the Massachusetts Peace Society, the Connecticut Peace Society, and the Philadelphia Peace Association of Friends. But there were numerous other types of organizations, devoted to peace only coincidently with other aims. As was to be expected from the rôle played by Mrs. Catt, delegates were sent by the two great suffrage organizations of the country—the National American Women's Suffrage Association and the Federal Suffrage Association. Representatives were also sent from the quite different quarter of the women's temperance societies—the National Women's Christian Temperance Union, the Colorado Women's Christian Temperance Union, and the District of Columbia Women's Christian Temperance Union. Further, delegates were present from educational organizations largely composed of women—the National League of Teachers' Associations, the International Kindergarten Union, and the Association of Collegiate Alumnae. Social workers' associations had their quota—the National Federation of Settlements and the Vital Conservation Association. A hue of economic liberalism was contributed to the motley group by the National Women's Trade Union League and the Woman's National Committee of the Socialist Party. At the same time there were represented such conservative organizations as the General Federation of Women's Clubs and the National Council of Women. Perhaps the most surprising participants in the conference in the light of their later attitudes were the National Society of the Daughters of the American Revolution and the Maryland Daughters of the American Revolution. One might say that the foregoing list represented the major part of American women as organized for reformist and cultural purposes. Pacifism provided a common ground upon which could meet American women from almost every important section of their organizational life.[2]

For a day and a half the assembled delegates discussed the principles and organization of the society which was to spring from this common ground. Mrs. Catt presided at the Sunday afternoon mass-meeting, and Miss Janet E. Richards, well-known parliamentarian, at the business sessions. The most important action of the conference was the adoption of a platform. The conference adopted the items of the platform in many cases by majority, and still more often, by unanimous vote. Such ease in securing agreement was evidently due largely to the fact that the delegates were resolved to disregard differences with respect to details of method for the sake of a united front of women in their protest against war.[3]

The platform adopted for the new organization was accompanied by a preamble, written by Mrs. Anna Garlin Spencer. Women are frequently prolix, but the following document is a model of brevity for party platforms:

WE, WOMEN OF THE UNITED STATES, assembled in behalf of World Peace, grateful for the security of our own country, but sorrowing for the misery of all involved in the present struggle among warring nations, do hereby band ourselves together to demand that war be abolished.

Equally with men pacifists, we understand that planned-for, legalized, wholesale, human slaughter is today the sum of all villainies.

As women, we feel a peculiar moral passion of revolt against both the cruelty and the waste of war.

As women, we are especially the custodian of the life of the ages. We will not longer consent to its reckless destruction.

As women, we are particularly charged with the future of childhood and with the care of the helpless and the unfortunate. We will not longer endure without protest that added burden of maimed and

---

[2] List of Charter Members of the Woman's Peace Party, MS, Jane Addams Peace Collection, Friends Historical Library, Swarthmore College.

[3] There are no records of the actual deliberations.

invalid men and poverty-stricken widows and orphans which war places upon us.

As women, we have builded by the patient drudgery of the past the basic foundation of the home and of peaceful industry. We will not longer endure without a protest that must be heard and heeded by men, that hoary evil which in an hour destroys the social structure that centuries of toil have reared.

As women, we are called upon to start each generation onward toward a better humanity. We will not longer tolerate without determined opposition that denial of the sovereignty of reason and justice by which war and all that makes for war today render impotent the idealism of the race.

Therefore, as human beings and the mother half of humanity, we demand that our right to be consulted in the settlement of questions concerning not alone the life of individuals but of nations be recognized and respected.

We demand that women be given a share in deciding between war and peace in all the courts of high debate—within the home, the school, the church, the industrial order, and the state.

So protesting, and so demanding, we hereby form ourselves into a national organization to be called the Woman's Peace Party.

We hereby adopt the following as our platform of principles, some of the items of which have been accepted by a majority vote, and more of which have been the unanimous choice of those attending the conference that initiated the formation of this organization. We have sunk all differences of opinion on minor matters and given freedom of expression to a wide divergence of opinion in the details of our platform and in our statement of explanation and information, in a common desire to make our woman's protest against war and all that makes for war, vocal, commanding and effective. We welcome to our membership all who are in substantial sympathy with that fundamental purpose of our organization, whether or not they can accept in full our detailed statement of principles.

PLATFORM

THE PURPOSE of this Organization is to enlist all American women in arousing the nations to respect the sacredness of human life and to abolish war. The following is adopted as our platform:

1. The immediate calling of a convention of neutral nations in the interest of early peace.

2. Limitation of armaments and the nationalization of their manufacture.

3. Organized opposition to militarism in our own country.

4. Education of youth in the ideals of peace.

5. Democratic control of foreign policies.

6. The further humanizing of governments by the extension of the franchise to women.

7. " Concert of Nations " to supersede " Balance of Power."

8. Action toward the gradual organization of the world to substitute Law for War.

9. The substitution of an international police for rival armies and navies.

10. Removal of the economic causes of war.

11. The appointment by our Government of a commission of men and women, with an adequate appropriation, to promote international peace.[4]

The foregoing is clearer than the great run of party platforms, yet there are certain phases of it which perhaps require annotation. The first point needing further explanation is the precise meaning of " the abolition of war," the general purpose of the organization. To the believer in the Kellogg Pact the outlawry of war means merely the abolition of aggressive war. But to these women the ideal of peace meant something much more. The abolition of war meant the elimination of all war in the present sense of the word—that is, of hostilities, whether offensive or defensive, conducted by a particular nation as such. In place of national defensive action the women proposed an international police force. Many of the group inclined towards the absolute pacificism suggested by the phrase, " to respect the sacredness of human life." That Miss Addams regarded " the sacredness of human life " as an absolute value is evident from an incident which occurred eleven months later, the famous Ballinger Baby Case. Miss Addams, making a public statement condemning the physician who refused to prolong the life of an extremely defective infant, insisted that " life can be taken away only by the One who gave it and should be prolonged at any cost." [5] To revert to the Woman's Peace Party, it was later to substitute economic and moral pressure for even the international use of armed force.[6] At this time, however, the group considered it either unjustifiable or impolitic to take so extreme a position.

The main burden of the preamble, however, is not the iniquity of war, which is assumed to be obvious to men and women of good will alike, but the justification of a separate women's peace movement. This is explained in general as the expression of woman's " peculiar moral passion of revolt

---

[4] Woman's Peace Party, *Preamble and Platform Adopted at Washington, January 10, 1915.*
[5] Quoted by Wilbur Marshall Urban in *Fundamentals of Ethics,* pp. 42-43.
[6] See below, p. 159.

against both the cruelty and the waste of war "—a thesis which had been impressed upon American women by Mrs. Pethick-Lawrence and Mme. Schwimmer. Ensuing ideas were statements of the reasons why women especially revolted against war. There were two principal reasons: that women as mothers were the "custodians of the life of the ages," charged not only with the future of childhood but also with the care of the helpless and unfortunate victims of war; and that women had built by their patient drudgery the basic foundation of the home and of peaceful industry. A women's peace movement was, however, implicitly related also to the fact that women, in their struggle against war, were led to demand at the same time a share in the settlement of questions concerning the life of both individuals and nations. This general demand was itemized by reference to the adjudications not only of the state but also of the home, the school, the church, and the industrial order; thus not merely woman suffrage but woman's rights in general were objectives. The Woman's Peace Party was, in sum, formed because women had both peculiar grounds of protest against war and peculiar social and political limitations upon their struggle against war.

Of the platform little need be said at this point, since it was merely an abbreviation of a full program, much clearer in meaning, which will be set forth and discussed shortly. In adopting so brief a statement of objectives for their chief medium of propaganda the women were carrying out their declared intention of emphasizing their protest against war and of welcoming to their membership all who were in substantial sympathy with that fundamental purpose whether or not they could accept in full the Party's detailed statement of principles. It is noteworthy that the planks of the platform are all, with one exception, directly related to the elimination of war. The exception is woman suffrage, which appeared to the women a major prerequisite of peace even though related to its promotion only indirectly. Another striking trait of the platform is that, while its first plank is devoted to immediate action in behalf of peace, most of it is concerned with the building up of permanent national and international institutions designed to make war impossible in the future. The institutions suggested, while inclusive of traditional peace ideas such as the replacement of war by law, are distinguished on the whole by their departure from pre-war formulae for world peace and by their orientation toward the ideal of a radically new world order.

The detailed principles of the Woman's Peace Party appeared in a " Program for Constructive Peace," which was also adopted at the January meeting. The program was prefaced by the statement that the Party adopted it in the belief that " such principles must find acceptance among peoples and governments to ensure the future peace of the world, and to this end recommends a nation-wide discussion of them." Because of its importance in the history of the organization, the program is to be considered in full:

PROGRAM FOR CONSTRUCTIVE PEACE

I. To SECURE THE CESSATION OF HOSTILITIES:

1. We urge our government to call a conference of representative delegates from the neutral nations to discuss possible measures to lessen their own injuries, to hasten the cessation of hostilities, and to prevent warfare in the future.

2. In case an official conference of the kind named above proves impossible or impracticable, we pledge ourselves to work toward the summoning of an unofficial conference of the pacifists of the world to consider points named.

II. To INSURE SUCH TERMS OF SETTLEMENT AS WILL PREVENT THIS WAR FROM BEING BUT THE PRELUDE TO NEW WARS:

1. No province should be transferred as a result of conquest from one government to another against the will of the people. Whenever possible, the desire of a province for autonomy should be respected.

2. No war indemnities should be assessed save when recognized international law has been violated.

3. No treaty alliance or other international arrangement should be entered upon by any nation unless ratified by the representatives of the people. Adequate measures for assuring democratic control of foreign policy should be adopted by all nations.

III. To PLACE THE FUTURE PEACE OF THE WORLD UPON SECURER FOUNDATIONS:

1. Foreign policies of nations should not be aimed at creating alliances for the purpose of maintaining the " *balance of*

power," but should be directed to the establishment of a
" *Concert of Nations,*" with

(a) *A court, or courts,* for the settlement of all disputes
between nations;

(b) An *international congress,* with legislative and administrative powers over international affairs, and with
permanent committees in place of present secret
diplomacy;

(c) An *international police force.*

2. As an immediate step in this direction, a permanent League
of Neutral Nations ("League of Peace") should be
formed, whose members should bind themselves to settle
all difficulties arising between them by arbitration, judicial, or legislative procedure, and who should create an
international police force for mutual protection against
attack.

3. *National disarmament* should be effected in the following
manner: It should be contingent upon the adoption of
this peace program by a sufficient number of nations, or by
nations of sufficient power to insure protection to those
disarmed. It should be graduated in each nation to the
degree of disarmament effected in the other nations, and
progressively reduced until finally complete.

4. Pending general disarmament, all manufactories of arms,
ammunitions and munitions for use in war should hereafter be national property.

5. The *protection of private property at sea,* of neutral commerce and of communications should be secured by the
neutralization of the seas and of such maritime trade
routes as the British Channel, the Dardanelles, Panama,
Suez, the Straits of Gibraltar, etc.

6. National and international action should be secured to remove the *economic causes of war.*

7. The democracies of the world should be extended and reinforced by general application of the principle of self-
government, including the extension of *suffrage to women.*

IV. IMMMEDIATE NATIONAL PROGRAM FOR THE UNITED STATES:

1. We approve the Peace Commission Treaties which our country has negotiated with thirty nations, stipulating delay
and investigation for the period of a year before any
declaration of war can take place. We express the hope
that all other countries will be included.

2. We protest against the increase of armaments by the United
States. We insist that the increase of the army and navy
at this time, so far from being in the interest of peace,
is a direct threat to the well-being of other nations with
whom we have dealings, an imputation of doubt of their
good faith, and calculated to compel them in turn to increase their armies, and in consequence to involve us in an
ever-intensifying race for military supremacy.

3. We recommend to the President and Government of the
United States that a commission of men and women be
created, with an adequate appropriation, whose duty shall

> be to work for the prevention of war and the formulation
> of the most compelling and practical methods of world
> organization.[7]

In this platform, the proposals which were of greatest
immediate importance to the organization were those designed
to secure the cessation of hostilities. Of the two proposals
so designed the first received the greater stress and engaged
much effort of the women through the first year of the Party's
history. The plan was, perhaps, the most interesting and
ingenious in the entire program; indeed it is difficult to find
precedent for it in traditional thought on international relations. It was known as a plan for " continuous mediation "
in view of the fact that the conference of neutrals was to
continue through the war to receive, consider, and present
proposals which might be a basis for successful mediation.
The " representative delegates " referred to in the program
were to be official only in the sense that governments appointed them. In reality they were, to quote Miss Addams,
" an International Commission of Experts . . . with scientific but no diplomatic function," appointed merely to " explore
the issues involved in the struggle in order to make proposals to the belligerents in a spirit of constructive internationalism." [8]

The idea of a conference of neutrals offering mediation
had been outlined by Rosika Schwimmer in the first month of
the war, but the details of the plan were developed later by
Julia Grace Wales, instructor in English at the University of
Wisconsin. Miss Wales wrote a pamphlet in the fall of 1914
entitled " International Plan for Continuous Mediation without Armistice." It defined the plan as providing for an
International Commission of Experts, to sit as long as the war
continued, with scientific function but without power to commit their governments. This commission was to undertake to
explore the issues involved in the war, to make propositions to
the belligerents in the light of this study and in the spirit of a

---

[7] Woman's Peace Party, *Program for Constructive Peace, January
10, 1915.*
[8] *Peace and Bread,* p. 8.

constructive internationalism, and, if the first effort failed, to
revise their original propositions and offer new ones until
some practicable basis for actual peace negotiation was found.
The following arguments were presented by Miss Wales for
the plan: that "humanity should be able to find some method
of avoiding prolonged wholesale destruction"; that on both
sides there were people who desired a right settlement; that
the only way to straighten the tangle was to employ the device
of placing conditional proposals ("will you—if the rest
will?") before the belligerents; that to place sane standing
proposals before the nations would tend to ripen the time for
peace; that delay was dangerous because it strengthened bitterness, the desire for revenge, and the power of the military in
all countries; and that the creation of "a world thinking
organ" at this juncture would open the possibility of establishing upon a deposed militarism the beginnings of world
federation.[9]

Before the formation of the Woman's Peace Party, Miss
Wales had submitted her plan to the Wisconsin Legislature.
The legislature had approved the plan and already sent it to
Congress with recommendation of its adoption.[10] Miss Wales
attended the meeting called to form the Woman's Peace Party
and presented her plan to the convention. Having been made
by the platform committee the first plank in its program,
"continuous mediation" was adopted as such by the Party.

The second plank, which called for a conference of the
pacifists of the world acting on their own initiative, was a
substitute in case governments should not adopt the commission's plan. The second idea was actually carried out within a
few months by an international congress of women which met
at The Hague, but in January the women had no foreknowl-
edge of their participation in that venture. Ultimately this
plank was also to influence many of the women in their support of the Ford project of a conference of neutrals.

---

[9] Julia Grace Wales, *International Plan for Continuous Mediation
without Armistice* (condensed statement). Pamphlet of Woman's
Peace Party.
[10] New York *World*, April 25, 1915.

Aside from the plan for continuous mediation, which had been advanced previously by individual pacifist writers, the program probably contained no proposal which had not already figured in the program of some other contemporary organization. Most of the proposals had in fact been incorporated into the platforms of a number of other groups. This fact was made manifest in the March 6 number of the *Survey,* which contained an article by George W. Nasmyth, director of the World Peace Foundation, analyzing the peace programs of ten leading European and American groups.[11] His comparison of the proposals with regard to the main issues of foreign policy and international organization led him to the conclusion that there was " a remarkable unanimity of the public opinion of all the countries represented, on the most essential points." [12] The programs considered were those of the Union of Democratic Control, the South German Social-Democrats, the American Socialist Party, the International Peace Bureau, the Chicago Emergency Federation of Peace Forces, the Dutch Anti-War Council, the World Peace Foundation, the New York Peace Society, the League of Peace (sponsored by the editor of the *Independent,* Hamilton Holt), and the Woman's Peace Party. The project of a concert of powers to replace the old theory of the balance of power as a method of preserving peace appeared in some form in all the programs. Nearly all of them called for reduction of armaments, an international police, consent of the population to the transfer of territories, and the democratic control of foreign policy. Other planks of the Woman's Peace Party appeared on one or several of the other programs. Thus woman suffrage was demanded by the American Socialist Party and the Chicago Emergency Federation of Peace Forces; removal of economic causes of war was a plank not only of these two groups but also of the Dutch Anti-War Council and the World Peace Foundation; the prohibition of war indemnities was advocated by the South German Social-Democrats, the Ameri-

---

[11] Nasmyth, " Constructive Mediation . . . ," *Survey* (1915), XXXIII, 616-620.
[12] *Ibid.*, p. 617.

can Socialist Party and the Chicago Emergency Federation;
the neutralization of seas, together with international owner-
ship and control of strategic waterways, figured in the
platform of the American Socialist Party. Even the conference of neutrals to offer mediation had been prefigured,
though without reference to continuous mediation, in the
platform of the Chicago Emergency Federation of Peace
Forces.

That the program of the Woman's Peace Party was not
novel was obvious to none more than to the leaders of the
organization itself. They emphasized their indebtedness not
only to Mme. Schwimmer, Mrs. Pethick-Lawrence, and Miss
Wales but also to the Union of Democratic Control. Moreover, the leader of the Woman's Peace Party had helped to
organize the Chicago Emergency Federation of Peace Forces
and had supported the incorporation in its program of most
of the objectives which were to form the program of the
Woman's Peace Party a month later.

Miss Addams did say in her book *Peace and Bread* that at
the time the program of the Woman's Peace Party was
" somewhat startling." [13] This statement, which was not a
claim for novelty, was justified. For the similar programs
of other organizations, though adopted before that of the
Woman's Peace Party, had not long antedated the latter but
had themselves been largely suggested by the experiences of
the World War. Moreover, with the exception of the Chicago
Emergency Federation of Peace Forces, which Miss Addams
headed, the groups which anticipated much of the program
of the Woman's Peace Party were European. With the one
exception mentioned, the Woman's Peace Party stood out
among American groups for the breadth and relative novelty
of its platform. Earlier and more fully than any other
national American organization it foreshadowed the international program which President Wilson was to advance in
his later development.[14] It is a preeminent illustration of the

---

[13] *Peace and Bread*, p. 8.
[14] For further discussion of this point see below, pp. 179-180.

4

truth of Professor Curti's observation that the peace societies paved the way for Wilson's international program.[15]

The women at the very outset determined upon ambitious efforts to promote the translation of their program into reality. A committee on plan of action, whose report was adopted, made a number of recommendations which promised vigorous activity to secure notice and favor for the program in both governmental circles and public opinion. With a view to the former, it was decided that the platform should be presented to all the embassies in Washington and that the organization should form both a national legislative committee and local legislative committees. Further, approval was given to the recently introduced Crosser bill, which called for government manufacture of military and naval equipment and forbade the export of privately produced munitions of war. The activities decided upon to influence public opinion were the following: the holding of mass meetings throughout the country, preferably simultaneously, to discuss the society's program; the promotion of peace propaganda through collaboration with existing organizations and through work in the public schools; and cooperation both with the press and with artists as a means to effective publicity. The last policy was first to be put into effect by the arranging for a production of Euripides' "Trojan Women" throughout the country. Finally, the conference resolved to send a commission abroad to study the effects of war on women.[16]

The only question which was not taken up with thoroughness was that which is usually primary at initial meetings— the form of the new society. Its organization was purposely left elastic, pending the careful consideration of a constitution. However, Mrs. Catt submitted a report in behalf of an organization committee, and in accordance with this certain tentative provisions were decided upon. The officers of the Party were to be a Chairman, a Secretary, a Treasurer and four Vice-chairmen, who together formed an Executive

---

[15] Merle Eugene Curti, *Peace or War; the American Struggle, 1636-1936*, p. 240.

[16] "A Woman's Party Full Pledged for Action," *Survey* (1915), XXXIII, 433-434.

Council. All these were elected at the annual meeting except the Secretary and Treasurer, who were to be appointed by the Chairman. The Executive Council was to appoint a Co-operating Council and Chairmen of States, the latter in turn to appoint Chairmen of their respective congressional districts. Members were to be of two categories: local groups wherever they could be organized, each to pay $5.00 annually to the National Treasury; and sustaining members, who individually were to pay $1.00 annually. National headquarters were to be established in Chicago. This selection was made as a matter of convenience for Miss Addams, who, despite her reluctance to undertake further duties, was elected national chairman. The other officers elected were Mrs. Anna Garlin Spencer, Mrs. Henry Villard, Mrs. Louis F. Post, and Mrs. John Jay White, as Vice-Chairmen and members of the executive board.[17]

On the last day of the conference, in connection with the Sunday mass-meeting, addresses were made by a number of women—Miss Addams, Mrs. Kate Waller Barrett, Mrs. Harriet Stanton Blatch, Mrs. Charlotte Perkins Gilman, Mrs. Pethick-Lawrence, Miss Janet E. Richards, Dr. Anna Howard Shaw, and Mme. Schwimmer. Some of the speakers brought into particularly sharp relief the purposes and attitudes that had led to the creation of the Woman's Peace Party. Thus Mrs. Catt touched upon the disillusionment of the women with the established pacifists:

The women of the country were lulled into inattention to the great military question of the war by reading the many books put forth by great pacifists who had studied the question deeply and who announced that there would never be another war. But when the great war came, and the women waited for the pacifists to move, and they heard nothing from them, they decided all too late to get together themselves and to try to do something at this eleventh hour.[18]

Mrs. Catt declared that the objective of the group was the formation not merely of a national but probably also of an international organization among women. This statement is

---

[17] Cited in *Woman's Peace Party Preamble and Platform.* Pamphlet of 1915.

[18] *Addresses Given at the Organization Conference of the Woman's Peace Party, Washington, D. C., January 10, 1915,* p. 4.

interesting for it shows that the international affiliation which later became so important for the party was contemplated in some form at the very beginning.

Mrs. Blatch's observations emphasized the disillusionment of the women with the pacifist efforts of men:

> Have we men big enough to do the work that would insure the peace of the world? If not, then we women are going to join internationally and try to do it. Practically every proposition that has been put out by men must wait until the end of the war to be put into operation.[19]

Continuing, Mrs. Blatch differentiated the program of the Woman's Peace Party from those propositions which involved waiting until the end of the war. The new program meant " immediate action " by this government, the calling of a conference of neutral nations which were to begin making some arrangements looking to the end of the war as well as to the formation of a great international government. If America had so acted at the beginning of the war, she declared, Turkey would not have drifted into the war and Italy would not be on the verge of drifting into it. She called upon the women to go forth " each one of us a center of influence." Then, despite the suffrage plank of the platform, she added: " Women, our men in political life are hampered by their political affiliations. You are free; rise to your opportunity." [20]

Not all who came to the conference were convinced at the outset, however, that women could only fulfil their opportunity through forming a separate peace organization. The arguments usually advanced to convince skeptics were later set forth by Mrs. Lucia Ames Mead in her report as National Secretary of the Party:

> Those who questioned why women should form a new society and not unite with men and women in the old organizations were shown that women held very few offices in the old societies and had some fresh methods of their own which they wanted to employ. Moreover, as women, they felt that they had a special work to perform in the interest of their suffering sisters beyond sea and in influencing great organized bodies of women whom the older societies have not yet reached. While abhorring needless duplication of machinery, it seemed to them that this organization need not duplicate any other,

---

[19] *Ibid.*, p. 13.   [20] *Ibid.*, p. 14.

but might reach with new methods into new fields, not detracting from, but rather adding to, the influence of the older societies with which it sympathizes and is glad to cooperate.[21]

Thus, when the women adjourned at midnight on January 10 they looked upon the founding of the Woman's Peace Party with the relief and inspiration which, in the words of Mrs. Mead, come from the creation of " what seemed destined to fill a real need." [22]   In point of numbers alone, to be sure, the new organization gave little basis for the confidence which Mrs. Mead also attributed to the founders.   There were only eighty-six charter members, two of whom, Mrs. Pethick-Lawrence and Mme. Schwimmer, were honorary members. On the other hand, all the delegates, while not committing by their membership the organizations which had sent them, signified by the very method of their coming the interest which many powerful organizations took in the new peace society. Moreover, the original membership of the organization represented in several senses an *élite* that held much more promise for the group than lies in mere numbers.   It included leaders of American women such as Miss Addams, Mrs. Catt, Dr. Anna Howard Shaw, and Miss Janet E. Richards; women of considerable academic or literary attainment such as Professor Anna Garlin Spencer and Mrs. Charlotte Perkins Gilman; women of important standing in the peace movement such as Mrs. Fannie Fern Andrews, Mrs. Lucia Ames Mead, and Mrs. Louis F. Post; women of prominent social or political connections such as Mrs. Joseph Fels, wife of the philanthropist and single-tax advocate, Mrs. Robert La Follette, wife of the Senator, and Mrs. Henry Villard, daughter of William Lloyd Garrison.[23]

Unpromisingly, however, the initial meeting of the Woman's Peace Party received almost no immediate attention from the public press.[24]   Doubtless this neglect was due in large part to the fact that the press was then occupied with the report-

---

[21] *Year Book of the Woman's Peace Party, 1916,* p. 42.
[22] *Ibid.*   [23] *Ibid.,* pp. 58-60.
[24] On January 11 a condensed statement of the program appeared in the *New York Post* and the *Washington Star.*   Other newspapers took notice of the party in connection with episodes of the ensuing months.

ing of a mammoth war beside which the protests of a group of women against the institution of war seemed insignificant as well as futile. Even the periodicals of the country were largely silent. One exception was the *Survey,* of which Miss Addams was an editor. It contained a long article entitled "A Woman's Peace Party Full Pledged for Action." [25]   Another exception to the neglect shown by the periodicals was the conspicuous notice and glowing praise accorded the meeting by Hamilton Holt, in the *Independent.* He remarked upon the fact that five out of six New York newspapers, the columns of which were full of war news, had taken no notice at all of the conference, which seemed to him so important that he published its declaration of principles and platform. The manifesto of the Party was characterized by him as " unsurpassed in power and moral fervor by anything that has been issued here or abroad since the Great War began." The platform, he declared, was " radical, sound, statesmanlike, constructive." The women readers of the magazine were urged to join the movement and their joining was facilitated by the publication of an application blank,[26] Moreover, the account of the conference was followed by an article entitled " Women and War," written by Anna Garlin Spencer, a vice-chairman of the Peace Party. In this article the readers of the magazine were familiarized with the motivating ideas of the new organization—the rising of a new social consciousness in women, the particular concern of women's moral sentiment for peace, the special injury of war to women's interests as well as ideals, and the mission of women at this time to make an effective protest against war.[27]

Another periodical which directed attention to the women's venture was the then young *New Republic.* The editorial article on the Washington conference was, however, much more reserved than the *Independent* in its praise of the women. It opened by observing that the women's horror of war was merely that of the spectator and would be " half-baked " until

[25] *Survey* (1915), XXXIII, 433-434.
[26] " Women for Peace," *Independent* (1915), LXXXI, 120.
[27] *Ibid.*, pp. 121-124.

they had tested it in the face of a personal crisis as had the women of Europe. Moreover, the writer suggested that an excellent chance to make such a test was offered by the Japanese question in California. Women, it was said, could not hope to intervene in Europe until they had shown what they could do in a state where women were powerful; nor could they evade domestic issues without meeting the great danger of all pacifist thinking—that it tends to oppose war in general and to ignore war in the concrete. However, after all criticisms had been made it was still to be conceded that " an organization like the Woman's Peace Party can perform a great service." This was the destruction of a " false notion of the value of human life " that led to inhumane statesmanship and ultimately to war, which the editorial writer, like the women, called " the sum of all villainies." [28]

The first step in the women's attack upon the sum of all villainies was very unmelodramatic—the practical task of installing and starting the machinery of their organization. This step was taken very quickly, for the national headquarters of the Peace Party were opened in Chicago on January 19. Mrs. Lucia Ames Mead, Mrs. William I. Thomas, and Miss Sophonisba P. Breckinridge were appointed, respectively, National Secretary, Treasurer, and Executive Secretary. Taking a lesson from the cooperation of militarists, Miss Addams at the outset effected a kind of coalition with the Chicago branches of the American Peace Society and the Church Peace Union— even to the extent of sharing headquarters. The first work undertaken by the National Office was the reprinting in its completed form of the platform and statement adopted at the Washington meeting. Then came the appointment of state chairmen. To some prominent woman in every state, known to be identified with the peace movement, was sent a letter inviting her to serve as chairman for the Woman's Peace Party. The responses were " somewhat discouraging," for as a result of the communications only twenty-eight women expressed a willingness to accept the official position.[29] In

[28] " The Sum of all Villainies," *New Republic* (1915), II, 36-37.
[29] *Year Book of the Woman's Peace Party, 1916*, p. 46.

February Mrs. Elizabeth Glendower Evans accepted the rôle of National Organizer and made trips in New England and the Middle States as a result of which some new chairmen were secured and some new branches organized. A cooperating council was formed which consisted of the presidents of many important women's organizations, including the International Woman Suffrage Alliance, the National American Suffrage Association, and the National Council of Women.

The main activity of the National Office was for some weeks the printing and distributing of literature to state chairmen and to the presidents of women's clubs. The literature consisted chiefly of brochures containing not only the platform of the Party and its full program but also items concerning its activities and recommendations to the state branches. Early publications reported the presentation of the results of the Washington conference to all embassies and legations at Washington as well as the transmission of these results, in translated form, to various foreign countries. It was further stated that Mme. Schwimmer, acting as International Secretary of the organization, was in direct communication with the women of seventeen nations. Recommendations were made to the state branches with reference to the holding of mass-meetings to protest against increase of armament in the United States, the stimulation of peace propaganda throughout existing organizations, the holding of peace meetings to discuss the platform of the Party, the teaching of pacifism and international cooperation in the schools, and the reading of pacifist literature.[30] After a time the National Office undertook, in addition to the circulation of the platform and program, the distribution of other publications, especially of the addresses at the Washington meeting and a " Group of Letters from Women of the Warring Nations." [31]

Even before progressing far with the problems of the organization and strengthening of the Woman's Peace Party itself, the officers of the group took an ambitious step. It was

---

[30] *Woman's Peace Party Preamble and Platform.* Pamphlet of 1915.
[31] *Year Book of the Woman's Peace Party, 1916,* p. 46.

to attempt the federation of all national forces favoring peace. Without this federation, it was realized from the outset, the hopes of the women would stand little chance of fulfilment. Thus, in the very month following the organization of the Party, its officers, in concert with Louis P. Lochner of the Chicago Peace Society, communicated with every public organization in the United States whose constitution contained a recognition of the desirability of international peace. Since peace was then a popular plank of organizational platforms, the list of communications numbered no less than twenty thousand and included everything from peace groups proper to mutual benefit societies. The call was an invitation to attend the National Emergency Peace Conference at Chicago which should effect a federation of peace forces.[32]

The conference met in the first week of March, and was attended by about three hundred men and women from communities all the way from New England to the Rocky Mountains. They represented an amazing diversity of groups: "commercial interests at the east and the national socialist party headquarters here at the west, newspapers and more than thirty colleges, fraternal orders and federations of labor, women's clubs and state and city governments, native Americans and foreign-born citizens from many lands, peace societies, and churches of different faiths."[33] In several ways the Woman's Peace Party played an influential if not a dominant rôle. Its chairman, Jane Addams, presided over the conference. In addition to Miss Addams, two members of the Party were on its executive committee, thus giving it a majority of the five women on the committee. Several of its members, including Rosika Schwimmer, spoke at the large mass meetings held in connection with the conference. A frequent theme of the addresses was the revolt of women against war. The interest of the conference centered in the project of continuous mediation which the Party had already sponsored. Miss Julia Grace Wales, the author of the plan, read a paper entitled " Mediation without Armistice." The

[32] *Ibid.*, pp. 43, 47, 49.
[33] Chicago *Daily News*, March 6, 1915.

conference petitioned the government of the United States to call immediately a conference of the neutral nations of the world to constitute a voluntary court of continuous mediation to bring about a peace both just and lasting. The platform adopted by the meeting contained most of the other objectives of the Woman's Peace Party—a concert of nations to replace alliances, reduction of armaments, democratic control of foreign policies, woman suffrage, substitution of law for war, and adoption of economic pressure and non-intercourse as the form of international sanctions. The conference resulted in the formation of a National Peace Federation, with Miss Addams as its chairman.[34] The meeting attracted considerable attention and, according to Mark Sullivan, to a considerable extent inspired Henry Ford to undertake his peace expedition to Europe.[35]

While collaborating with other organizations through the Federation, the Woman's Peace Party at the same time went on in the immediately succeeding months of 1915 with educational activities of its own. In the early spring of 1915 the women experimented with various propaganda techniques. Some of their methods were, to say the least, unusual. A poem entitled " Five Souls," which had appeared in the London *Nation,* appealed to them so much that they had it set to Beethoven music and employed three young Englishwomen to sing it on various stages throughout the country. The work, Miss Addams indicates,[36] especially expressed an idea entertained by herself and others who had worked among people of many nationalities living harmoniously together: namely, that the common soldier was a peace-loving man who was fighting because of governmental propaganda. When one reads the words it becomes apparent that the poem was chosen for its expression of a poignant emotion rather than for its literary construction:

---

[34] " For a Peace Conference of Neutral Nations," *Survey* (1915), XXXIII, 597-598.
[35] Mark Sullivan, *Our Times—The United States, 1900-1925,* V, *Over Here,* p. 163.
[36] Addams, *The Second Twenty Years,* p. 122.

FIRST SOUL

I was a peasant of the Polish plain;
  I left my plow because the message ran:
Russia, in danger, needed every man
To save her from the Teuton; and was slain.
  I gave my life for freedom—This I know;
  For those who bade me fight had told me so.

SECOND SOUL

I was a Tyrolese, a mountaineer;
  I gladly left my mountain home to fight
Against the brutal, treacherous Muscovite;
And died in Poland on a Cossack spear.
  I gave my life for freedom—This I know;
  For those who bade me fight had told me so.

THIRD SOUL

I worked at Lyons at my weaver's loom;
  When suddenly the Prussian despot hurled
His felon blow at France and at the world;
Then I went forth to Belgium and my doom.
  I gave my life for freedom—This I know;
  For those who bade me fight had told me so.

FOURTH SOUL

I owned a vineyard by the wooded Main,
  Until the Fatherland, begirt by foes
Lusting her downfall, called me, and I rose
Swift to the call—and died in fair Lorraine.
  I gave my life for freedom—This I know;
  For those who bade me fight had told me so.

FIFTH SOUL

I worked in a great shipyard by the Clyde,
  There came a sudden word of wars declared,
Of Belgium, peaceful, helpless, unprepared,
Asking our aid; I joined the ranks, and died.
  I gave my life for freedom—This I know;
  For those who bade me fight had told me so.[87]

Doubtless a more effective contribution of the women to both art and peace was their promotion of a production of Euripides' "Trojan Women," for which the Carnegie Endowment for International Peace gave them a grant of five thousand dollars. The play was given in many cities throughout the country and eventually at the Panama Exposition at San Francisco. Jane Addams has recorded the impression that "an audience invariably fell into a solemn mood as the age-

---

[87] *Ibid.*, pp. 122-123.

old plaint of war-weary women cheated even of death, issued
from the darkened stage, reciting not the glory of War, but
' shame and blindness and a world swallowed up in night.' " [38]
Others than those sponsoring the production gave testimony
to its appeal. Thus the dramatic critic of the *Chicago Evening Post* observed:

The experiment of bringing such art as this to the people of a country as a means of arousing them to full imaginative realization of
the horror of war is one to be watched with interest, and aside from
the fact that the Greek drama was originally the possession and the
education of the people at large, is probably unique. Propagandists
have lectured and preached, and they have written thesis plays; one
course has been more or less useless, and the other, if it has done
good to morals, has hurt art.
But here is a play of the most exquisite beauty bringing, through
Gilbert Murray's magic translation, Greek and modern together in
the realization of what life may hold. Before the war the play had
its appeal to all people of fine imagination. That the aroused imagination of the nation which is brought into such close contact with
war again should have this means of crystallizing itself is a boon
for which we cannot be too grateful to the Woman's Peace Party.[39]

Ironically enough, Gilbert Murray, whose translation was
used, was not at all in sympathy with the pacific ideas of
Jane Addams and her co-workers. He wrote Miss Addams a
letter to this effect.[40] He also wrote to an acquaintance, Re-
bekah Wheeler Baker, a note on the subject which was printed
in the *New York Times*. Murray declared:

For my own part, great as is my admiration of Miss Addams and
her work in social matters, I cannot help thinking that her views on
the war are vitiated by the fact that she will not consider the question of justice or of right. She considers nothing but peace. Peace
is in my opinion almost the greatest and most fundamental of human
blessings. But there are cases, and I believe this one of them, in
which men should be prepared to fight and die rather than submit
to triumphant wrong. We worked for peace to the last moment.[41]

But to the women the words of Euripides, despite those of his
translator, spoke the necessary union of peace and justice.

A major purpose underlying the early educational activity
and organizational work of the Woman's Peace Party was to
bring to bear upon the Government such great pressure of

---

[38] Addams, *Peace and Bread*, p. 12.
[39] *Chicago Evening Post*, April 12, 1915.
[40] MS, Jane Addams Peace Collection, Swarthmore College Library.
[41] *New York Times*, October 23, 1915.

public opinion in behalf of the Party's first plank that it would be induced to call a conference of neutral nations to offer continuous mediation to the belligerents. A month after the organization of the group there was introduced in Congress a resolution which invigorated such efforts by providing a basis for governmental action in the direction desired. On February 8, Senator La Follette of Wisconsin introduced a joint resolution which authorized the President " to convey to all neutral nations the desire of this Government for an international conference for the purpose of promoting by cooperation and through its friendly offices the early cessation of hostilities and the establishment of peace among the warring nations of Europe, and for other purposes." [42] The collateral purposes included armament limitation, nationalization of the manufacture of military equipment, the prohibition of the export of such equipment, the establishment of an international tribunal, and the neutralization of certain waters and maritime trade routes. In his chief purpose, the calling of a conference of neutrals, Senator La Follette had doubtless been influenced by the action of the Wisconsin Legislature in submitting to Congress Julia Grace Wales' plan for continuous mediation. That the Senator intended continuous mediation is clearly indicated by the following words from his supporting speech of February 12:

It devolves upon the peoples who are not in this conflict, who can still exercise a calm and dispassionate judgment, to confer together and strive, and strive again and yet again, as the unbiased friend of each of the belligerents, to bring about a cessation of hostilities through the offers of mediation.[43]

Only a few newspapers took the trouble to voice praise of the resolution, but the pacifists who had been advocating a conference of neutrals showered Senator La Follette with enthusiastic telegrams. Harriet P. Thomas, Executive Secretary of the Women's Peace Party, wired the Senator as follows: " Please accept the gratitude and appreciation of the Woman's Peace Party." The others who wired similarly in-

---

[42] *Congressional Record*, 63d Cong., 3d sess., p. 3230.
[43] *Ibid.*, p. 3631.

cluded Louis P. Lochner, Secretary of the National Peace Federation, Rosika Schwimmer, and several prominent members of the Woman's Peace Party.[44]

Only a few weeks after the introduction of the La Follette resolution one similar in design but without the element of continuous mediation was introduced by Senator Newlands of Nevada. Both resolutions were referred to the Committee on Foreign Relations and while they reposed there served at least to keep alive among the pacifists hope of governmental action.[45]

The first months of life of the organization brought a marked growth in its membership. While most of the branches developed in the large cities of the eastern seaboard, there were flourishing affiliates in Minnesota and California as well. One of the most successful of the eastern branches was that in Boston, which, with a membership of twenty-five hundred, carried on a vigorous campaign for both reasonable peace terms and the early termination of the war. A number of the leading women's organizations became affiliated branches of the Woman's Peace Party. " Women everywhere," writes Miss Addams, " seemed eager for literature and lectures, and as the movement antedated by six months the organization of the League to Enforce Peace, we had the field all to ourselves." [46] With reference to this early period of success, Miss Addams records a bit deprecatingly that " the members of the new organization scarcely realized that they were placing themselves on the side of an unpopular cause." [47] At the time the cause was not, indeed, unpopular; the period was that in which one of the most popular of popular songs was " I Didn't Raise My Boy to be a Soldier."

At the end of February an even more promising chapter in the history of the Woman's Peace Party loomed into view. An invitation was received from Europe to attend an international congress of women pacifists at The Hague, an oppor-

---

[44] *Ibid.*, pp. 3633-3634.
[45] Addams, *The Second Twenty Years*, pp. 126-127.
[46] *Peace and Bread*, p. 10.
[47] *Ibid.*

tunity to organize that international movement of women for peace of which the founders of the organization had dreamed at the very outset. Happy over this opportunity, the women scarcely realized that its seizure was to initiate them into the real tribulations and unpopularity of the pacifist. Indeed, the brief time behind them since the formation of the party was the only period of their history which ended upon a bright and promising note.

CHAPTER III

WOMEN OF THE WORLD UNITE

The Hague International Congress of Women to which the Woman's Peace Party was invited initiated an international pacifist movement in which the American organization was to take a leading part throughout its history. The groups and persons responsible for this meeting, however, were European rather than American and in fact were largely identical with those who had given the initial impetus to the formation of the Woman's Peace Party. The congress was the culmination of a moral revulsion from the European War on the part of women in both belligerent and neutral countries who for the most part were members of the groups of the International Woman Suffrage Alliance which had delegated Mme. Schwimmer to come to the United States.

At the very outset this organization, the president of which was Carrie Chapman Catt, had indicated its belief that the European War was incompatible with the interests and ideals of women as feminists and humanitarians. On July 31, the morrow of the first declaration of war, an International Manifesto of Women, an urgent appeal " to leave untried no method of Conciliation or Arbitration " to avert the war, was delivered by the women to the Foreign Office and foreign embassies in London.[1] After the war became general there emerged from the ranks of the suffrage organization individual women and groups of women who now held that the white flag of pacifism was even more important for the time being than the banner of woman's rights. These women sought to import into the fight for peace the same method of separate action as women that they had used in the fight for the vote. They also strove to retain the same international unity of women that had marked the campaign for woman

[1] *Report of the International Congress of Women, The Hague, 1915*, p. ix. The story of the background of the congress is taken mainly from the authoritative accounts in this work.

suffrage. An illustration of this internationalism of the suffragist pacifists was the international petition of women in
behalf of a conference of neutrals, which Mme. Schwimmer
brought to the United States. Still further, the women
desired to maintain the communication essential to those who,
though separated by war between their countries, retained
a sense of moral solidarity. They utilized for this purpose the
columns of *Ius Suffragii*, the organ of the International
Suffrage Alliance. But the lack of personal contact with their
co-workers in foreign countries remained a privation, and for
this reason the suffragists looked forward to the biennial
convention of the organization, planned before the war to take
place in Berlin in June 1915.

It was a real disappointment when, in September 1914, the
German Union for Women Suffrage regretfully felt compelled
by the war to withdraw their invitation. Dr. Aletta H.
Jacobs, president of the Dutch suffrage society, wrote to
numerous suffrage leaders that it was highly important that
the meeting be held, even if in some neutral country, in view
of the fact that in times of war and hatred " women have to
show that we at least retain our solidarity and that we are
able to maintain mutual friendship." [2] Dr. Jacobs was not
the only woman to raise her voice about this time in behalf
of the maintenance by women of their solidarity and mutual
friendship. And the most striking of such appeals were those
made by women of belligerent countries, who demonstrated no
little courage. An Englishwoman, Emily Hobhouse, well
known for her courageous humanitarianism during the Boer
War, attracted worldwide attention by sending a " Letter of
Christmas Greeting " to the women of Germany and Austria.
There were others who called upon the women of Europe not
only to maintain Christian feelings toward each other but
to meet in conclave to discuss the reestablishment of peace on
earth and good will among men. One was Lida Gustava
Heymann, leader of the German woman suffrage movement,
who issued a " Call to the Women of Europe " to meet somewhere in Europe to raise their voice in protest against the

---

[2] *Ibid.*, p. xxxvii.

continuation of a war of such terrible destruction. Another was the Scottish woman lawyer Chrystal Macmillan, a secretary of the International Woman Suffrage Alliance, who, in supporting Dr. Jacobs' proposal for a meeting of the Alliance in a neutral country, urged that in addition to its own meeting the Alliance should through its president convene a meeting of delegates from women's societies, national and international, to be held immediately after the business meeting of the Alliance. The purpose of this special meeting should be to discuss questions of international peace. Miss Macmillan, who seems to have provided the seed of the idea of the Hague Congress, suggested as subjects of discussion international arbitration, control of foreign policy by public discussion and parliaments, principles on which territory should or should not be transferred, the reduction of armaments, international federation—all subjects which were later discussed by the Hague Congress. Miss Macmillan further proposed that should the Alliance decide not to call such a meeting it be convened by a number of internationally known women on their own initiative.

Though Dr. Jacobs' letters elicited much encouragement, the Alliance, sensible of all the practical and psychological difficulties, decided not to call even its own meeting. About the time when the internationalist suffragists received this disappointment, many of them were also becoming impatient with the failure of the neutral governments to act upon their appeal for a conference to offer mediation.[3] Under such circumstances, Dr. Jacobs decided to invite a few women from both the belligerent and neutral countries accessible to Holland to a meeting at Amsterdam on February 12 and 13, with a view to taking action in line with Miss Macmillan's suggestion for a women's congress on international affairs.

To the meeting at Amsterdam there came numerous women from The Netherlands and in addition four Belgian, five British and four German women. This meeting, merely on the initiative of those present, arranged the ambitious plan of

---

[3] "Women and War," *Outlook* (1915), CIX, 676.

the international women's congress. The women decided upon the subject-matter of the resolutions which were to be presented and appointed a subcommittee, which was to be enlarged by the addition of delegates from various countries, to frame these resolutions. Furthermore, they determined the general conditions of the congress: that membership was to be open both to individual women and to women delegates from women's groups or mixed societies; that a necessary condition of membership was the expression of general agreement with the resolutions on the preliminary program; and that discussions on the relative national responsibility for or conduct of the war should be banned from the deliberations of the congress. The congress was to be held at The Hague, traditional citadel of peace. The Dutch women were authorized to form a special committee to issue the invitations to the congress and to make all other arrangements.

It was the Executive Committee formed at Amsterdam, headed by Dr. Aletta Jacobs, which in February 1915 issued the invitation to the Woman's Peace Party to attend an international congress of women at The Hague from April 28 to May 1. The invitation, vitalized by the women's sense of their high purpose, was in reality an appeal, almost a summons:

From many countries appeals have come asking us to call together an International Women's Congress to discuss what the women of the world can do and ought to do in the dreadful times in which we are now living.

We women of the Netherlands, living in a neutral country, accessible to the women of all other nations, therefore, take upon ourselves the responsibility of calling together such an international congress of women. We feel strongly that at a time, when there is so much hatred among nations, we, women, must show that we can retain our solidarity and that we are able to maintain a mutual friendship.

Women are waiting to be called together. The world is looking to them for their contribution towards the solution of the great problems of the day.

Women, whatever your nationality, whatever your party, your presence will be of great importance.

The greater the number of those who take part in the congress the stronger will be the impression its proceedings will make.

Your presence will testify that you, too, wish to record your protest against this horrible war, and that you desire to assist in preventing a recurrence of it in the future.

Let our call to you not be in vain! [4]

---

[4] *Report of the International Congress of Women, The Hague, 1915*, p. 280.

With the invitation was sent the preliminary program of the congress, indicating its proposed principles. At the same time Miss Addams was invited to preside over the conference. This selection was probably due to her chairmanship of a woman's peace organization in a great neutral country, free from European commitments. Miss Addams and Mrs. Fannie Fern Andrews were asked to be the two American members of the executive committee of the congress.

In the tentative program of the conference there were numerous proposals which could not but enlist the interest and sympathy of the Woman's Peace Party. First of all there was an appeal to the belligerent governments to call a truce with a view to defining their terms of peace. The Woman's Peace Party as we have seen was already committed to seeking an approach to early peace through a conference of neutrals offering continuous mediation. Other principles which the international group shared with the American women pacifists were the repudiation of war, the support of arbitration and conciliation as substitutes for war, democratic control of foreign policy, popular consent as prerequisite of territorial transfers, and, of course, woman suffrage. The receptiveness created by this similarity of principles was reenforced by the realization of the women that, to quote Miss Addams, " one obvious task was to unite with other organizations in setting out a constructive program with which an international public should become so familiar that an effective demand for its fulfilment could be made at the end of the war." [5]   What coalition was better from the point of view of the Woman's Peace Party than union with like-minded women of all nations?

Thus the invitation was answered with an acceptance, doubtless given with a certain pride that the leader of the American group had been honored with the chairmanship of the international gathering. Miss Addams and Mrs. Andrews undertook to bring a delegation from the United States, consisting not merely of representatives of the Woman's Peace Party but

[5] *Peace and Bread*, pp. 10-11.

also of other organizations which might be interested. But
between formal acceptance of the invitation and the formation
of a delegation there was, under the circumstances, no little
distance. This was no invitation to a clubwomen's pink tea.
The Americans knew that all who went would have to pay
their own expenses, would be compelled to venture through
perilous lanes of the sea, and would be staking their efforts
upon a difficult and uncertain undertaking. Since the announcement of the enterprise there had been, in various
countries and even among peace groups, no little criticism of
the proposed congress as being both inappropriate and impracticable.

Forty-seven undaunted women, however, decided to undertake the precarious venture. The majority of them were
members of the Women's Peace Party but only two, Miss
Addams and Mrs. Louis F. Post, were official representatives
of the Party as a national organization. Some of the Woman's
Peace Party members were delegates from various branches of
the society, some participated in a purely individual capacity,
and many acted as delegates of other organizations. The
number and diversity of organizations other than the Woman's
Peace Party in the delegation were great and indicated that
there was wide interest in the congress. Some of these
organizations selected members of the Woman's Peace Party
as their representatives, others sent women outside the Party.
To cite only some of the organizations, there were delegates
from the American Peace and Arbitration League, the Universal Peace Union, the Immigrants' Protective League, the
Committee on Organization of Department Store Workers
of New York City, the National League of Teachers' Associations, the Oregon State Federation of Women's Clubs, the
Woman's Lawyers Association, the Woman's Trade Union
League, the National Federal Suffrage Association, the National Society of Daughters of the American Revolution, and the
American Federation of Labor. As individuals the members
of the delegation also formed a distinguished list, representing
the achievement of women in many fields of professional and

social endeavor. To mention only types, there were Grace Abbott, director of the Immigrants' Protective League, Fannie Fern Andrews, veteran peace worker, Emily Greene Balch, professor of economics and sociology at Wellesley College, Madeleine Z. Doty, prominent lawyer and Juvenile Court investigator, Elizabeth Glendower Evans, leading suffragist and woman's trade union organizer, Dr. Alice Hamilton, vice-president of the American Medical Association, Mary Heaton Vorse, author, and Julia Grace Wales of the University of Wisconsin, author of a plan for continuous mediation.[6]

The inclusion of so many prominent women in the list of delegates did not prevent the announcement of the congress from provoking much criticism and even ridicule. Theodore Roosevelt, then engaged in an attack on Wilson's pacifist policies, was one of the most vehement assailants of the women and brought their undertaking into general discussion. In a letter which was originally printed in the *Chicago Herald* and was quoted by many other newspapers, the Colonel expressed his unflattering opinion of the venture to Mrs. George Rublee of Washington, D. C., a member of the District branch of the Woman's Peace Party, who was a delegate to The Hague and had rather innocently sent Mr. Roosevelt a prospectus of the congress. The party platform of the women pacifists seemed to the Colonel to be " both silly and base." Not wishing these adjectives to reflect too harshly on the women belonging to the group, he then qualified his statement by saying that this did not mean that all those signing and championing it were silly and base. It was, he admitted, unfortunately true that some of the very worst movements in human history, " such as the effort to break up this Union in order to perpetuate slavery," have had very high-minded men and women enlisted in their support. He went on to assail not merely the pacifist movement but the motives of many of its adherents. He compared the Woman's Peace Party to the Copperhead Movement:

---

[6] *Report of the International Congress of Women, The Hague, 1915*, pp. 266-270.

. . . a very large proportion of the peace at any price or copper-head sympathizers were undoubtedly physical cowards, and equally undoubtedly a very large proportion of ultra-pacifists of today who uphold such views as those outlined in the paper you inclosed, in championing peace without regard to righteousness, are really most influenced by physical cowardice. They fear death or pain or discomfort beyond anything else and like to hide their fear behind high sounding words.[7]

Finally Mr. Roosevelt turned from personal invective to the ideas which underlay his rejection of pacifism:

I speak with scientific accuracy when I speak of this movement as both base and silly. It is silly because it is absolutely futile. It proposes to go on with just the same kind of futile agitation which, by the experience of a century, and above all, by the experience of the last thirty years has proved wholly useless and on the whole slightly mischievous.

Not one particle of good will be obtained by any such action as that outlined in that paper you sent. But this is not all. It is base as well as futile. There is nothing more repulsive than to see people agitating for general righteousness in the abstract when they dare not stand up against wickedness in the concrete. On the whole, there is nothing that does so much damage to a church as to have a minister who thunders continually against wrong in the abstract or against wrong committed by the Pharisees a couple of thousand years ago, but who cannot be persuaded to stand up against present-day wrong in the concrete; and the professional pacifist leaders in the United States are in exactly this position.[8]

The Colonel then specified the present-day concrete wrongs which, by not opposing, the women seemed to him to be indorsing. They were the injuries which had been done to the Belgians, injuries which could have been answered by this heroic people only by war. Yet the pronouncement of the women pacifists not only failed to protest against the injuries but denounced war in such fashion as to include in the condemnation the Belgians just as much as the oppressors of Belgium. In conclusion Roosevelt suggested to the women a course of action which seemed to him more meritorious than entering into "vague and hysterical demands for right in the abstract coupled with the unworthy and timid refusal to allude to frightful wrongs that are at the very moment being committed in the concrete." To show that they were really striving for righteousness, the women should act as follows:

---

[7] "Is the Women's Peace Movement 'Silly and Base'?" *Literary Digest* (1915), L, 1022.
[8] *Ibid.*

Let the people who advocate the platform and principles you enclosed hold a meeting specifically to denounce the invasion of Belgium by Germany and to demand that in the interests of peace the United States do what it can to put a stop to those wrongs. Let them denounce Messrs. Wilson and Bryan for trying to force through the Ship Purchase Bill, which was in the interest of the Power that wronged Belgium and in spite of the fact that their action might tend to bring us into war with the Powers that have sought to defend Belgium.[9]

Naturally the women pacifists proposed to do nothing of the sort. They did not, however, see fit to leave unanswered a public attack from so distinguished a source. Mrs. Amos Pinchot, chairman of the New York City branch of the Woman's Peace Party, wrote to the *New York Times* a letter marked by more restraint and objectivity than the Colonel's. She declared that the women did not mind having their program called silly and base, for they " consider that Colonel Roosevelt's public services in the past have been so conspicuous as to give him the right to call it anything he pleases, an opinion in which the Colonel evidently heartily coincides." This observation, however, was merely the prelude to a thoroughgoing criticism of Mr. Roosevelt's militarist doctrine, the publication of which seemed to Mrs. Pinchot a more serious matter than his invective because " like all half-thought-out proposals, it is accompanied with danger." Mrs. Pinchot saw as the basic premise of this militarism the doctrine that war was self-starting and that any effort to examine its causes with a view to diminishing them in the future by rational means of adjustment was both foolish and noxious. This doctrine, Mrs. Pinchot observed, showed an ignorance of the fact that the causes of war " can be influenced by the spread of healthy, constructive, humane ideas, and especially by the realization of a spirit of world-citizenship in politics and in commercial action." Women in particular were not disposed to take a defeatist attitude toward war, even though called cowards when they protested against it. " No, it is not for ourselves that we fear, but for the children of the whole world, for the future of the race," Mrs. Pinchot affirmed. The purpose of the Woman's Peace Party was " to help open

---

[9] *Ibid.*, p. 1023.

the first tiny wedge in the thick walls of prejudice and precedent, to let humanity come into its promised land of good
faith and international brotherhood." [10]

Mrs. Henry Villard was another leader of the Woman's
Peace Party who answered the Colonel's animadversions. She
observed that the charge of base motives was a strange one
to apply to " a movement which seeks to conserve human life,"
and the accusation of cowardice a curious one to level against
Jane Addams and the other women " who have devoted their
lives to the work of improving social conditions for working
people." The sweeping condemnations, she pointed out, included the European women who remained earnest workers
for peace though they had given their husbands and sons to
fight for their country. Though it would not be forthcoming,
Mr. Roosevelt " owed an apology to the women of the world."
In this view Mrs. Villard was supported by the *Pittsburgh
Gazette-Times*, which quoted her answer with the observation
that Colonel Roosevelt had not added to his laurels by his
published attack on the participation of American women in
the prospective congress at The Hague.[11]

However, there were other assailants of the women's venture, both individuals and organs of public opinion. Perhaps
the most bitter came from a woman, Mrs. William Lowell
Putnam, sister of President Lowell of Harvard University.
It was marked by an amusing acerbity:

The Woman's Peace Party is one of the most dangerous movements
which has threatened our emotional people for some time. It was
founded by an ex-militant, a woman who had been several times con-
victed of criminal acts which were far from peaceful.[12] This woman,
to whom notoriety was the breath of her nostrils, got the ear of
several emotional women whose hearts are so large that many people
have mistaken them for heads. They were told that, though they did
not bear arms they bore the armies, and similar catch-phrases. These
good women, of whom the most prominent are childless, and many
of whom are spinsters against whom no breath of scandal has ever
been raised, were lined up together and photographed as " mothers of
men " and no one saw the absurdity of it all.[13]

---

[10] *Ibid.*
[11] *Pittsburgh Gazette-Times*, April 19, 1915.
[12] The reference is probably to Mrs. Pethick-Lawrence.
[13] Quoted from the *Boston Herald* by the *New York Times*, April
29, 1915.

Jane Addams was apparently quite able to survive the agitation which the idea of a women's international peace congress had created. The speeches and interviews which she gave on the eve of sailing reflect serenity of spirit. Nor did she evince an excessive hopefulness with regard to the success of the undertaking. Thus, speaking after a performance of " Trojan Women," she declared:

We do not think we can settle the war. We do not think that by raising our hands we can make the armies cease slaughter. We do think it is valuable to state a new point of view. We do think it is fitting that women should meet and take counsel to see what may be done.[14]

The women delegates sailed from New York on the *Noordam,* a Holland-American liner, on April 13. From the mast of the vessel floated a flag on whose field were blue letters spelling " PEACE." It was a homemade substitute for the emblem which Mayor John Mitchell of New York had promised the women but had failed to deliver.[15] There was something a little pathetic and at the same time defiant about that homemade standard. It seemed to recall to the women not only the fact that their mission was not even supported by official sanction but also the rude reply which Assistant Secretary of State Lansing had made to Jane Addams when she inquired if the State Department would permit the display of the American emblem. Lansing's telegram reminded her that the *Noordam* was a Dutch vessel and then ended with this flippant sentence: " Officially we can say nothing but fly ahead." [16] Just before sailing the women were heartened by a gracious message from Queen Wilhelmina of Holland who cabled: " If we can be of service to you command us." [17]

The voyage was not the idle interlude of the ordinary trans-Atlantic vacationer. As Emily Greene Balch has recorded, " sunny weather and a boat steadied by a heavy load of grain made it possible for the delegates to meet and study and

[14] *Chicago Record-Herald,* April 13, 1915.
[15] Hoboken *Hudson-Observer,* April 14, 1915.
[16] New York *Morning Telegraph,* April 13, 1915.
[17] *New York Press,* April 14, 1915.

deliberate together during the voyage." [18]   The Secretary of
the Chicago Peace Society, Louis Lochner, who accompanied
the delegates, gave a brief course of lectures on peace questions.
After these were over the women, some days meeting morning,
afternoon and evening, considered the question of the ac-
ceptability of the preliminary program submitted to them by
the committee which had met at The Hague.

Though preserving the general framework of the program
worked out by the European resolutions committee, the American delegation nevertheless determined upon certain suggestions for change which would bring the platform of the
congress into closer accord with that of the Woman's Peace
Party.   The most important was the proposal that, in case
the belligerent governments did not call the truce suggested
by the international committee, they should avail themselves
of continuous mediation without armistice.   It was added that
the neutral countries be immediately asked to take steps to
create a conference of neutral nations which would have the
function of offering continuous mediation.   Other proposals
recommended as addenda were the establishment of an international congress to deal with non-juridical issues, the
limitation of international sanctions against aggressors to
economic and moral pressure, the immediate publication of all
existing treaties, ratification by legislatures of all future
treaties, nationalization of the manufacture of armaments, the
principle that investments in other countries should be made
solely at the risk of the investor, abolition of all preferential
tariffs, neutralization of the seas and of important maritime
trade routes, and condemnation of the denial of equal protection of laws to resident aliens.[19]

The women had just succeeded in working out their proposals by the time they sighted land.   " It was well we had

---

[18] Jane Addams, Emily G. Balch, Alice Hamilton, *Women at The
Hague*, p. 3.
[19] " Preliminary Programme of the International Women's Con-
gress, with the Suggestions Offered by the American Delegation on
Board the Steamship *Noordam*."   Mimeographed sheet in Jane
Addams Peace Collection, Swarthmore College Library.

done so," writes Miss Balch, "for though we were on the *Noordam* for five days longer, we were hardly placid enough to work to advantage." Dramatic events supervened to remind women of the proximity of war. Miss Balch writes:

> We were first stopped one evening under the menace of a little machine gun trained full upon us by a boat alongside while two German stowaways were taken off and searched and carried away. . . . One prisoner, with a rope about him to prevent his escaping or falling overboard, shouted *Hoch der Kaiser, Deutschland über Alles* before he stepped upon the swaying ladder over the ship's side; . . . . Every now and then out of the darkness a new vessel drew up to us. At one time five were alongside.[20]

At last they were allowed to proceed, but not for long. For the next morning, which was four days before the date set for the opening of the congress, the *Noordam* came to an inexplicable standstill in the English Channel near Dover. And it remained motionless for four days.[21] The passengers were not allowed to land, to have anyone come aboard, or to indicate their whereabouts in the telegrams which they sent. Ambassador Page replied to their urgent dispatches that the matter was in the hands of the Admiralty and that he could do nothing.[22] His inability to render assistance doubtless did not weigh on the Ambassador too heavily for privately he gave the congress of pacifist women the name of the "Palace of Doves."[23] While they awaited the action of the impenetrable Admiralty, the distraught women could hear the booming of the cannon. They watched dispatch boats, torpedo boats, and destroyers whiz by. A dirigible floated above them. They saw a loose mine explode. English newspapers, which were brought aboard by a fisherman, contained news of the hostility with which the congress was viewed.[24] The delegates read that they were called "Peacettes" and that their enterprise was bombarded with ridicule.[25]

---

[20] *Women at The Hague*, pp. 4-5.
[21] *New York Tribune*, April 30, 1915.
[22] New York *Evening Post*, April 26, 1915; *New York Times*, April 27, 1915.
[23] Sullivan, *Our Times*, V, p. 162.
[24] *New York Tribune*, April 30, 1915.
[25] Addams, *Peace and Bread*, p. 13.

At last, twenty minutes after they had received one of Ambassador Page's irritating telegrams, they were "released as mysteriously as [they] had been stopped." [26] They landed at Rotterdam in the afternoon, went through the customs and took the train to The Hague. Just as the women in charge of the conference were becoming frantic over the non-appearance of their president, the American delegation finally arrived, barely in time for the first session in the evening.

While the British government was making difficulties for the American pacifists it was treating the English delegates even worse. The British government, despite the pressure of apparently more momentous affairs of state, displayed an unusual interest in the proposed peace mission. The English pacifists who had accepted the invitation to the conference were 180 in number, but the Secretary for Foreign Affairs advised the Home Office to limit the issuance of passports to 24. Reginald McKenna, British Secretary of State for Home Affairs, explained this limitation in the House of Commons by saying that the Secretary for Foreign Affairs believed that so large a number of Englishwomen in a city so near the war arena and so overrun with the enemy's spies would constitute a danger for Great Britain.[27] The chosen twenty-four waited in vain at Folkestone, first for boats, then for airplanes, neither of which ever came. The communications between England and Holland had been stopped shortly after the pacifists received their passports. Whether this new rule had been formulated with special reference to the delegation is still a matter for speculation. In any event, only three of the British delegation succeeded in getting to the congress. These were Kathleen Courtney and Chrystal Macmillan, who were members of the Resolutions Committee and had reached The Hague a week before the congress opened, and Mrs. Pethick-Lawrence, who had come over with the American women.

The women of Canada did not present as great a problem

---

[26] *Women at The Hague*, p. 6.

[27] Mary Chamberlain, "Women at The Hague," *The Survey* (1915), XXXIV, 220; New York *World*, April 28, 1915; *Gazette de Holland*, April 29, 1915.

to their government. Although two Canadians attended the meeting they were there in unofficial capacity only. Canadian women regarded the congress as "untimely peace propaganda." [28] When the invitation to attend the meeting was received, a public reply prepared by the executive secretary of the National Committee of Patriotic Service of Canada, a federation of nationally organized women societies, was circulated among Canadian club women. This Canadian response, which according to the *Toronto Mail Empire* received "unanimous endorsement of Canadian women," [29] set forth the reasons why no delegates from Canada would join in the international peace congress. The main motive of this attitude is to be found in the last paragraph of the letter:

> When Germany has learned that right is stronger than might, when the mailed fist no longer threatens Europe, then may we hope for peace which our children's children may inherit. And with such a peace we may hand on, unbroken, the great traditions of our Empire—honor unstained, liberty safeguarded, justice vindicated.[30]

The secretary of the National Committee for Patriotic Service sent this manifesto to The Hague addressed to Jane Addams. It was accompanied by a letter which amplified the explanation of the Canadian women's position, emphasizing the wrong done to Belgium and the consideration that acquiescence in this wrong would be a horror greater than the horrors of war.[31]

Others who showed aloofness toward the congress were women groups in France and Russia. The Conseil National des Femmes Françaises and the Union pour le Suffrage des Femmes framed a manifesto, addressed to the women of the neutral and Allied countries, which expressed their disagreement with the purpose of the meeting in no uncertain terms:

> In order that future generations may reap the fruit of this magnificent display of self-sacrifice and death, French women will bear the conflict as long as it will be necessary. At this time united with those who battle and die, they do not know how to talk of peace.[32]

---

[28] *Toronto Mail Empire*, April 23, 1915.
[29] *Ibid.*   [30] *Ibid.*   [31] *Ibid.*
[32] *Report of the International Congress of Women, 1915*, p. 314; *New York Times*, April 25, 1915.

Although the manifesto doubtless represented the vast majority, some individual French women did express their sympathy with the congress.   One letter signed by Mme. Gabrielle Duchène, chairman of the Section du Travail du Conseil National, and fifteen industrial workers, offered to the delegates good wishes and the assurance that they were ready to work ardently with them to prepare the " peace of tomorrow." [33]

From Russia, where the organized peace movement had always been weak and where the recipients of the letter probably feared their government, came a manifesto which echoed the sentiments of the French declaration.

The attitude of the Belgian groups was also unsympathetic, especially in view of the invitation of delegates from the Central Powers.   However, five Belgian women decided that they would go to the congress to protest against any measure, such as the calling of an armistice, which they deemed unjust to Belgium.   Strangely enough, the German authorities gave them permission to attend.   Their journey was, to say the least, difficult.   They travelled by automobile to Esschen. There they were thoroughly searched.   Then they walked two miles to Rosendahl across the Dutch border.   From there they travelled by train to The Hague.

As though to symbolize the transcendence of governmental hostilities, Dr. Anita Augspurg of Germany welcomed the Belgian women to a seat on the platform.   From the Central Powers forty-three delegates attended—twenty-eight from Germany, nine from Hungary, and six from Austria.   However, they did not manage to arrive without enduring governmental suspicion and bitter journalistic criticism.[34]   In Germany the delegates were threatened with social boycott.[35]   Among the German delegates were Dr. Anita Augspurg and Lida Gustava Heymann of Munich, initiators of the suffrage movement in Germany, who lost their property by confiscation and are in

---

[33] Chamberlain, p. 222.
[34] *Ibid.*
[35] Emily G. Balch, " The International Congress of Women at The Hague," *Home Progress* (1915), V, 111.

1939 in Switzerland because of Hitler's failure to appreciate pacifists.

Of the large European neutral countries, Italy alone was not well represented—doubtless because after it contemplated entrance into the war restrictions were placed on the Italian peace movement. Rosa Genoni of Milan, lecturer and writer, was the sole delegate from Italy. Twelve delegates came from Norway, twelve from Sweden, and six from Denmark. The largest number of delegates came, of course, from Holland, which, disproportionately to all the other nations, sent a thousand women. The size of the delegation was due, however, not merely to the location of the congress but also to the strength of pacifist sentiment among the Dutch people.

The 1136 delegates, gathered from twelve nations, represented not only women's groups but also mixed societies which sent women representatives. The great bulk of the organizations represented were woman suffrage or peace societies, but in Europe as in the United States there were other groups which had sent delegates—for example, the Danish Social Democratic Women's Union, the Woman's Cooperative Guild, and the National Women's Labor League. The interest aroused by the congress is not, however, to be measured simply by the countries and groups which had sent representatives. Expressions of sympathy were received from large women's organizations in ten countries not represented, including Argentina, British India, Bulgaria, and South Africa. Numerous women's groups in the countries represented contented themselves with sending greetings; expressions of sympathy from the United States alone fill many pages of the official account of the congress.[36] One of the most noteworthy of the greetings came from the international congress of socialist women that had been held in the preceding month at Berne— a congress which provided a precedent for the Hague meeting by virtue not only of its organization by women but also of the pacifist and international elements of the program adopted.

[36] *Report of the International Congress of Women, 1915*, pp. xliii-xlv.

But more than any other message to the congress Jane Addams seems to have treasured a letter from a young soldier in which he appealed: " It is clear why the men are holding back, but why do not women make a statement so many of us are longing for ? " [37]

In the last few days before the opening of the congress the attention of the press in many countries was directed upon it. An example of the unfavorable reaction that was predominant in belligerent countries was a sarcastic editorial which appeared on April 26 in the *Temps*. It declared that the Hague Congress imparted " a note of comedy to these war-darkened days." The French journalist found it laughable that neutral women should meet to settle difficulties which must, he declared, be fought out by the warring nations. He went on to say that the fact that Englishwomen were taking part only indicated " that the British people suffer less directly than the French and Belgians." " If," the writer concluded, " the resolutions are defended with the vigor peculiar to English suffragette eloquence we expect that the comic note will become one of frank gaiety." [38] Even in the United States there was some merrymaking, the more effective because it was obviously not the product of national bitterness. Thus the *Elgin News* observed with unconcealed sarcasm :

In a few days we may learn that Kaiser William, King George and Emperor Nicholas have capitulated to the women and agreed to leave the settlement of all the issues at stake to them. Then the newspapers will scream, " Map of Europe changed by Miss Jane Addams and Susie Smith! " Unlike Teddy, we bid the ladies good luck.[39]

Not even good wishes were extended by the Newark *Morning Star*, which expected " a flood of well-meant but futile resolutions." [40] The *New York Times* spoke of the congress as the " mad plan " and thought that its only effect would be a discrediting of the woman suffrage movement.[41]

[37] *The Second Twenty Years*, p. 129.
[38] Quoted by the *New York Times*, April 27, 1915.
[39] *Elgin News*, April 29, 1915.
[40] Newark *Morning Star*, April 29, 1915.
[41] *New York Times*, April 28, 1915.

6

On the other hand, some of the editorials were kindly. The *Charlotte Observer* expressed the view that the enterprise was not to be taken lightly even if it was not easy to see how deliberations unsupported by military power or gold could have any appreciable effect in halting the carnival of slaughter. The newspaper paid tribute not merely to Miss Addams personally but to the dignity of her undertaking:

And yet for all the apparent hopelessness of their cause, theirs is an inspiring rôle, as idealism is always inspiring. That the war should end they have no doubt. That, therefore, it is their duty to do what they can to consummate that end, they are equally positive. And hence they are off on this stupendous mission, the unofficial spokesmen for the millions of women and children who are being bereft of all that makes life worth living. They may not succeed in restoring peace, but they will at least have given voice to the humane instincts of the world and they will have been true to their own conception of duty. And that, in itself, will be an example of vast value.[42]

Already so largely prejudged, the women opened their novel conclave on April 28. The meetings were held in the Direntuin, the largest hall in The Hague. Four morning and one afternoon sessions were devoted to business discussions, and in the evenings large public propaganda meetings were held to hear addresses by the most prominent of the women delegates on "Women and War" and "Woman Suffrage and War." Some of the sessions were attended by as many as two thousand visitors, all of whom paid an entrance fee but were not allowed to take part in the deliberations. During the first part of the congress the galleries were filled with police.[43]

On the first evening a stirring address of welcome was given by Dr. Aletta Jacobs, president of the Dutch committee. After commenting on the atmosphere of sadness which overhung the meeting she said: " . . . we will not endure in this twentieth century civilization, that governments shall longer tolerate brute force as the only method of solving their international disputes." She refuted the objections which had been made to the holding of the meeting during the war by pointing out how much more difficult it would be to discuss

[42] *Charlotte Daily Observer*, April 29, 1915.
[43] *Peace and Bread*, p. 14.

the prevention of future wars in a congress which included women from the conquering and conquered nations. And she added that far from being premature the making of a women's protest against war had been delayed too long. "Those of us who have convened this Congress," she continued, "have never called it a *peace congress*, but an international congress of women to protest against war, and to discuss ways and means whereby war shall become an impossibility in the future." Then, paying tribute to a cause which in the women's interest was outranked only by the ideal of peace, she said:

We consider that the introduction of woman suffrage in all countries is one of the most powerful means to prevent war in the future. . . . But to accomplish this we need political power. . . . The Governments of the world, based on the insight of the [male] half of humanity, have failed to find a right solution of how to settle international disputes. . . . Only when women are in the parliaments of all nations, only when women have a political voice and vote, will they have the power effectively to demand that international disputes shall be solved as they ought to be, by a court of arbitration or conciliation.[44]

The next morning the discussion of the resolutions began, conducted in English, French, and German. At the outset the congress accepted the recommendation of the Resolutions Committee that the expression " in general agreement with the resolutions," the qualification for membership in the congress, should be interpreted to imply two convictions: " That international disputes should be settled by pacific means "; and " that the parliamentary franchise should be extended to women." It was also decided that resolutions dealing with the rules under which war should in future be carried on would be outside the scope of the congress.[45] The ensuing discussions were conducted with considerable difference of opinion in regard to details but very little in regard to fundamentals. The deliberations were also notable for the general absence of acrimonious dissension. On one occasion, it is true, Mme. Rosika Schwimmer displayed strong resentment over the assertion of an American delegate, Mrs. Louis F. Post, that the congress asked only that there should be no war except one wished by the people of the world.[46] And once the pre-

---

[44] *Report of the International Congress of Women, 1915*, pp. 5-8.
[45] *Ibid.*, p. 73.   [46] *Ibid.*, pp. 96-97.

siding officer was obliged to reprimand the delegates as they hissed an Englishwoman who insisted that the average woman was no more pacific than the average man! [47]

The resolutions adopted by the congress were the product primarily of the deliberations of the resolutions committee, which had changed the preliminary program in many respects to include suggestions submitted later; yet a number of the proposals were due to amendments presented from the floor. The program is interesting not as a novelty in the contemporary peace movement but rather as a compendium, formed of ideas drawn from previous programs of many nations and groups. The women, however, affixed to the resolutions a preamble which was distinctive in expressing their attitude and purpose in this novel coming together:

We women, of many nations, in International Congress assembled, raise our voices above the present hatred and bloodshed, and however we may differ as to means we declare ourselves united in the great ideals of civilization and progress.

We come together both from the warring and the neutral countries not to place the responsibility for the present conflict upon one government as against another, not to consider the rules of warfare but impelled by profoundly humane forces, and bound together by the beliefs that women must share in the common responsibility of government and that international relations must be determined not by force but by friendship and justice, we pledge ourselves to resist every tendency to rancour and revenge, to promote mutual understanding and good-will between the nations and to work for the reconciliation of the peoples.

We declare the doctrine that war is inevitable to be both a denial of the sovereignty of reason and a betrayal of the deepest instincts of the human heart. With a sense of our share in the failure to prevent the wars of the past and of the present and in sorrow for the suffering, the desolate and the oppressed, we, the members of this Congress, urge the women of all nations to work for their own enfranchisement and unceasingly to strive for a just and lasting peace.[48]

The preamble was followed by two resolutions on "Women and War," the first voicing the protest of women against "the madness and the horror of war" and the second the protest of women "against the odious wrongs of which women are the victims in time of war, and especially against the horrible violation of women which attends all war." [49]

---

[47] *Ibid.*, p. 129.
[48] *Report of the International Congress of Women, 1915*, p. 35.
[49] *Ibid.*, pp. 35-36.

The second group of resolutions concerned the problem which was of greatest immediate importance to the women, the action to be taken towards an immediate peace. This group was moved as a substitute for that in the preliminary program which called for an immediate truce. Miss Chrystal Macmillan, in her official review of the congress, explains this substitute as follows: " The difficulties of members who did not wish to ask for peace if there were any doubt as to the justice of that peace, and of those who felt that the whole Congress would be a failure, if no demand was made to end the war, were met by putting into one resolution the demand for an end to the bloodshed, for the beginning of peace-negotiation and for the establishment of peace based on the principles of justice adopted by the Congress." [50] The justification of this demand, strikingly similar to a pronouncement of President Wilson, was to the effect that all belligerents were fighting for the same ends and therefore had a common basis for peace discussion.[51] The second resolution under " Action towards Peace " embodied the American proposal of " Continuous Mediation." This resolution was proposed by Rosika Schwimmer as an answer to the question of what could be done immediately.[52] It was seconded by Julia Grace Wales, author of the widely distributed pamphlet " Continuous Mediation without Armistice," who decried the immemorial but anachronistic custom of stopping all communication between belligerents once war had begun.[53] The resolution was as follows:

This International Congress of Women resolves to ask the neutral countries to take immediate steps to create a conference of neutral nations which shall without delay offer continuous mediation. The Conference shall invite suggestions for settlement from each of the belligerent nations and in any case shall submit to all of them simultaneously, reasonable proposals as a basis of peace.[54]

The third group of resolutions concerned the " Principles of a Permanent Peace," which was also a leading topic in the Woman's Peace Party's " Program for Constructive Peace."

---

[50] *Ibid.*, p. xlvi.
[51] *Ibid.*, p. 36.
[52] *Ibid.*, pp. 154-155.
[53] *Ibid.*, p. 155.
[54] *Ibid.*, p. 37.

These principles, to quote their abbreviated form, were as follows:

> That no territory should be transferred without the consent of the men and women in it, and that the right of conquest should not be recognized.
> That autonomy and a democratic parliament should not be refused to any people.
> That the Governments of all nations should come to an agreement to refer future international disputes to arbitration or conciliation and to bring social, moral and economic pressure to bear upon any country which resorts to arms.
> That foreign politics should be subject to democratic control.
> That women should be granted equal political rights with men.[55]

The American delegates gave especially strong support to the foregoing proposals, which were also in the platform of the Woman's Peace Party. Miss Breckinridge introduced the resolution regarding international sanctions, saying in her accompanying speech that it meant only spiritual forms of pressure. The British delegate, Mrs. Pethick-Lawrence, however, amended the resolution to a form specifying non-military pressure. Another resolution introduced by an American delegate was that concerning non-transfer of territory without consent of the people residing in it. The statement of every people's right to autonomy and a democratic parliament, which was introduced by a Polish delegate, was supported by a speech of an American, Miss Grace Abbott. The inclusion of the right of women to suffrage in the principles of permanent peace was unusual but natural in view of the background of the delegates. In the full resolution the enfranchisement of women was presented as releasing one of the strongest forces for the prevention of war—the combined influence of the women of all countries. Woman suffrage was also said to be an element in the democratic control of foreign relations.[56]

" International Cooperation " was a fourth heading in the resolutions of the congress. It covered points that related not so much to the peace settlement as to the institutions of international society that were to be built up by governments after the termination of the war. It was demanded, first, that a third Hague Conference be convened immediately after the

---

[55] *Ibid.*, pp. 36-37.   [56] *Ibid.*, p. 38.

war. Second, two agencies of international organization were called for. One was a permanent international court to settle questions or differences of a justiciable character. The other, meeting the desires of the American delegation, was a permanent international conference to deal with practical proposals for further international cooperation, to formulate and enforce the principles ensuring justice to the weaker countries, subject communities, and backward peoples. The international conference was to appoint a permanent council of conciliation and investigation for the settlement of non-juridical differences. A third demand was for general disarmament, to be approached through the nationalization of the manufacture of arms and munitions and through control of international traffic in such equipment. A fourth resolution favored general liberty of commerce, freedom of the seas, equality in the use of trade routes, and the principle, first suggested by Sophonisba Breckinridge, that international investments of capitalists should be made at their own risk. A fifth resolution proposed the voiding of secret treaties, the legislative ratification of future treaties, and the institution of commissions and conferences for the scientific study of the principles of permanent peace. It demanded further that, both nationally and internationally, women share all civil and political rights and responsibilities on the same terms as men.[57]

A fifth heading, " The Education of Children," covered a resolution urging the necessity of directing the education of children towards the ideal of constructive peace. Under a sixth, " Women and the Peace Settlement Conference," the Peace Conference was urged to pass a resolution in favor of woman suffrage in all countries and also to invite to its deliberations representatives of the people, including women delegates.[58]

The final heading, " Action to be Taken," embraced resolutions which are important in relation to the further history of the women's pacifist movement. One resolution provided that " an international meeting of women shall be held in the same

---

[57] *Ibid.*, pp. 38-40.   [58] *Ibid.*, pp. 40-41.

place and at the same time as the Conference of the Powers which shall frame the terms of the peace settlement after the war for the purpose of presenting practical proposals to that Conference." The other gave practical embodiment to the determination of the congress to strive for present action and to bring its influence to bear on governments at once. " In order to urge the Governments of the world to put an end to this bloodshed and to establish a just and lasting peace," the congress delegated envoys to carry the message expressed in the congress resolutions to the rulers of the belligerent and neutral nations of Europe and to the president of the United States. The envoys, who were to be women of both neutral and belligerent nations, were to be appointed by the International Committee of the congress. They were to report the results of their missions to the International Women's Committee for Constructive Peace and these reports were to serve as a basis for further action.[59]

A most important action was also taken to provide for the future, with particular reference to the meeting of women to be held simultaneously with the peace conference. The congress, while " recognizing the desirability of the cooperation of men and women in the cause of peace," resolved to form a committee of women of all countries which would have two objects: the ensuring of the holding of the proposed international congress and the organization of support for the resolutions passed by the Hague Congress. This committee was to be called the " International Committee of Women for Permanent Peace." It was to be permanent and was to consist of the members of the International Committee of the congress, and others selected by them. Each country was to be represented by not more than five members. The congress recommended the adhesion to this international body of national committees or branches in each country. Membership in these groups was to be open to those who supported the extension of the parliamentary franchise to women and the settlement of international disputes by peaceful means,

[59] *Ibid.*, p. 41.

and who were in general agreement with the resolutions adopted by the International Congress of Women. It was suggested that the women of each country should either join existing organizations which favored such objectives or should start new ones.[60]

Through acceding to the resolution forming the international body, the American delegates tentatively committed the Woman's Peace Party to membership in the International Committee of Women for Permanent Peace. At its first annual convention, in January 1916, the American organization ratified this action of the delegates by adopting a constitution providing for the international affiliation and changing the name of the national body to " The Woman's Peace Party: The Section for the United States of the International Committee of Women for Permanent Peace." [61]   Miss Addams was made president of the International Committee.

On the last day of the congress Miss Addams read a press cutting from a United States paper reporting a most encouraging comment of President Wilson on the women's meeting. After questioning the President on the subject of the congress, the paper had reported as follows:

While the United States Government was not consulted in connection with the Int. Women's Peace Conference at the Hague, the President indicated to-day that the movement had his sympathetic support. Although the meeting has no official status, Mr. Wilson said he understood the delegation had not asked for official authority, because they preferred to act unofficially.[62]

By resolution of the congress, a telegram was sent to President Wilson in reply to his good wishes.

Jane Addams closed the congress with the following words:

This, the first International Congress of women, met in the cause of peace in the necessity brought about by the greatest war the world has ever seen. We have been able to preserve good will and good fellowship, we have considered in perfect harmony and straightforwardness the most difficult propositions and we part better friends than we met.

---

[60] *Ibid.*, pp. 42-43.
[61] *Constitution of the Woman's Peace Party, Adopted January 8, 1916*, Jane Addams Peace Collection, Swarthmore College Library.
[62] *Report of the International Congress of Women, 1915*, p. 178.

It seems to me most significant that women have been able to do this at this moment and that they have done it, in my opinion, extremely well.[63]

A less restrained approval was given by the editor of the *Cambridge Magazine,* who declared: " The International Congress at the Hague has not only brought a breath of fresh air into the unhealthy atmosphere which envelopes the most terrible calamity the world has known; it has established a precedent in history." [64]   However, most comment in the belligerent countries hardly agreed with this opinion. According to Emily G. Balch, in England the congress was reported to be managed in the interest of Germany, while in Germany the delegates were threatened with social boycott for attending a pro-British meeting.   In many European countries, she further states, the meetings were reported to have been practically unattended or to have closed in a row.[65]

Nor was press opinion in the United States by any means entirely in accord with Miss Addams as to the accomplishments of the congress.   The venture was regarded by the Detroit *Free Press* as " the excursion of innocents," by the *New York Herald* as " a silly proceeding," and by the Pittsburgh *Gazette-Times* as " a disappointing failure." [66]   The *Outlook* hoped that the congress had not " inadvertently put another weapon into the hands of those doubters who assert that women are emotional and unfit to take an active part with men in matters of great public import." [67]   At the 1915 convocation exercises of Bryn Mawr College, President M. Carey Thomas deprecated the action of Jane Addams and the other delegates to The Hague as being " ill judged," and the product of misinformation.   She reiterated the most commonly used point of the critics when she said: " No peace

---

[63] *Ibid.,* p. 179.
[64] Quoted in a pamphlet published by the Woman's Peace Party: Jane Addams, *The Revolt Against War,* p. 7.   Jane Addams Peace Collection, Swarthmore College Library.
[65] *Women at The Hague,* p. 14.
[66] " Was the Women's Peace Congress a Failure? " *Literary Digest* (1915), L, 1139.
[67] " Women and Peace," *Outlook* (1915), CX, 50.

could be made now save one that would favor Germany and would provide no indemnity for ravished Belgium." [68]

On the other hand, the *Chicago Daily News* remarked that at least the congress had called attention to the fact that "there are in the world a goodly number of people sane enough to desire peace and brave and optimistic enough to labor for it, effectively or otherwise." [69] The *Indianapolis News* was hopeful enough to feel that the protest of the women was not likely to die out.[70] The *Chicago Herald* declared that "he is lacking in imagination who sees in this conference only an isolated feministic event." It seemed to this paper "part and parcel of the great manifestation of national feeling which this war has awakened in America, and independently of what it actually accomplishes it will have historical importance." [71] The *Springfield Republican* asserted: "The significance of the event is to be found in the fact that such a thing never happened before, while the fact that it can now happen shows that women's influence in opposition to war is but just beginning to be feebly mobilized as a force capable sometime of powerful restraint upon the destructive fighting energies of the civilized world." [72] The Baltimore *Evening Sun* also expressed a favorable opinion: "The Hague Congress did not accomplish the impossible, but its protest has not been thrown away, and its quiet influence may be felt with others ultimately in shortening the duration of a fruitless international deadlock." [73]

For the women the Hague Congress was not a final gesture of protest but a beginning of action. The next task was to try to accomplish "the impossible."

---

[68] *Philadelphia Bulletin*, September 30, 1915.
[69] Quoted by the *Literary Digest* (1915), L, 1139.
[70] *Ibid.*
[71] *Ibid.*
[72] *Ibid.*
[73] Baltimore *Evening Sun*, July 9, 1915.

CHAPTER IV

VISITS TO STATESMEN

From the point of view of the Woman's Peace Party, the resolution of the Hague Congress which was of greatest immediate importance was that adopting the plan for continuous mediation by a conference of neutral nations. More than anything else this plan for attaining an early peace had spurred the Americans to organization, had received emphasis in their early pronouncements, and had been urged by them upon the Hague Congress. Now it had not only been accepted in theory by an international organization of women pacifists but was by way of being placed before the governments of the world. For the Hague Congress had decided that its resolutions, especially that on a conference of neutrals, should be transmitted by a committee of its members from neutral countries to the premier and the minister of foreign affairs of each of the belligerent countries, and by another committee to the same officials in the neutral countries.

In view of the importance attached to the rôle of the United States in mediation, it was natural that an American woman was placed on each of the two committees. The committee to visit the belligerent countries consisted of Jane Addams, Dr. Aletta Jacobs, and two unofficial delegates—Frau van Wulfften Palthe of The Hague and Dr. Alice Hamilton of the United States. The other committee comprised the British delegate, Chrystal Macmillan, Rosika Schwimmer, Mme. Cor Ramondt-Hirschmann of Holland, and Emily G. Balch of the American delegation; during a portion of its travels Julia Grace Wales acted as secretary of this second committee.[1]

Resolved to lose no time in setting about their momentous undertaking, the two committees started their travels in May only about a week after the end of the congress. There is surely no episode of the war period stranger than this journey made by a few women, seeking peace in the name not of

---

[1] *New York Times*, May 11, 1915.

governments but of members of their sex gathered from twelve nations. Perhaps the strangest thing about the venture may seem the belief of the women that they had a chance to succeed; but it is pointed out by Miss Balch that they were "neither impulsive nor very optimistic." She writes: "We meant to leave no stone unturned but I doubt if any one of us was even hopeful of success." [2]

The experiences of the women did not, however, confirm that skepticism which, at the announcement of their undertaking, laughed at the attempt of private individuals to achieve contact with and make some impress upon the statesmen of Europe. Visiting fourteen countries in scarcely more than five weeks, the women could say of themselves at the end:

They were received gravely, kindly, perhaps gladly by twenty-one ministers, the presidents of two republics, a king, and the Pope. All, apparently, recognized without argument that an expression of the public opinion of a large body of women had every claim to consideration in questions of war and peace.[3]

Moreover, as Miss Addams has written, it was possible for them as women from belligerent and neutral nations alike "to carry forward an interchange of question and answer between capitals which were barred to each other." [4]

What the envoys proposed to the statesmen may be inferred in part from the memorandum on their mission prepared at its conclusion by Rosika Schwimmer and Chrystal Macmillan. According to this memorandum, the women, while laying before the statesmen all the resolutions of the congress, laid special emphasis upon the resolutions urging the summoning of a neutral conference for continuous mediation. As this resolution was rather general and vague the interpretation of it given in the memorandum casts valuable light on the probable content of the discussion. The resolution was said to mean the following:

(a) Invitations to send delegates to the Conference should be sent to the Governments of all neutral Sovereign States.

(b) The work of the Conference should be to formulate concrete

---

[2] A letter to the author.
[3] *Women at The Hague*, p. 110.
[4] Addams, *Peace and Bread*, p. 16.

proposals of possible terms of peace as a basis for suggestions and objections on the part of the belligerent governments and for public discussion. In other words, it should frame the outlines of a possible peace treaty to be submitted to the belligerent governments and to be publicly discussed in the different countries.

Further, on the basis of the suggestions and objections received from the belligerents, the Conference should modify the original proposals, and submit them again thus modified to the belligerents. It should in this way *continuously develop the original proposals* in the line of further suggestions and objections made by the belligerent governments or arising out of the public discussion of the successive proposals in the different countries. It should continue in this way until the proposals have reached a point when the belligerents of both sides find in them sufficient common ground themselves to meet for the final settlement of the peace treaty.[5]

Thus the interpretation of the resolution was in accord with the Julia Wales plan for continuous mediation, which provided further that the delegates, though representing governments, should be without power to commit them.

The women initiated the venture by a comparatively easy undertaking. As the meeting which framed the points had been held in the capital of Holland, they sought their first interview with the Dutch Prime Minister, Cort van der Linden. He was waited upon not by the appointed committee but by a group of the congress leaders—Jane Addams, the Italian delegate, Rosa Genoni, Dr. Jacobs, Chrystal Macmillan, and Rosika Schwimmer. There are no available records of that interview.[6] The *New York Times* merely reported

---

[5] "Memorandum by Rosika Schwimmer and Chrystal Macmillan, members of the delegations to the governments of Europe from the International Congress of Women, The Hague, April 28th to May 1st, 1915, on the proposal for a conference of neutral nations." MS, Jane Addams Peace Collection. This will henceforth be referred to as "Memorandum by Schwimmer and Macmillan."

[6] There are unfortunately other gaps in the records. The sources chiefly relied upon in the following account are the above-mentioned "Memorandum by Schwimmer and Macmillan" and Jane Addams' notes on the trip, both of which are in the Jane Addams Peace Collection. Use of these documents, however, has been supplemented by several other sources. Of such the fullest is a book written by K. D. Courtney, the British pacifist, entitled *Extracts from a Diary during the War*, printed for private circulation in December 1927. This book is to be found in the United States in the Jane Addams Peace Collection. It contains notes written on July 23, 1915, on the author's recollections of a report which Jane Addams had given orally on the preceding day to a London committee affiliated with the Hague Congress. Other sources used were the contemporary

that the Prime Minister declined to comment on the women's visit.[7] That the reception was not unfavorable may be surmised from the fact that two months later he again received a number of the delegates when they returned from the Scandinavian countries.

After the interview with the Dutch statesman the more hazardous and dramatic part of the adventure began. Miss Addams, Dr. Jacobs, and Mme. Genoni journeyed to London to talk with Asquith and Grey. The time of their visit was most inauspicious, for only two days before their arrival in the English capital the *Lusitania* had been sunk. That disaster inspired in the English a hatred of the Germans which was so bitter that Parliament had decided to intern German subjects living in London. The very air was charged with intense bitterness toward the enemy. Nevertheless, Ambassador Page, although thoroughly unsympathetic with the women's mission, was willing to arrange for them interviews with both ministers. Despite the unfavorable background, including the indifference of the English press toward the women, the committee was received cordially by the statesmen. A precise report of Asquith's reactions is not available. But in a newspaper interview which she gave on her return to New York, Miss Addams divulged the fact that Grey had told her that the war would have to go on to a finish. He declared, she said, that any departure from this policy on the part of England would look like a weakening and that for the same reason no other belligerent power could broach the question of peace. He was willing to concede, however, that the neutral nations might submit a number of propositions, one of which might serve as an opening wedge for further negotiations.[8] In response to a remark that neutrals think they have to wait till the right moment comes before taking

---

items on the mission in the *New York Times*; the "Manifesto" issued by five of the women envoys on October 15, 1915; and the book *Women at The Hague*, written by Jane Addams, Emily G. Balch, and Alice Hamilton, and published under the auspices of the Woman's Peace Party in 1915.

[7] *New York Times*, May 8, 1915.

[8] *New York Times*, July 6, 1915.

action towards mediation, he "indicated his astonishment by asking when they did think that the right moment would come." [9]

The next interview took place in Berlin while the news of the *Lusitania* was being celebrated. The women again faced an American ambassador who considered them "cranks," but he, too, arranged for their audiences with the heads of the government—meetings to which, according to Gerard, the statesmen "looked forward with unconcealed perturbation." [10] The women first spoke with Foreign Minister von Jagow. Having read the resolutions presented to him, he assured the visitors in a gracious tone that he regarded it as quite natural that women should be engaged in such a work and expressed surprise that they had not done this thing sooner. To be sure, he showed his caution by speaking of the feeling of German soldiers that the war must be fought to a conclusive end, and of German women that any peace, however desirable that it come soon, must safeguard the national integrity. Moreover, he showed some resentment in discussing the selling of munitions by the United States to the Allies. He pointed out that, while American citizens had a legal right to do this, the practice was causing hard feelings on the part of Germany toward the United States.[11] Nevertheless, the main entry of the women regarding von Jagow's attitude toward the conference was favorable:

. . . Herr von Jagow said he thought it very desirable that peace should come soon but thought that the first steps should be taken by the neutrals because it could not be taken by them. When asked if he thought the United States should take the first steps to invite the neutrals, he asked whether the United States was neutral. He said that the neutral countries should form a conference such as the delegation proposed as soon as possible.[12]

After the von Jagow interview, the women saw Chancellor von Bethmann-Hollweg. Whether or not because he had lost a son in the war, Bethmann-Hollweg took their mission more seriously than had the Foreign Minister. He displayed inter-

---

[9] MS, Memorandum by Schwimmer and Macmillan.
[10] James W. Gerard, *My Four Years in Germany*, pp. 412-413.
[11] Courtney, p. 43; *New York Times*, June 24, 1915, July 6, 1915.
[12] MS, Memorandum by Schwimmer and Macmillan.

est in the plan for continuous mediation and was willing to
talk with the women about it. He said that he believed that
the neutral countries were playing too feeble a rôle in the
current international scene and that they should begin to
make propositions in regard to peace terms. Agreeing with
Grey's obvious point, the Chancellor declared that no belligerent could take this step. Then, following von Jagow's
policy of caution, he made a number of rambling comments
on other subjects. He delivered some nationalistic utterances
on Germany's humanity and urged Miss Addams to go to
Belgium to see what outstanding social legislation the Germans had introduced there.[13] An interesting entry of Miss
Addams covers the rest:

> He said he had never heard a German say he wanted to crush
> England. I said I had never heard an Englishman say he wanted
> to crush Germany, but that they wanted to crush German militarism.
> He said that was a distinction but not a difference. The army in
> Germany is part of the government, and he went on to talk in that
> half mystical way they do—so difficult for us to understand. It is as
> if their feeling for the army was that of a church for its procession.
> It is a part of it.[14]

A few days after their interview with the German statesmen
the delegates went to Vienna, the capital which had taken the
first steps toward the war. In this city they saw the ghastly
effect of privation—an experience which was to influence
greatly their subsequent feeling about the peace terms. The
committee first interviewed Prime Minister Stürgkh, a " large,
grizzled, formidable man." After the women had finished
their presentation he said nothing. Miss Addams then ner-
vously remarked: " It perhaps seems to you very foolish that
women should go about in this way; but after all, the world
itself is so strange in this war situation that our mission may
be no more strange and foolish than the rest." The minister
banged his fist on the table with a thud which rattled the
objects in the room:

---

[13] Courtney, p. 44; *New York Times*, May 24, 1915.
[14] Jane Addams Notes on the Mission to the European Governments.
MS, Jane Addams Peace Collection. This will be referred to as
" Jane Addams Notes."

Foolish? Not at all. These are the first sensible words that have been uttered in this room for ten months. That door opens from time to time, and people come in to say, "Mr. Minister, we must have more men, we must have more ammunition, we must have more money or we cannot go on with this war." At last the door opens and two people walk in and say, "Mr. Minister, why not substitute negotiations for fighting?" They are the sensible ones! [15]

This incident was to be carefully cherished by the women as a high spot of their mission and was much emphasized in their public pleas for the neutral conference.

Miss Addams and Dr. Jacobs were received on May 27 by the Minister of Foreign Affairs for Austria-Hungary, Count Burián.[16] This statesman, too, was favorable to the idea of continuous mediation but expressed doubt whether the United States should take the initiative. The entry of the women with regard to this interview was as follows:

May 27th. Graf Burián, the Foreign Minister, said that he thought that a conference as proposed should be brought together as soon as possible. He did not think that America should begin because America did not know enough about European interests. He thought that America should send a representative to such a Conference but that it ought to be someone who understood European interests. Mr. Wilson's way of offering mediation was impossible because it was only offered, if the belligerents wanted it. Both parties were obliged to say no. He did not consider that the right way to offer mediation. He thought that definite propositions should be made to both parties. The neutrals can come again with proposals, if the first are not accepted.[17]

This meeting did not terminate the efforts of the women in the Dual Monarchy. Paying heed to the national consciousness of the Hungarians the delegates decided that Prime Minister, Count Tisza, should also be interviewed. At this point in the journey the two Dutch women went on to Berne to attend a peace meeting, and the Americans went alone to Budapest. The women found that the atmosphere in the Hungarian capital differed from any other which they had experienced during their journey. Whereas in other countries the interview with the prime minister had been arranged for privately, in Hungary it was secured by the Suffrage Society.

[15] *Women at The Hague*, pp. 96-97; Courtney, pp. 43-44.
[16] *New York Times*, June 2, 1915.
[17] MS, Memorandum by Schwimmer and Macmillan.

This society also arranged for a large dinner and a public meeting, both of which were well and favorably reported by the Hungarian press. The Americans found Prime Minister Tisza very friendly. An ardent Presbyterian, he expressed his grief over the shock to religion which the war had brought about. He also declared that, despite the fact that Austria-Hungary was fighting Russia, the Hungarians liked the Russian people. Russia could be assured that the Austro-Hungarian Empire would not be unreasonable about peace terms, he declared.[18] The notes of Miss Addams contain the following entry:

Count Tisza, of Hungary, expressed the feeling that the Hungarians were getting nothing out of the situation. Let Germany settle with the Belgians. He would welcome negotiations.[19]

The next interviews took place in Berne. Miss Addams and Dr. Jacobs first saw President Motta, who, though he expressed approval of the idea of continuous mediation, declared that Switzerland could not take the initiative in such a plan. He said that not until the other neutral countries had agreed to send delegates would his country participate in such a peace conference. He also expressed the opinion that the opportune moment for negotiations had not arrived.[20] The next interview, which was with Foreign Minister Hoffmann, proved even more discouraging. He greeted the women with cool politeness. After they had explained their plan he said nothing. They were soon out of his office.[21]

The delegates then set out for Rome. On the way they stopped at Milan, which was under martial law. The city had other ominous indications of the militarism which, after the declaration of war, was entrenching itself in Italy. The flags of the five Allies decked the streets and the shop windows displayed large photographs of a Belgian child with a neatly amputated hand. In Rome, also, flags were flying everywhere. Soldiers in new uniforms were crowding the streets. In Italy the delegates were to feel that so far as the government and public opinion were concerned they had accomplished nothing

---

[18] Courtney, p. 44.
[19] MS, Jane Addams Notes.
[20] *New York Times*, June 4, 1915.
[21] Courtney, p. 44.

more than the formal carrying out of their project. A new war ministry had come into power. Prime Minister Salandra and Foreign Minister Sonnino both received them, but the latter spoke lightly and the former declared that it was too early to talk about peace terms.[22]

However, the women found hope in another quarter—the Vatican. The Papal Secretary of State, Cardinal Gasparri, to whom the women had a letter from the Primate of Hungary, told them that the Vatican deeply deplored the awful havoc of war and that it seemed time for women to move in the direction of peace.[23] With respect to the Vatican's assistance the women recorded the following:

> The Vatican was not supposed, he said, to want to go into anything that failed. That was not so, at least in this case. They would go into this undertaking. We discussed the possibility of a group which would not attempt to conclude the war but would conceivably create some basis on which we could go ahead. The Vatican was eager to go into such an undertaking and thought the President should be the leader.[24]

After the conference with the Cardinal, the women had an encouraging audience with the Pope. It was reported by Miss Addams as follows:

> We had an interesting half hour with the Pope, who spoke of the war being a throwback for the church, after its teachings through all the ages. He thought the President of the United States ought to lead. If asked to send a representative to a conference of neutrals he would appoint, he said, a neutral and a secular. We took it that he meant that he would accommodate himself—would not stand on ecclesiastical grounds.[25]

The next capital which the committee visited was terror-stricken Paris. It had neither time nor patience for pacifists, and everywhere they went the women were followed by police. Although even in France they were received by the governmental leaders, the interviews did not greatly help their cause. When they spoke with the militaristic Delcassé he declared that France would have nothing to do with peace negotiations,

---

[22] *New York Times*, June 11, 1915; Courtney, p. 44.
[23] *New York Times*, June 11, 1915, June 24, 1915, July 6, 1915; Courtney, p. 44.
[24] MS, Jane Addams Notes.   [25] *Ibid.*

even the best.   Unable to foresee Hitler, he avowed that it was
the desire of France to beat down Germany to the point where
that country would not be able to regain its strength for a
hundred years.[26]   After their reception by this jingoistic
gentleman the women interviewed Viviani, newly elected
Prime Minister, on June 14.   This formerly active Socialist
listened more patiently to them and even declared that he had
drunk in pacifism with his mother's milk.[27]   Then he said
that France would " not resent " the formation of a neutral
conference for the offering of continuous mediation such as
the women proposed.[28]   The delegates also had interviews with
laymen.   Some were former pacifists who they found had
become " more militaristic than the military." [29]   Only a few
French men and women, most of them young people, had
remained in the peace movement.

From Paris the women journeyed to the seaside near Havre,
where the Belgian Government was housed in hotels and villas.
On June 14 they saw Foreign Minister Davignon, who
appeared to take their mission very seriously but declared that
Belgium was in the hands of the Allies and must leave all
negotiations to its protectors.   He added, however, " that
Belgium would rather have the enemy leave their country
as the result of negotiations than have the armies fighting over
it a second time." [30]   After this interview, in view of the fact
that the Havre police gave even greater difficulty than had
the Parisian constabulary, the delegates found it expedient
to abandon their plans for remaining overnight in Havre and
hastened back to the French capital.[31]

The interviews with the Belgians completed the assignments
of the committee until the resolutions could be presented to
President Wilson.   But as the delegates had a week to spare
before the time for departure from Liverpool, they spent the
interim conferring with statesmen and other prominent figures

[26] Courtney, p. 44.
[27] Interview described by Miss Balch in a letter to the author.
[28] MS, Memorandum by Schwimmer and Macmillan.
[29] *Women at The Hague*, p. 50.
[30] MS, Memorandum by Schwimmer and Macmillan.
[31] Courtney, p. 46.

in England. Before reaching England Miss Addams wrote to
Sir Edward Grey, hoping for the opportunity to present her
impressions to him. On June 20 he wrote her that owing to
trouble with his eyes he would not be able to return to London
till the following month. Therefore he had sent her letter to
the Foreign Office, with the request that they communicate
with her. However, he had begun by words showing a personal interest:

> I have received your letter and I should personally be most inter-
> ested to hear the impression gained by you of the views of Statesmen
> in other belligerent countries.
> I think it is also important that these should be known to the
> British Government; but this latter object can best be effected by
> your seeing one of the Ministers or some responsible person in
> London.[32]

The attitude of the English officials with whom the women
talked, Lord Crewe, Lord Robert Cecil, and Lloyd George, was
not dissimilar to that of Delcassé. Lloyd George in particular
was rampant for the crushing defeat of Germany.[33] In the
hope of finding at least the Church more sympathetic, Miss
Addams sought an audience with the Archbishop of Canterbury and the Bishop of Winchester. Both prelates questioned
her closely and they were especially interested in the Pope's
reaction to her mission.[34] Whether or not they committed
themselves to the plan is not reported.

Before sailing Miss Addams gave an interview to a reporter
of the *New York Times* in which she summarized the impressions of her travels. Among other things, she said:

> In going into the belligerent countries we naturally did not try to
> force peace talk any more than in going into a home in turmoil
> a caller would attempt to give advice. But our mission in going to
> the Continent was apparently quite well known, and the talk drifted
> easily to our peace efforts. We met with no molestation anywhere;
> in fact, we found the officials ready to help us along. That does
> not mean that the officials gave the impression that they sympathized
> with the idea of bringing about a speedy peace, for they expressed
> only the idea that the war must be pushed to a decisive end.[35]

---

[32] Grey to Jane Addams, June 20, 1915, MS, Jane Addams Peace
Collection.
[33] Courtney, p. 46.   [34] *Ibid.*
[35] *New York Times*, June 24, 1915.

While the Jane Addams Committee was carrying out its mission in the belligerent capitals, the second committee had taken the plan to the northern countries. There is available no detailed report of the interviews of the latter committee, but Miss Balch has described the mission in its general outline.

From Amsterdam the committee set out for the Scandinavian countries. "What we are asking the Scandinavian countries," Miss Balch wrote Louis Lochner on June 1, "is 'Would you three with Switzerland and Holland send out an invitation to a neutral conference if you knew that the United States would be glad to respond?'" [36] Miss Balch added that this question was on the supposition that the present state of public opinion in Germany excluded the United States as the first mover. One may cite in this connection the Schwimmer and Macmillan memorandum, which, suggesting the same procedure of a joint invitation, stated:

> The advantage of having the invitation issued by a group instead of by an individual government is that, on the one hand, the group acting jointly would give confidence to the belligerents of both sides, and, on the other, would help to safeguard the neutrality of the individual governments signing the invitation.
> This would be so because the sensitiveness of the belligerents might lead them to suppose that some of the neutrals might lean to one side and some to the other, so that the invitation signed by the group would assure the belligerents of the disinterestedness of all the signers.[37]

The first city visited by the committee was Copenhagen. There they were received by Prime Minister Zahle and Foreign Minister de Scavenius. In this city, according to the letter written by Miss Balch to Louis Lochner, Mme. Schwimmer had an interesting discussion with the German Ambassador. Talking quite frankly, he expressed his opinion that President Wilson had acted very badly. He did not have reference to the supplying of ammunition to the Allies. His criticism was, to the women's amazement, that a great neutral

---

[36] Emily G. Balch to Louis Lochner, June 1, 1915, MS, Jane Addams Peace Collection.
[37] MS, Memorandum by Schwimmer and Macmillan.

country like the United States had not come forward in such a world war.[38]

From Copenhagen the committee journeyed to Christiania, where, doubtless because of the strength of the feminist and pacifist movements in Norway, the women were received by King Haakon. The King seemed deeply interested in the plan for mediation, giving them an audience of an hour and three quarters.[39] In Christiania the delegates were also received by Prime Minister Knudson and Foreign Minister Ihlen. In Norway they were accorded the most formal recognition which can be given to unofficial persons. They were received in the Parliament House by the President and Vice-President of the *Storthing*, the Parliament composed by the coordinate chambers meeting in joint session, and by other legislative leaders. The women then went to Stockholm, where they had an interview with Foreign Minister Wallenberg. This statesman, who was also a wealthy banker, was of all the men seen by this committee the most enthusiastic for the plan for neutral mediation.[40] Among the Swedes outside the official world who showed their sympathy and interest in the pacifists' project was Selma Lagerlöf.

The next capital to which the delegates traveled—an exception to their assignment to neutral countries—was that of a belligerent country, Russia. Before the departure for Petrograd the place on the committee of Rosika Schwimmer, who was technically an enemy, was taken by Baroness Ellen Palmstierna, a distinguished Swedish woman. In Petrograd the delegates had an interview of nearly an hour with Foreign Minister Saznoff, who promised to give the memorandum his careful attention. He said that it would not be unacceptable to Russia if the neutral governments called a conference to offer mediation and to make proposals of possible terms of peace to the belligerents but that he did not think that it would be useful.[41] While Saznoff indicated that Russia

[38] Emily G. Balch to Louis Lochner, June 1, 1915, MS, Jane Addams Peace Collection.
[39] *Women at The Hague*, p. 101.
[40] Personal information of Miss Balch to the author.
[41] *New York Times*, June 18, 1915; MS, Memorandum by Schwimmer and Macmillan.

would at least put no obstacle in the way of the plan, the attitude of the Russian press toward the peace-makers was less open-minded. A dispatch from Petrograd to the London *Morning Post* reported that for the most part the press ignored the delegation but that the *Bourse Gazette* carried an editorial which declared that their mission was futile and that " to talk to us now of peace is pure mockery." [42]

The pacifists journeyed back by way of the Scandinavian countries. In Sweden the return of the delegates was greeted by a set of simultaneous peace meetings held in three hundred and forty-three places. Each meeting heard the same address and passed the same resolution, affirming most of the planks of the Hague Congress, including its call for mediation. One of the five meetings in Stockholm was attended by thirty-two hundred people, while eight hundred could not gain admittance. [43] In that city Foreign Minister Wallenberg was again interviewed by the women. So warmly interested did he show himself in the plan that the women felt constrained to change all their plans and to go beyond their mandate by extending their efforts to Holland, England, and the White House. [44] In Christiania the delegates again spoke with Foreign Minister Ihlen. The warm reception accorded to the women in the Scandinavian countries reflects the great sentiment for early peace in these nations, which, though neutral, were deeply affected by repercussions of the war.

In Holland, their starting place, the women had interviews with the Minister of Foreign Affairs and the Prime Minister. Soon they were joined in Amsterdam by some members of the other committee and the two delegations exchanged reports. The reports of visits to the belligerents were to the effect that the belligerent governments were open to proposals but thought that only the neutrals could take the first step toward mediation. On the other hand, the second committee had learned that the neutral governments " seemed to be afraid that the immediate calling of a neutral conference might be

---

[42] *New York Times*, June 17, 1915.
[43] *Women at The Hague*, pp. 104-105.
[44] Personal information of Miss Balch to the author.

considered inopportune or unfriendly by the belligerents." [45]
The women, therefore, considered it important to revisit at
least one of the important governments on each of the belligerent sides in order to gain assurances which they could
convey to the neutral governments. Thereupon Mme. Schwimmer and Mme. Ramondt-Hirschmann returned to Berlin while
Miss Balch and Miss Macmillan journeyed to London.

Von Jagow, interviewed again on July 15, reassured the
women that Germany would not find the calling of a conference of neutrals unfriendly, although he warned against
formulating too many illusions about it. There was another
statement of von Jagow which suggested his desire for the
conference:

In response to a remark of our delegation that, if the side in the
strongest position were to ask for peace the weaker side would
resent mediation because it would be thought that the stronger
wanted to dictate terms; while, were the weaker side to ask for
peace, it would be considered as a confession of defeat. Acknowl-
edging the truth of this Herr von Jagow said: " But at this moment
neither side is strong enough to dictate terms and neither side is
so weakened that it has to sue for peace." [46]

In London Miss Macmillan and Miss Balch were briefly
received by Sir Edward Grey. On July 14 they had an interview with Lord Crewe. The content of this interview is
revealed by a letter confirming it from Sir Eric Drummond
to Miss Macmillan. Lord Crewe made it clear in the first
place that the British Government could not invite the formation of a conference of neutrals because this might be thought
equivalent to an indirect proposal for peace. But, as Sir Eric
recalled, he did authorize Miss Macmillan to " say that the
Government would not place any obstacles in the way of the
formation of such a body or make any protest against its
existence if it should come into being." [47]

Later the information secured from the belligerent governments was placed by European members of the committees
before the neutral governments. By the end of July, the

[45] MS, Memorandum by Schwimmer and Macmillan.
[46] Ibid.
[47] Eric Drummond to Chrystal Macmillan, July 22, 1915, MS, Jane
Addams Peace Collection.

members of the two committees were convinced, in the light of the attitude of the governments visited, that the neutral conference for continuous mediation was not impracticable. The memorandum of Rosika Schwimmer and Chrystal Macmillan, submitted to the International Committee of Women for Permanent Peace in Amsterdam on August 2, proposed in consequence of this conviction that the initiative be taken immediately either by The Netherlands or by Sweden, one of the two inviting the other four neutrals to a preliminary meeting, which in turn was to issue a joint invitation to the conference.

At this point we may well pause to consider the significance of the data which the women envoys had gathered. The general accuracy of their reports seems unassailable in view not only of the high character of the witnesses but also the concurrence of the multiple testimony. As to the significance of what the statesmen said to them, there is, naturally, some room for debate. The women envoys themselves believed that as a result of their efforts the plan of starting mediation through the agency of a continuous conference of the neutral nations was being seriously discussed alike in the cabinets of the belligerent and neutral countries.[48] This assumption was not so bold and sweeping as it might seem for it did not involve any assertion that the belligerent governments would take a step towards mediation on their own initiative. But, while always making clear that the initiative must come from the neutral nations, the women did have the idea that the belligerent nations would quite possibly welcome a mediating conference of neutrals if it came about in such a way as to save their face. Yet even this idea, though derived from things which the statesmen interviewed had said to the women visitors, is one that must be viewed with reserve. For it is quite possible that the statesmen were simply, to use the vernacular, jollying the women along in order to make the best impression upon a large section of public opinion, with the conviction that nothing could come of their impetuous wanderings.

---

[48] See their manifesto, cited below, pp. 119-121.

Certain individuals, possibly in a better position to understand the situation than the women pacifists, have expressed the opinion that the latter were building their hopes upon a foundation of sand or upon no foundation at all. Colonel House wrote to President Wilson to this effect on July 17, 1915, in connection with his announcement to the latter of an approaching visit from Jane Addams. His words with reference to her plan were brief but unequivocal:

She has accumulated a wonderful lot of misformation in Europe. She saw von Jagow, Grey, and many others, and, for one reason or another, they were not quite candid with her, so she has a totally wrong impression.[49]

Viscount Bryce was of the same opinion. He wrote to House on November 26, 1915, that Jane Addams, " who ought to have known better after her journey around Europe," and other women had been trying to engineer a movement for mediation but might have spared themselves the trouble.[50]

On the other hand, there is the problem raised by Ray Stannard Baker, in his biography of Wilson, of whether Grey and other British statesmen had been quite candid with House in discouraging American effort in behalf of peace.[51] When at last Sir Edward Grey saw fit to encourage mediation, he wrote a letter to House on August 26 which conveys a much more favorable impression of the efforts of the pacifists. The letter said in part:

. . . Several neutrals have pressed me about a Conference of neutral States to be formed so that it may be ready to undertake mediation whenever it is opportune. I have said that no one could resent any efforts of neutrals which were impartial and independent to promote peace, but I did not think a Conference of neutrals would be of much use unless the United States was in it.

If the end of this war is arrived at through mediation, I believe it must be through that of the United States. . . .

. . . I look forward to the help of your country under the guidance of the President and impelled by this section of public opinion in those larger conditions of peace, which looking to the future, interests neutrals as much as belligerents.[52]

[49] Charles Seymour, *The Intimate Papers of Colonel House*, II, 22.
[50] *Ibid.*, p. 111.
[51] Ray Stannard Baker, *Woodrow Wilson, Life and Letters*, VI, 123 n.
[52] *Ibid.*, pp. 88-89.

It is very probable that the " several neutrals " referred to at the beginning included the three envoys of the International Committee, Jane Addams, Dr. Aletta Jacobs, and Rosa Genoni. Miss Addams' previously quoted account of what he said squares in substantials with his own statement. In any event, it is evident from Grey's letter to House, unless the letter itself was disingenuous, that he at least was favorable to a conference of neutrals in which the United States would take the lead. As to the attitude of the other statesmen visited by the women, there is too little clear information to permit of any certain judgment with regard to the issue. The truth of the matter probably lies somewhere between the extreme skepticism of their critics and the women's acceptance of the assurances of the statesmen at their face value.

What attitude would Americans, in particular President Wilson, take towards the news garnered by the women? This was the problem which weighed upon the American delegates as they left European shores. There were two of them, however, whose haste to be home to find the answer was to be sorely tried by an episode of the war-ridden ocean. Julia Wales and Lola Lloyd, two delegates to the Hague Congress, were passengers on a Scandinavian-American liner which on June 6 was stopped off the Hebrides by the British warship *Cedric* and compelled to put to port at Stornaway, where the ship was held for three and a half days before being allowed to proceed to New York. The two women were none the less indignant for being ardent pacifists and circulated among the passengers a petition of protest to President Wilson. The petition called upon him to take steps to end such treatment by Great Britain and pointed out that it went far beyond the justified right of search. They complained of the interference with the course of the ship, the transference of the passengers from safety to a danger zone, and the holding them incommunicado for several days. Then, realizing that the petition might be interpreted as inconsistent with their pacifism, the women took a milder tone:

While expressing our vehement protest against this injustice, we disclaim any intention of urging our Government to use military measures. We recognize the wisdom of your policy in keeping our country out of war, and we pray that nothing will change this policy in the future.

But is it not time to use all our moral force toward ending the war in Europe? [53]

The protest of the pacifists called forth from the *New York Times* a rather satirical editorial. It presented as " curious " the fact that the only incitement to making a serious row about the incident came from two women returning from the pacifist congress at The Hague. Noting the women's final disclaimer of any appeal for force, the editorial remarked: " Seemingly these dear ladies want what they think their rights firmly asserted, but not for worlds would they have these rights maintained ! " [54]

The next event which brought the enterprise of the women pacifists to the attention of the American public was the arrival home of their leader, Jane Addams. On the morning of July 5, through the heaviest part of a long thunderstorm, the American liner *St. Louis* slid up to her pier in North River, New York. A group of about fifty people, most of them representatives of peace societies, had been waiting at the dock. Many of them wore a white ribbon inscribed " Welcome to Jane Addams." After disembarking, Miss Addams spoke briefly at the pier. She emphasized as facts of great significance the meeting of fifteen hundred women at The Hague during time of war and the courtesy everywhere accorded their representatives by officials of the countries subsequently visited. [55] However, the *New York Times*, in an editorial on Miss Addams' return, declared that the true significance of her effort, designed to end the war before democratic nations had triumphed, was that it assisted not peace but war.[56] On the other hand, the *Public* believed that the return of Jane Addams marked " the completion of the initial steps of one of the world's great movements." [57]

[53] *New York Times*, June 19, 1915.
[54] *Ibid.*, June 21, 1915.
[55] " Jane Addams Back," *Survey* (1915), XXXIV, 327.
[56] *New York Times*, July 6, 1915.
[57] Quoted by the *Friends' Intelligencer* (1915), LXXII, 505.

Four days after Miss Addams' arrival a huge mass-meeting was held in her honor at Carnegie Hall. Three thousand people attended and thousands were turned away. When she appeared on the stage the throng rose and cheered. The woman before them was a symbol not only of humane revulsion from war but of the hope that earnest cooperative effort might bring the present slaughter to an early end. Miss Addams' address dealt primarily with the women's congress at The Hague and their visit to the European capitals, but this was merely a point of departure for a stirring discourse on the revolt against war. This revolt, her observations had convinced her, had so broad a popular basis that even the belligerent governments were inclined to view favorably the proposed conference of neutrals to offer mediation. The revolt was expressed, it seemed to Miss Addams, particularly in the widespread feeling that the war was an old men's war. In connection with this part of her address Miss Addams spoke certain words which were to become notorious:

The soldiers themselves call this " the old men's war." Many of the young fellows in the trenches think that war as a method of settling international difficulties is out of date. Hand-to-hand fighting seems to them contrary to every teaching of civilization. This detestation of violence is typical of the generation. We were told by young men everywhere who had been at the front, that men had literally to be stimulated to a willingness to perform the bloody work of bayonet charges. The English are in such cases given rum; the French, it is said, absinthe; the Germans, more scientifically perhaps, inhalations of ether.[58]

These words, which were only incidental to the main theme of the address, were discussed up and down the land and from the point of view of two issues. The first, suggested by the remark about the old men's war, was whether or not the war could validly be blamed on old age. The *Cedar Rapids Times* agreed with Miss Addams and brought to her support the alleged fact that nearly every general in Europe was above sixty or around seventy.[59] The New York *Evening Globe,* putting the matter in ideological terms, declared that the present war was " the logical outcome of the peculiar romantic

[58] Quoted by Linn, *Jane Addams,* pp. 313-314.
[59] *Cedar Rapids Times,* June 15, 1915.

ideas of those who gained their views of life in the middle nineteenth century." The younger generation, however, seemed to the *Globe* different in that young people were more concrete in their thinking and believed life to be more real and valuable than abstractions. " They might fight like tigers in defense of actual things that were dear to them," the editorial asserted, " but they would never go to war of their own accord for things they do not believe exist." [60]

Most journalists found the idea of Miss Addams distasteful or silly. Thus the *New York Times* felt that, although the guiding and controlling men in the various fighting countries were rather well along in years and not a few were really old, " they exercise power only through the permission or submission of the younger generation, where the real strength lies—in everything except mentality, at least—and the contention that the younger generation is notably pacifist and anti-military needs better proof than that Miss Addams has heard of youths who ' didn't believe in war ' and committed suicide rather than render a service that involved shooting." [61] The *Hudson Republican* waxed sarcastic over the phrase of Miss Addams with " a great big thought behind it, which was undoubtedly worth the trip to The Hague." [62]

However, the controversy over an " old men's war " was trivial compared with the furor which was raised by Miss Addams' assertion that there was an artificial stimulation of soldiers before a bayonet charge. Richard Harding Davis, devotee of the romantic notion of war, wrote to the *New York Times* a seething letter which charged that Miss Addams had by implication told the children of slain soldiers: " Your father did not die for France, or for England, or for you; he died because he was drunk." The war correspondent, who had only a hearsay account of Miss Addams' words, branded them as an unworthy, untrue, and ridiculous " insult " flung by a complacent and self-satisfied woman at the memory of those

---

[60] New York *Evening Globe*, July 12, 1915.
[61] *New York Times*, July 12, 1915.
[62] *Hudson Republican*, June 23, 1915.

who had died for women.[63] The *New York City Town Topics*
rasped that Miss Addams was "a silly, vain, impertinent old
maid, who may have done good charity work at Hull House,
Chicago, but is now meddling with matters far beyond her
capacity." [64] The *Philadelphia Inquirer* loftily and contempt-
uously remarked that "the trouble with Jane Addams seems
to be that, being a woman, she can't understand how men can
possess sufficient physical courage to charge into a cloud of
shot and shell unless 'soused to the gills.' " [65] The *Springfield Sun*, scarcely stopping short of personal insult, spoke of
Miss Addams' idea as "her brand of dope" and likened her
imagination to the "impossible imagination of an opium
smoker." [66]

To the wrathful utterances of American newspapers were
added the shocked expostulations of the Canadian press. The
Ottawa Journal, irritated already with Miss Addams for a
peace congress which "would have put a seal of success upon
the German crime against Belgium," now suggested that the
"fiasco" of the congress had "upset completely in Miss
Addams a mental status which never could have had much
balance." [67] Twenty years later, in editorial comment on her
death, a number of Canadian journalists still remembered this
one "grave error."

But the error was the misunderstanding of her intent, which
was merely to convey her belief that soldiers were too sensitive
and decent to kill without artificial beclouding of their senses.
In referring to the attacks upon her she wrote some years
afterwards:

This stormy experience was at least a preparation for the raging
tempest which was to come later, after the United States had
entered the war, and perhaps fortified us in advance. At any
rate, it was at this time that I first learned to use for my own
edification a statement of Booker Washington's, "I will permit no
man to make me hate him." We realized that it would be insup-

---

[63] *New York Times*, July 13, 1915.
[64] *New York City Town Topics*, July 15, 1915.
[65] *Philadelphia Inquirer*, July 20, 1915.
[66] *Springfield Sun*, August 18, 1915.
[67] *Ottawa Journal*, July 13, 1915.

8

portable that an advocate of peace should become embittered with those who differed, when he based his whole cause on the right to differ! [68]

There remains, of course, the question whether Miss Addams took the best method of dealing with her opponents in making a remark so provocative and subject to misinterpretation.

The episode was not, in any event, the most auspicious beginning for the ambitious plan which Miss Addams had returned to American soil to forward. Nevertheless, undaunted, she journeyed to New Hampshire to discuss it with Colonel House and then to Washington to present the Hague resolutions to President Wilson. No immediate response was, of course, given or expected. From Washington Jane Addams returned to her home city, Chicago, where she was given a rousing welcome. Whether from pacifist sympathy or mere pride in a native daughter, a committee of aldermen met her at the station.

On July 24 Miss Addams addressed a packed Chicago auditorium. In her speech she explained the ideals which had motivated the delegates to the Hague Congress and had made them unwilling to accept the conventional assumptions in regard to the possibility of getting an immediate peace. Some of her words are to be quoted for their revelation of the foundation of her pacifist credo:

I am reminded of the old story Tolstoi told me years ago. In Russia there is a sect of Doukhobors, a religious sect who do not believe in going to war. They are like the Quakers. When the young men become of military age and refuse to serve, they are arrested, punished, sometimes exiled or executed. One of the young men was brought before a humane judge, who felt sorry for him. The judge told him that he was very foolish to put himself up against a powerful government. The young man gave the judge a homily upon the teachings of Jesus in regard to non-resistance, and the judge, being Orthodox, said: " Of course, we all believe in that but the time has not come to put it into practice." The young man answered, " The time may not have come for you, Your Honor, but the time has come for me." Something of that is what the women felt when they went to The Hague.[69]

---

[68] Addams, *The Second Twenty Years*, p. 133.
[69] Address by Jane Addams made in Chicago Auditorium, July 24, 1915, MS, Jane Addams Peace Collection.

The period was one in which the actualization of peace seemed a real possibility to the women by virtue of their faith in President Wilson, who then had the Hague resolutions before him. " I have unlimited faith in President Wilson," [70] Miss Addams had said in a London interview two months before. She and her associates thus believed that the President would be inclined to adopt the plan of the Hague Congress for continuous mediation. This belief rested upon his obvious love of peace, his declaration early in the war that the United States was the great " mediating " nation, and his refusal to be stampeded into war by the *Lusitania* incident. Eager for confirmation of her expectations, Miss Addams visited President Wilson in August to receive his opinion about the Hague resolutions.[71] He withheld any definite answer but did speak words that she cherished. At an international congress of women in 1919 she reported them as follows:

He drew out the papers I had given him, and they seem to have been much handled and read. " You see I have studied these resolutions," he said, " I consider them by far the best formulation which up to the moment has been put out by any body." [72]

These words, combined with the optimistic preconceptions about Wilson, seemed to mislead Miss Addams and her co-workers with regard to the attitude of the President. Again and again through the fall months they visited not only Wilson but Lansing and House in behalf of the plan for continuous mediation, unable for some time to see through the careful evasions of Wilson and unwilling to be discouraged by the more candid reactions of Lansing and House. The visits are to be viewed in connection with the critical memoranda that these shapers of American foreign policy exchanged with each other in regard to the women pacifists besieging them. The first visit to Lansing occurred on August 6 and was made by Miss Addams in conjunction with other peace leaders. The

[70] *Ottawa Journal*, July 13, 1915.
[71] Addams, *Peace and Bread*, p. 59. The exact date of the visit is not given.
[72] *Report of the International Congress of Women, Zurich, 1919*, p. 196.

group included Lillian D. Wald and Oswald Garrison Villard, who were interested in the Union Against Militarism. The pacifists presented to the Secretary of State a memorial demanding " the immediate initiation of a peace movement by the United States as the natural leader of the neutral nations." [73] The plan for continuous mediation adopted by the Hague Congress of women was described in detail. Lansing declined to make any comment upon the memorial but forwarded it to the President.

Wilson returned it next day to Lansing with a note which, aside from a rather patronizing attitude toward the women, scarcely indicated any reaction. He merely asked:

Have [you] . . . any opinion about this proposal that you would be willing to express to me? I ask because I know these good people are not going to let the matter rest until they bring it to a head in one way or another. I must, I suppose, be prepared to say either Yay or Nay.

Lansing left no doubt as to what he thought the President should say. He answered:

I do not believe that it is true that the civil leaders of the belligerents would at the present time look with favor on action by the neutral nations; and, even if they did, the military branches of the belligerent governments dominate the situation, and, they favor a continuance of the war.

After stating his opinion that the Central Powers would demand territorial and financial compensation on the basis of their military success, while the Allies would hold out in the hope of ultimate victory, Lansing concluded:

Holding these views I would strongly favor discouraging any neutral movement toward peace at the present time, because I believe it would fail and because, if it did fail, we would lose our influence for the future.[74]

On August 19 Wilson responded: ". . . I entirely agree. . . ." According to Ray Stannard Baker, his biographer, he was particularly impressed by Lansing's argument—also advanced by House—that the United States must safeguard its influence by never moving toward mediation until success was guaran-

---

[73] Baker, VI, 122.   [74] *Ibid.*, pp. 122-123.

teed. However, Baker states his own opinion that " scorn of any direct movement because of the opposition of the leaders of the warring nations was not wholly warranted " and cites as evidence the letter from Grey to House that has been noted above.[75]

Other efforts of the women pacifists to influence the Administration by personal contact also occurred in August. On August 18 Wilson received Professor Emily G. Balch, one of the committee appointed by the Hague Congress to bear to the President its resolutions. The nature of the discussion, which lasted about an hour, is revealed by a letter which Miss Balch wrote to Miss Addams on August 19. The most important statement made by Wilson, and the most gratifying to Miss Balch, who feared that he meant to stand aside, was that " he would not wait to be asked to mediate, if he saw any opportunity to be of use he would take it." Miss Balch told him of the prospective visit of Dr. Jacobs, who had called the Hague International Congress of Women and was now vice-president of the International Committee of Women. Wilson, though at first reluctant to receive her because the newspapers might misinterpret his reception of a foreigner, finally indicated that his mind was open and that he would consider the interview further.[76]

Dr. Jacobs arrived in this country on August 25 and immediately wrote to Miss Addams a bit of news which showed that the efforts of the women, combined with other circumstances, did have some effect upon governmental circles. As

[75] *Ibid.*, p. 124.
[76] Emily G. Balch to Jane Addams, August 19, 1915, MS, Jane Addams Peace Collection. To the account of the interview in the text may be added that given by Miss Balch in a letter to the author. " Miss Addams had told the President of my experiences and he wanted to see me. I had a rather long tête-à-tête interview with him. I told him my whole story and he was interested. As I remember it he told me that if he called such a conference he would have to call in the South American countries which would be an embarrassment or make the meeting too confused or cumbrous (I forget just how he worded his objection). I got the impression he preferred to act alone and be free to take his own line and to judge when the right time had come. This is as I recall it. I am afraid I never wrote this down."

an "important message" Dr. Jacobs told Miss Addams the following:

> Our Government wants to know unofficially the attitude of Pres. Wilson concerning the Congress of neutral governments. Most of the 5 Europ. neutral governments want that the Dutch Government should take the initiative to call the 5 Europ. neutrals together and that they together shall ask Pres. Wilson and other neutrals to join them. But our Government wants to know, before it takes any step in that direction, if perhaps Pres. Wilson likes to take the lead and if not, is willing to join the Europ. neutrals in sending representatives of the U. S. to such a conference. Our Premier, Cort V. D. Linden, believes that such a question should be asked and answered in the same unofficial way as we get the other statements.[77]

Dr. Jacobs, a few days later, went to Washington in company with Miss Balch, and from Washington to New York to see Colonel House. The only available record of this series of visits is the very general one given in Colonel House's diary under the date of September 1. After identifying Dr. Jacobs as the woman who called the Hague Congress of Women, the Colonel wrote:

> They had just been to Washington and the President, in a letter which they showed to me, referred them to Lansing and to me. Their interview with Lansing was thoroughly unsatisfactory from their viewpoint. They claimed he was pro-Ally and very unsympathetic with their suggestion that the United States should call together all neutral countries in order to make peace overtures. I tried to show them how utterly impracticable their plan was, while evidencing the deepest sympathy with their general purpose.[78]

Dr. Jacobs was apparently neither convinced by House's arguments nor discouraged with regard to the President. To obtain answers on the points interesting the Dutch Prime Minister she visited Wilson on September 15. The President was, Dr. Jacobs wrote to Miss Addams, "very kind and manlike as well as gentlemanlike" but his answers were most "diplomatique." They were summarized by the Dutch pacifist as follows:

> The U. S. were now in such great difficulties with the belligerents that a definite answer in one way or another was impossible. The

---

[77] Aletta H. Jacobs to Jane Addams, August 26, 1915, MS, Jane Addams Peace Collection.
[78] Seymour, II, 94.

Pres. was very thankful for the informations [*sic*] I brought, but about his attitude towards peace he could not say a word. Every day that attitude could be changed, according to the circumstances, and even a quite unofficial statement in one way or another could bind him in a certain degree. He wants to remain free to act in the best way as he sees the things himself.[79]

The words of the President are interesting as indicating not merely his aversion to even informal commitments but also his diplomatic policy in handling a group which he did not wish to antagonize. While his note to Lansing shows that he had already decided against calling a conference, he did not say as much to Dr. Jacobs but left her with the impression that he was simply undecided.

Thus it is understandable that the Woman's Peace Party continued to work in behalf of the conference of neutrals. They devoted the first week in September to a campaign designed to acquaint the public with their plan for ending the war. This campaign was assisted in considerable measure by the Chicago Peace Society, which from the outset had cooperated with the women's group. Dr. David Starr Jordan, president of the American Peace Society, also lent his aid. Over three thousand letters were sent out from the Chicago office, and with them the text of a petition to President Wilson.[80]

Much of the educational work in behalf of the peace plan was contributed by three European visitors from the International Committee—Dr. Jacobs, Mme. Schwimmer, and Miss Macmillan. Emphasizing the factors favorable to a peace conference which prevailed in Europe, these women gave interviews and spoke at mass-meetings organized by the Woman's Peace Party. Most important of all, on October 15, 1915, the three European pacifists joined Miss Addams and Miss Balch in a public manifesto regarding the plan for the neutral conference. The manifesto was issued simultaneously in New York and Amsterdam. It was put forward as the " united and deliberate conclusions " of the women envoys

---

[79] Aletta H. Jacobs to Jane Addams, September 15, 1915, MS, Jane Addams Peace Collection; *New York Times*, September 16, 1915.
[80] *Year Book of the Woman's Peace Party, 1916*, p. 50.

as the result of their missions to the European capitals. The manifesto stated that the belligerent governments, while averse as a matter of prestige to initiating negotiations or even to expressing willingness for them, "would not be opposed to a conference of neutral nations." It also declared that " the governments of the European neutrals we visited stand ready to cooperate with others in mediation." The women believed that, of the five European neutral nations visited, three were ready to join in such a meeting and two were contemplating the calling of such a conference. Evidence in the form of declarations by statesmen was cited to substantiate these contentions.

For the rest, the manifesto presented the arguments of the five signatories in favor of taking advantage of this alleged readiness of the governments visited. The manifesto considered first the objection that no negotiation should be started until one or another party had won a victory or, at least, until some new military balance was struck. The answer given was " that every delay makes more difficult the beginning of negotiations, more nations become involved, and the situation becomes more complicated." Another objection dealt with was that a conference called when one side had met some military advantage would favor that side. The women answered that the proposed conference would start mediation at a higher level than that of military advantage; this evidently meant that the conference would proceed on the principle of equity rather than on that of maintenance of the present status. A third objection cited was to the effect that the proposed conference would bind the neutral governments participating in it. The refutation of this point was based on the peculiar character which was proposed for the members of the conference: individuals assigned as experts " not to problems of their own governments, but to the common service of a supreme crisis." In other words, as was emphasized in the original plan of Miss Wales, continuous mediation was to be offered by those who, while appointed by governments, had no power to bind them.

The last part of the manifesto appealed to the neutral governments to respond to the will of vast sections of their people and take action to end the war. In conclusion it challengingly declared:

> The excruciating burden of responsibility for the hopeless continuance of this war no longer rests on the will of the belligerent nations alone. It rests also on the will of those neutral governments and people who have been spared its shock but cannot, if they would, absolve themselves from their full share of responsibility for the continuance of the war.[81]

The issuance of the manifesto was shortly followed by a renewed appeal of the Woman's Peace Party for public support of the conference of neutrals. On November 8 numerous letters were sent out urging and giving directions for the holding of simultaneous mass-meetings throughout the country, together with the sending of appeals to the President. In connection with this movement, two large mass-meetings were held in Chicago and over a thousand telegrams were sent to Washington.[82]

One of the most important achievements of the women was their securing the endorsement of the Fifth International Peace Congress, which was held in San Francisco from October 10 to 13 in connection with the Panama-Pacific International Exposition. Dr. David Starr Jordan was commissioned to take a resolution to the White House urging the President to initiate a neutral conference for continuous mediation.[83]

Dr. Jordan and Louis Lochner, who had been secretary of the Resolutions Committee, went to see Wilson on November 12, 1915. Lochner has described Wilson's reaction to their request as follows:

> The President, who assured us that he had revolved the proposal in his mind dozens of times, voiced two main objections: (1) That America might, in a neutral conference, be outvoted by other neutral governments which in some cases were out of sympathy with their own peoples, and therefore not truly representative; and (2) that one side (the Allies) might object to mediation as a partisan measure.

---

[81] *Manifesto, Issued by Envoys of the International Congress of Women at The Hague to the Governments of Europe and the President of the United States*, October 16, 1915. Jane Addams Peace Collection.

[82] *Year Book of the Woman's Peace Party, 1916*, p. 50.

[83] Louis P. Lochner, *Henry Ford—America's Don Quixote*, pp. 6-7.

In the course of the discussion which followed, however, we felt that we were meeting the objections to his satisfaction. Indeed, we felt so confident of having scored our point that we were encouraged to say to him at the close of the interview, "Then may we take the message with us that you will act?"

The President's rather informal manner suddenly changed. He was the cautious statesman now. "No, that is for me to say when the right moment, in my judgment, arrives," he replied.[84]

Perhaps largely as a result of this interview, the leaders of the Woman's Peace Party came about this time to the realization that Wilson did not intend to act. At a meeting of the Woman's Peace Party, held on November 19 and 20 with a view to formulating a policy to be submitted to the annual meeting in January, they made the discouraging report that, despite the favorable attitude shown by European statesmen the United States was disinclined to offer mediation.[85] This impression was confirmed by an interview which Miss Addams, Miss Wald, and Mme. Schwimmer had with Colonel House on November 21. They put before him what the Colonel called in his diary "the same old story of trying to get the President to appoint a peace commission jointly with other neutral nations." This time the Colonel told the women definitely that "the President could not do this officially." [86] The impression of the women, derived from an interview with Bryan when he was Secretary of State, was that the reasons restraining the United States were its hesitancy to ignore any of the South American countries, who were too many for all to be invited with any convenience, and its unwillingness to call a conference when the Central Powers had the military advantage.[87] They thought that they had successfully answered these objections and consequently were mystified by the continuing reluctance. But one of the pathetic features of the relations of public groups with government is the aptness of the former to be ignorant of the real factors determining the attitude of statesmen toward their proposals. The women could not know then what is well known now—that at

---

[84] *Ibid.*, pp. 8-9.
[85] Addams, *Peace and Bread*, p. 26.
[86] Seymour, II, 96.
[87] Addams, *Peace and Bread*, pp. 26-27.

the time of their interview with House both he and Wilson were engrossed with a quite different plan for dealing with the war, a proposal which had been suggested by House about the middle of October. It provided, first, that the Allies be asked to let the United States know unofficially whether it was agreeable to them that this country demand a cessation of hostilities. If a favorable response was received, the United States was to demand in behalf of the rights of neutral countries that peace parleys be started on the basis of both military and naval disarmament. The Allies, as parties to the intrigue, would accept the mediation. If the Germans accepted, the war would be over. If not, it was proposed that the United States should break off diplomatic relations and ultimately join the Allies in the conflict.[88] Even if House had not been prejudiced against the women's plan at the very outset, he would not at this time, when his own more devious and Machiavellian scheme was in the very course of discussion with Great Britain, have encouraged the consideration of something else. Not knowing that Wilson concurred with House's reasoning, the women felt that they still had one chance to interest the government in calling a conference of neutrals. This chance lay in bringing to bear a tremendous pressure of public opinion upon the officials in Washington. But the difficulty here was that, as Miss Addams was well aware, the newspapers were closed to the pacifists so far as concerned the serious advocacy of any such plan of solving Europe's difficulties.[89] Then immediately after the November meeting a way out of the impasse suddenly presented itself.

It was an offer of help from Mrs. Henry Ford, whom Mme. Rosika Schwimmer interested in the women's plan on November 19 while visiting Mr. Ford. The indomitable Hungarian prevailed upon Mrs. Ford to donate $10,000 to make possible a telegraphic campaign of messages from the mothers of America to the White House in favor of continuous mediation. The telegrams were to be sent on November 26, the day on which Wilson promised to see Mme. Schwimmer and Mrs. Philip Snowden of England, a delegation representing the

---

[88] Seymour, II, 85.　　　[89] Addams, *Peace and Bread*, p. 27.

war-suffering mothers of Europe. Mrs. Ford signed and gave
to the press the following statement:

Happy in my own motherhood and sympathizing with the bitter
sorrow of the mothers bereaved by war, I want to foster a demonstration enabling American women to go on record as favouring a
conference of neutral nations working toward a just settlement of
the great European tragedy.[90]

The demonstration was organized by the Woman's Peace
Party. It was, by grace of Mrs. Ford's money and of the
telegraph, one of the quickest mobilizations of public opinion
in behalf of peace that had ever been managed. Only a few
days intervened between the start of the undertaking and the
date on which Wilson was to receive the two women. Ninety
stenographers and clerks and eighty messenger boys worked
in relays all day and half of the night to send out about ten
thousand telegrams. The telegrams, signed by Jane Addams
as president of the Woman's Peace Party, were sent to the
women's organizations of the country. Miss Addams asked
them to support the appeal of Mme. Schwimmer and Mrs.
Snowden to the President by wiring to President Wilson in
support of the proposed conference of neutrals.[91] Although
the telegrams to the President were not paid for by the Party
the response was a great success. By November 26 twelve
thousand telegrams, two thousand more than asked for, had
poured into the White House.[92] All the telegrams contained
the words: "We work for peace. The mothers of America
pray for it." [93] President Wilson's eyes were not strained but
the White House had to engage two extra clerks to receive the
telegrams. In consequence of the demonstration President
Wilson, ten thousand women's organizations, and the newspapers were impressed with the fact that the proposal of a
conference of neutrals was a matter of widespread interest to
American women.

Applying a method designed to influence both public and

[90] Louis P. Lochner, p. 15.
[91] Addams, *Peace and Bread*, pp. 27-28; *New York Times*, November
24, 1915.
[92] Addams, p. 28.
[93] *New York Times*, November 27, 1915.

official opinion, the Woman's Peace Party on November 26
held in Washington a mass-meeting simultaneously with the
visit to the President of the two delegates. As an indication
of the political connections of the women, the presiding officer
of the mass-meeting was Mrs. Louis F. Post, wife of the
Assistant Secretary of Labor. As another indication, Mrs.
George Rublee, wife of a member of the Federal Trade Commission,[94] moved the resolution to be adopted by the assemblage in behalf of the conference of neutrals. The resolution
cited as its reasons the information gathered by the women
envoys about the favorable attitude of the belligerents, the
fact that the belligerent nations themselves were unable to
take the initiative, and the suffering of women as well as men
from the devastation of war. It then declared that "we,
members of the Woman's Peace Party and others assembled
in Washington, urge that the President of the United States,
the head of one of the principal neutral countries of the
world, call upon the other neutral nations to appoint representatives to assemble in conference for constant mediation,
without armistice, and dedicated to finding a just settlement
of this conflict." [95]

While a group from the mass-meeting waited outside, Mme.
Schwimmer and Mrs. Ethel Snowden of England talked with
President Wilson for about an hour. Upon leaving the conference the women professed to be encouraged. The President, they declared, regarded the information which they
gave him about European readiness for peace as new, and
informed them with earnestness and sympathy that he would
be heard from at the suitable time. But, when asked as to
whether he had given a yes or no answer in regard to the calling of the conference of neutrals, they all admitted that he
had not committed himself.[96]

The women had now learned that even the pressure of public opinion would not bring the President, at least not before

---

[94] Mr. Rublee is known to the public as Director of the Inter-
governmental Committee on Political Refugees.
[95] *Ibid.*
[96] *Ibid.*

his own good time, to the adoption of their program.   Insofar as the project of a conference of neutrals had been based upon the expectation that the United States Government would take the initiative, it had been grounded upon a false hope. The leaders of the Woman's Peace Party now realized this but yet they did not despair.   For, only a few days before their appeal to the President failed, a new path to peace had opened up to them.   Forgetting all the labor spent upon the old, they now turned to this more promising approach with the indefatigable zeal which Providence gives idealists.

CHAPTER V

HENRY FORD AND THE PEACE MOVEMENT

On November 24, 1915, Henry Ford announced to a group of startled reporters that he had chartered a ship and was going to try to get the boys out of the trenches by Christmas. If the world was amazed, the leaders of the Woman's Peace Party were not. Miss Addams had been present when the idea was first discussed. In fact, although Mr. Ford's announcement considerably distorted its character, the idea— not the peace ship itself but the main instrumentality, to which the ship was but an incident—was the intellectual child of the Woman's Peace Party. They had seen no chance of bringing it before the world until the eloquence of Rosika Schwimmer, honorary member of the Woman's Peace Party, persuaded the auto magnate to take the plan under the wing of his impressive fortune. He did so just about the time when the women had become discouraged in their efforts to convert President Wilson to the project of a governmental conference of neutrals.

The Ford Peace Mission is usually thought of almost entirely in terms of its most sensational feature—the sailing of a group of pacifists to Europe on the *Oscar II*. The fact is overlooked that the hope of getting the boys out of the trenches was based primarily upon what the pacifists were to undertake after arriving in Europe—the setting up of a conference of neutrals to offer continuous mediation. The plan differed from the one hitherto emphasized by the Woman's Peace Party since the conference was to be called and conducted upon purely private initiative. Nevertheless, the private conference had figured in the original platform of the Woman's Peace Party as a desirable alternative in case the governments did not call the official conference. The course of events was such that the alternative recommended itself to the women more and more until, by the time of Mr. Ford's expedition, many of them were glad to cooperate with the auto magnate as individuals even if not as members of the Woman's Peace Party.

The story of Mr. Ford's high-geared venture into pacifism has been told by Louis Lochner, its manager, but even Mr. Lochner's careful account does not discuss adequately the most important element in its background—namely, the gradual conversion of leaders of the Woman's Peace Party to the belief that an unofficial conference should receive their first consideration. Yet without this conversion of the women Mr. Ford would never have attempted to make peace. The conversion of the women was not due entirely to the failure of the governments to act upon the proposal of an official conference. The germinal idea, so far as Miss Addams was concerned, was the realization, even when the official conference was being urged, that the inclusion of some unofficial experts in the conference would be inherently a good thing. Thus, while Miss Addams was on her mission to the European capitals, she reacted favorably to the suggestion in a private communication that each neutral send two representatives— one governmental, the second representing the people. " Miss Addams felt," it is recorded, " that the non-official element in such a communication was important, if you take anyone representing the United States, he would think of the United States all the time; and it would tend to make the whole work heavy and constricted [sic]." [1]   Moreover, she told Mr. Norman Angell that it was commercial, scientific, artistic groups which had true international experience, which were " on all four legs in the world at large." Thus Miss Addams felt personally that some of the delegates to the conference should not be governmental—should " rather represent the great commercial, labor and scientific groups which have international relationships apart from the ordinary governmental divisive channels." [2]

By the month of August Miss Addams had apparently advanced so far along this line as to favor a conference made up entirely of unofficial delegates, even if it should be a conference called by, or approved by, the neutral governments. This is the implication, at least, of the letter which Miss Balch wrote to Miss Addams on August 19, after her interview with

---

[1] MS, Jane Addams Notes.   [2] *Ibid.*

President Wilson. Describing to her associate this interview, Miss Balch said:

> Speaking of a conference of neutral governments I said that you now felt differently towards this plan, that your mind turned toward an unofficial body. He said that he had heard so that when you and Miss Wald were with him Miss Wald had wanted you to develop this point but that you had preferred to merely give your report. . . . With regard to an unofficial body he spoke of some of those who would be the natural persons to be on such a body being perhaps not quite well fitted to serve successfully. The out and out pacifist, seeking a solution in terms of right could not understand sympathetically and deal with those who came at the problem from the point of view of military advantage. [3]

One may note incidentally that Wilson was later to give to Ford the same advice about not using absolute pacifists.[4] But, so far as concerns the implication of the above words with respect to Miss Addams, it is evident that while inclining towards an unofficial body she had not at this time come to the point of excluding the official conference and confined herself to reporting to the President as representative of the international body committed to the official conference.

As has been already noted, in both October and November Miss Addams and the Woman's Peace Party continued to work for the official conference—official at least in the sense that it should have governmental approval. Yet in a resolution favoring continuous mediation, circulated by the Woman's Peace Party in September, reference is made to the possible appointment of the delegates to some private body in case the President should find it impossible to consider the other proposition.[5] Then, after two months of fruitless waiting for the President to consider the proposition favorably, there came a time when the alternative to the official conference seemed both to Miss Addams and her associates to be the only practicable plan under the circumstances. Their arrival at this point of view is described in words of Miss Addams at the January 1916 annual meeting of the Woman's Peace

---

[3] Emily G. Balch to Jane Addams, August 19, 1915, MS, Jane Addams Peace Collection.
[4] Lochner, p. 74.
[5] "Resolution in Favor of Mediatory Commission of Neutrals." Mimeographed sheet, Jane Addams Peace Collection.

Party. She said that in consequence of the decision of the United States Government not to call an official conference, "there developed among the members of the Woman's Peace Party, as well as among other people, a plan for a possible conference of neutrals that should be non-governmental, not to take the place of a governmental conference but to prepare the way for it."[6] Shortly before this plan became crystallized Miss Addams, Miss Wald, and Mme. Schwimmer touched upon it as a possibility in their interview with Colonel House on November 21. House recorded that the women raised the issue after he had explained to them that the President could not carry out the plan of the official conference:

They then wanted to know whether he would object to an unofficial commission doing it, and I thought he would not. As usual, I got them into a controversy between themselves, which delights me since it takes the pressure off myself.[7]

Whatever controversy there was between the women was due to the fact that they took the plan quite seriously. Miss Addams saw various factors as promising the success of the conference—the unwillingness of both sides to "dig in" for another winter of trench warfare, the discouragement of governmental authorities over the tremendous daily loss of life unaccompanied by any change of military position, and the fact that most normal minds at that time had not yet become habituated or morally reconciled to the long continuation of the war. The great obstacle seemed that of expense, but according to Miss Addams the women had "hoped that a sum large enough to defray all the general expenses of such a conference might initiate it as a private enterprise."[8]

This was to hope for a miracle, but one of Miss Addams' associates was indeed a miracle-worker. The remarkable associate was Rosika Schwimmer, who had formulated a plan for neutral mediation immediately after the outbreak of war, had received the title of honorary member through her part in

---

[6] *Year Book of the Woman's Peace Party, 1916*, p. 21.
[7] Seymour, II, 96.
[8] Addams, *Peace and Bread*, pp. 29-30.

organizing the Woman's Peace Party, and had served on one committee of the Hague Congress to the governments in the interest of the plan for continuous mediation. Her greatest achievement was to ensue after she came to Detroit in November 1915 to deliver a lecture. Mr. Ford had announced his conversion to pacifism on August 22 and somewhat later made it public that he would give half his fortune to shorten the war by one day. Mme. Schwimmer, who thought she knew how to shorten the war by many days, on November 18 called on this likely "prospect" for her cause. What is more surprising, she gained admittance. Of what passed between the two there is no record, but from Mr. Ford's later utterances it would appear evident that Mme. Schwimmer talked to him about continuous mediation in both the official and unofficial forms, and particularly emphasized the recent work of the Hague Congress of women and the International Committee of Women for Permanent Peace. While she was with Ford there arrived on the scene another persuasive pacifist, Louis Lochner. Mr. Lochner, who with Miss Addams had formed the National Peace Federation in February 1915 and had accompanied the American women on their journey to the Hague Congress, had just come to Detroit from an unsuccessful appeal to President Wilson by Dr. Jordan and himself in behalf of an official conference of neutrals. Mme. Schwimmer and Lochner converted the eager, impulsive industrialist very quickly. What they converted him to is indicated by the remark which Ford, according to Lochner, made to other petitioners for peace funds who visited him the same day: "I'm going to back the work of the International Committee of Women." [9]

On November 20 the newspapers announced that the auto magnate, after conferences with Mme. Schwimmer, had decided to visit President Wilson to discuss "the plan to have the United States join a conference of neutral nations for the purpose of bringing about peace in Europe." [10] The idea was thus still to have the official conference if possible. On No-

---

[9] Lochner, p. 16.
[10] *New York Times,* November 20, 1915.

vember 21 Ford left for New York City to confer with leading pacifists who favored the plan for continuous mediation. He was accompanied by Mr. Lochner, who, with Ford's approval, issued a statement attacking the Carnegie Endowment for its staid preoccupation with the " governmental mind " and its failure to promote peace by more vigorous methods.[11] Ford arrived in New York City on the very day the conference of the Woman's Peace Party adjourned. At a luncheon he met not only Miss Addams but also Oswald Garrison Villard, Dean George W. Kirchwey of Columbia University, and Paul Kellogg of the *Survey*. All corroborated the statement of Lochner and Mme. Schwimmer—that they advocated the sending to Europe of a mediatory commission, by official appointment if possible, but if not, by private initiative.[12] " We were very grateful," Miss Addams writes, " when Mr. Ford became interested in the idea of a conference of neutrals and expressed his willingness to further it." [13] Miss Addams had not attached any importance to the idea of a peace ship, which, as a semi-humorous suggestion of Mr. Lochner's, first came up at this luncheon. But Mr. Ford, encouraged by Mme. Schwimmer, seized upon an idea so congenial to the advertising spirit. By the evening of that day—so quickly did Mr. Ford move—the *Oscar II* had been chartered.

The next step in furthering the conference was a visit to President Wilson, whom Ford saw on November 23. Ford told the President that he favored the proposal of the Woman's Congress at The Hague and urged him to take the necessary steps for the appointment of a neutral commission. He offered unlimited financial backing for defraying the expenses of the undertaking. Wilson replied ambiguously that he was not saying that the plan for continuous mediation was not the best yet offered but that, as the head of a neutral nation, he must preserve neutrality of judgment in dealing with various proposals regarding the war. If he should commit himself to the women's plan, he would be prevented from adopting a better one which might come later.[14]   Mr. Ford

---

[11] *Ibid.*, November 22, 1915.   [12] Lochner, p. 19.
[13] *Year Book of Woman's Peace Party, 1916*, p. 22.
[14] Lochner, pp. 19-20.

then told the President challengingly that he had chartered a ship, that he offered it to the President to transport delegates to Europe, and that if the President would not use it he would.[15] Thereupon, according to Ford, the President told him he was within his rights in financing a neutral conference and wished him all success.[16]

On the evening after his return from Washington, Mr. Ford reported to Miss Addams and the rest of the committee consulting with him a momentous decision. Since the President had refused to appoint official delegates, Ford had decided to form a conference of private citizens. To Miss Addams this news, however welcome, was somewhat spoiled by another announcement—that of the chartering of the *Oscar II*. It was the first time she had heard of it and she immediately expressed opposition. She insisted that "it would be easy enough for the members of the conference to travel to Stockholm or The Hague by various steamship lines, paying their own expenses; that we needed Mr. Ford's help primarily in organizing a conference but not in transporting the people."[17] Mr. Ford answered that the more publicity the better and that the sailing of the ship itself would give the conference the most effective publicity it could receive. Miss Addams was unconvinced but she was not so certain of the importance of the issue of the ship as to dissociate herself from the undertaking. She consented to sail with the ship, though not as representative of the Woman's Peace Party.

On November 25 the announcement of the Ford Peace Mission, which was to sail on the *Oscar II* on December 4, appeared on the first page of the papers of the country. Mr. Ford's announcement, perhaps written by Mme. Schwimmer, contained not only the ideas of the Woman's Peace Party and its international affiliate but references to them by name. He said in part:

> We are going to get behind the work done by the Hague peace conference of women and carry that work forward. It is my earnest

---

[15] *Ibid.*, p. 28.
[16] Addams, *Peace and Bread*, p. 33. Miss Addams here reports Ford's version of what Wilson said.
[17] *Ibid.*, p. 34.

hope to create a machinery where those who so desire can turn to
inquire what can be done to establish peace and begin relations with
those who also desire peace. Even recent dispatches from Germany
say that now is the time to establish such a clearing-house. It is
an experiment in the right direction.[18]

When asked about the destination of the peace ship, Mr. Ford
declared that he was not certain but that the conference might
take place at the headquarters in Amsterdam of the Woman's
Peace Party (he had in mind the International Committee of
Women for Permanent Peace).[19]

The association thus established in the public mind between
the Ford venture and the Woman's Peace Party was reenforced when, on November 26, he addressed the Washington
mass-meeting of the party.[20]   Explaining that this was the
first time he had ever faced a public audience, he spoke only
a few words:

I simply want to ask you to remember the slogan, "Out of the
trenches by Christmas, never to go back," and I thank you for your
attention.[21]

Mrs. Post, presiding officer, repeated the slogan dramatically
after him.   On the same day Ford made the statement to the
press that in viewing so optimistically the prospects for peace
he was relying upon the accomplishments of the International
Committee of Women.   Saying that he had assurances that
the governments would have no objection to a conference at
The Hague, he explained that some of these assurances were
received immediately after the Women's Peace Congress at
The Hague, some at different times later—evidently an allusion to the assurances received by the two travelling committees of women.   Setting a precedent which Mme. Schwimmer
followed later, he refused to make the documents public,
holding that if made public they would become the "play-
things of diplomacy" and cause embarassing denials.[22]

On the following day Mr. Ford apparently passed the acid
test of his interest in the women's work.   He agreed, according

---

[18] *New York Times*, November 25, 1915.
[19] *Ibid.*
[20] See the preceding chapter.
[21] *New York Times*, November 27, 1915.   [22] *Ibid.*

to Mme. Schwimmer, to donate $200,000 for the work of the International Committee of Women for Permanent Peace. Mme. Schwimmer wired Dr. Aletta Jacobs in Amsterdam of this windfall and said that she would send $20,000 immediately. The Amsterdam executives were overjoyed, especially since the international organization had been crippled by lack of funds.[23]

The National Woman's Peace Party received no financial donation,[24] but their work and especially their plan of continuous mediation shared in a publicity perhaps greater than given to any other peace enterprise in modern times. On the other hand, they learned that this new-found limelight entailed the payment of a heavy price in the form of various embarrassments. Miss Addams found that the Peace Ship was not the only idea to which she would have to adjust herself. Mr. Ford's slogan, popularly referred to as " Get the Boys out of the Trenches by Christmas," was even harder to swallow. As soon as she heard of it she telephoned Mr. Lochner in New York and begged him to keep the enterprise in hand. Miss Addams not only realized the naïve over-optimism of the slogan but feared with reason that it would strike the belligerent governments as treasonable. She was scarcely reassured by Mr. Lochner's defense of Ford's belief in direct appeal to "the boys" and catchy advertising.[25] What was worst of all, however, was the deterioration of the Ford Party in the character of its personnel. Miss Addams had participated on the first day in the drawing up of a tentative list of guests and had even then evinced discomfort at certain of Mr. Ford's selections. The inclusion of representatives of college youth seemed to her of no direct usefulness to the conference even if it was symbolic of youth's revolt against war. But the original list did include people of substantial reputation, even though some of these like Colonel House, whom Miss Addams

---

[23] *New York Times*, January 20, 1916.
[24] The New York branch, however, received a thousand dollars from Mr. Ford. *New York Times*, December 29, 1915.
[25] Addams, *Peace and Bread*, p. 36.

selected,[26] were out of the question at the outset.　As Mr. Ford's enterprise took on sensational features which the press turned into roaring comedy, many of these people thought discretion the better part of pacifism, whether from devotion to their own dignity or to the dignity of the peace movement. While these declined and their inferiors pressed for admittance, the passenger list became, as even the gentle Miss Addams noted, " with many notable exceptions, a group of very eccentric people." [27]　Among the esteemed exceptions were several prominent members of the Woman's Peace Party, including Mrs. Joseph Fels and Mrs. William Bross Lloyd, who were officials of the Expedition.

But among those who declined Mr. Ford's invitation was Mrs. Anna Garlin Spencer, vice-president of the Woman's Peace Party.　Her letter of declination, which was published in the press, shows the reasons why many members of the party held aloof:

I cannot conscientiously accept your invitation unless positively assured beforehand that at least ten men well known and deservedly trusted as peace advocates of experience and good judgment form the leadership of the expedition.　As an officer of the Woman's Peace Party I am deeply grateful for the confidence you show in the purposes of that organization; and the calling of a conference of neutral nations is a part of our program.　We are also committed to trying to secure an unofficial conference of neutrals and peace workers, provided no Governmental sanction can be secured.　It would therefore be a great disappointment if your backing of our program should prove fruitless.　Any gathering, however, whether official or unofficial, in the interest of a speedy close of this war and the prevention of future wars should be preceded by careful private conference as to the personnel of those invited, plans of procedure in the United States, and methods of securing foreign assistance.[28]

Numerous friends urged Miss Addams to resign from a ship that threatened to sink from a torpedo of humor before it left port.　But Miss Addams, while recognizing all the dangers they pointed out, adhered to her original decision.　Her reasons for remaining faithful to a venture which caused her so many doubts reveal her great—perhaps too great—intel-

[26] Letter from David Starr Jordan to Jane Addams, January 6, 1916, MS, Jane Addams Peace Collection.
[27] Addams, *Peace and Bread*, p. 39.
[28] *New York Times*, November 30, 1915.

lectual tolerance. In the first place, Miss Addams felt that the question of method was one which must be viewed broadly, with reference to the soundness of the entire plan rather than merely of certain of its details. Thus she wrote subsequently:

> I was so convinced of the essential soundness of the conference of neutrals and so confident of European participation, that I was inclined to consider the sensational and unfortunate journey of the American contingent as a mere incident to the undertaking, for after all the actual foundations of the conference itself would have to be laid on the other side of the Atlantic. It became clearer every day that whoever became asociated with the ship would be in for much ridicule and social opprobrium, but that of course seemed a small price to pay for a protest against war.[29]

In the second place, while her inveterate instinct was against sensational methods of promoting social ideals, Miss Addams was not convinced that such methods did not have their place as necessary popularizations. The Woman's Peace Party itself represented a novel and sensational attempt to dramatize peace, even if it is true that in her previous career, as her biographer states, Miss Addams had carefully held aloof from showmanship.[30] Now Louis Lochner and others supporting Mr. Ford's enterprise used arguments which for the time being shook her preference for slow, dignified educational methods. As Miss Addams states, these people believed that " the anti-war movement throughout its history had been too quietistic and much too grey and negative; that the heroic aspect of life had been too completely handed over to war, leaving pacifists under the suspicion that they cared for safety first and cherished survival above all else; that a demonstration was needed, even a spectacular one, to show that ardor and comradeship were exhibited by the non-militarists as well." [31] Under the influence of these arguments, Miss Addams and some of her associates began to wonder whether the appeal of Ford was not " more natural and normal, more fitted to the situation than that which we had so eagerly been advocating." [32] Even in his appeal to the boys to come out of

---

[29] Addams, *Peace and Bread*, pp. 39-40.
[30] Linn, pp. 316-317.
[31] Addams, *Peace and Bread*, p. 37.
[32] *Ibid.*, p. 38.

the trenches Miss Addams saw "a touch of what might be called the Christian method, 'cease to do evil,' you yourself, just where you are, whatever the heads of the church and state may dictate." [33]   That it was a slang version did not weigh much beside the fact that it expressed the Christian spirit. The version of one who himself knew the rank and file of workingmen, was it perhaps not the only one which could win the simpler people who made up the great bulk of armies and of populations?   It was the idea of a Billy Sunday pacifism which Miss Addams acquiesced in at this juncture just as evangelistic methods have at times won the acceptance of religionists of decorous tastes.

The trouble was, however, that the Ford Mission in practice represented anything but the simplicity of the evangelist. Whether Miss Addams could have tolerated steamship and grand-tour pacifism in person is, as she herself intimates,[34] doubtful.   From this point of view it was fortunate for her, at least, that she was not able to make the attempt.   Accident intervened to save her from the danger to which her lack of selfish discretion exposed her.   Three days before the Ford ship sailed Miss Addams developed a serious illness in Chicago, and the ship left without her.   Many newspapers, ignoring all statements made by Miss Addams and her physicians, said that she was only pretending to be ill.   But in fact during the following weeks tuberculosis of the kidney set in, and doomed her to a year of semi-invalidism.[35]   Years later the notion that her illness had been merely diplomatic persisted in certain accounts; Walter Millis in *The Road to War* gave it credence [36] and Mark Sullivan in *Our Times* only failed to further the impression by including in his footnotes the protest of Miss Addams herself, who read the pages, against the implication of his statement that she "plead illness." [37] In Miss Addams' reminiscences one reads between the lines, especially in her regret that "what might have occurred"

---

[33] *Ibid.*, p. 40.   [34] *Ibid.*
[35] Information of Dr. Alice Hamilton, who was Miss Addams' physician, to the author.
[36] Millis, p. 244.   [37] Sullivan, V, 171.

must be veiled from us by the intervention of " our physical limitations," a certain belief that if she could have participated in the expedition its fate might have been somewhat different.[88]

To be sure, the ridicule heaped on the voyage, based so largely upon the distortion and exaggeration of minor incidents, was for the most part inevitable. Yet certainly Miss Addams could have discouraged some of the methods used on the expedition; she shows plainly her disapproval of all its more ostentatious elements.[39] Mme. Schwimmer, the guiding brain of the venture, has been accused of serious errors of judgment in connection with it even by those who recognize the sincerity of her purpose. In the opinion of Louis Lochner, General Secretary of the Ford Mission, her direction of the expedition was a failure, owing to her own shortcomings such as her domineering attitude and her secretiveness. Both Lochner and Elmer Davis, who accompanied the group as correspondent for the *New York Times,* lay particular blame upon Mme. Schwimmer for her use of the documents which were associated with the visits of the Hague Congress envoys to the statesmen of Europe. Davis declares: " On the basis of the very cautious encouragement which Miss Addams had been able to get for the idea of official neutral mediation, she built up the grandiose fiction of the ' documents ' in her black bag guaranteeing that the warring Governments were eager to welcome the mediation of those tassels of the lunatic fringe who sailed on *Oscar II.*" [40] For some time Mme. Schwimmer refused to show these documents, saying that they were the property of the International Committee of Women for Permanent Peace.[41] Prodded constantly by the press, she arranged to show a delegation the vaunted papers, only to withdraw the invitation on the date set because a new insult had been thrust at her by the jeering newspapermen. When, at a later date, the nature of the contents of the black bag were finally divulged,

---

[88] Addams, *Peace and Bread*, p. 40.   [39] *Ibid.*, p. 41.
[40] Elmer Davis, " Henry Ford's Adventure with the Lunatic Fringe," *New York Times Book Review*, October 4, 1925, p. 3.
[41] *New York Times*, January 21, 1916.

they proved to be only the very general and cautious statements by Sir Edward Grey, von Bethmann-Hollweg, Count Burián, Count Tisza, and others, described in foregoing pages, indicating that the formation of a conference of neutral governments to offer mediation would not be unwelcome. It seemed to Elmer Davis that the discovery of this fact " discredited the whole enterprise." [42]

What did the International Committee of Women, the acknowledged inspirers of the peace expedition, think of the undertaking? The answer to this question must be prefaced by narration of a comedy of errors, again involving Mme. Schwimmer. The European members of the Committee had been made well-disposed toward the Ford Mission by the financial contribution about which Mme. Schwimmer, eager to assure for the Ford Party as cordial a welcome in Europe as possible, had cabled to them from New York. On the basis of these promises Dr. Jacobs entered into financial expenditures to revive the drooping activities of the organization. But Mr. Ford never paid to Mme. Schwimmer even the $20,000 which was to be sent to Amsterdam immediately, and Mme. Schwimmer did not answer the several inquiring cables which Dr. Jacobs sent to the *Oscar II*. Whatever chances for getting the money remained were ruined by an occurrence which intervened between the departure of the Peace Ship and its arrival in Norway. Upon the inquiry of Scandinavian members of the International Committee as to the position to be taken toward the Ford Party by the International Committee, Dr. Jacobs cabled to Miss Addams as president for instructions. Miss Addams' reply, which on account of her illness did not come till the day before the arrival of the peace pilgrims in Christiania, spoke first of the advisability of postponing the meeting of the Committee till the middle of January, when she could be present. She then said: " Keep the International Committee distinct from Ford enterprise." [43]

---

[42] Davis, *loc. cit.* It is understood that Mme. Schwimmer is now writing her memoirs, and their publication may, of course, bring to view data or arguments which will modify the judgments here set forth.

[43] *New York World*, January 20, 1916.

Later Miss Addams explained to the press that she had meant merely that the Committee should be kept distinct from the Ford venture till the meeting of the Committee, which alone could take action on the matter; and that she had desired the members of the Committee to cooperate in any event as individuals.[44]   She made the same explanation to Mme. Schwimmer, adding that she had originally inserted the words "until then" but that in the interest of brevity the words had been removed.[45]   However, the European women misunderstood Miss Addams' cable and, when the Ford Party arrived in Scandinavia, they kept the Woman's Committee not merely distinct but aloof.   Doubtless irritated by the cool treatment received from the Committee in Christiania, Mme. Schwimmer, on arriving in Amsterdam and being questioned about the $20,000, dismissed the incident by resigning from the International Committee.   Thereupon Dr. Jacobs, in an interview with an American correspondent, denounced Mme. Schwimmer and expressed her belief that the Ford Mission could not succeed with Mme. Schwimmer as its leader.[46]   However, some other European women on the International Committee cooperated with the Ford Mission generously.[47]

Mme. Schwimmer and Mr. Ford suffered another disappointment in the form of public statements by Miss Addams regarding the relations of herself and the Woman's Peace Party to the Ford Expedition.   They were prompted by an interview given by Mr. Ford on January 4 in which he declared that it was Jane Addams who had first brought to his attention the movement for peace which he was supporting. Miss Addams flatly denied this.   She said that she had not talked to Mr. Ford until after Mme. Schwimmer had interested him in the movement and that she knew nothing of the *Oscar II* plan until after the ship had been chartered.   The next day Miss Addams made clear the position of the Woman's

---

[44] *New York Times*, January 20, 1916.
[45] Jane Addams to Rosika Schwimmer, February 18, 1916, MS, Jane Addams Peace Collection.
[46] *New York World*, January 20, 1916.
[47] Julia G. Wales to Jane Addams, January 14, 1916, MS, Jane Addams Peace Collection.

Peace Party toward Mr. Ford. She began mildly by prais-
ing his sincere devotion to peace and his ability to publicize
the cause of peace. Then she declared:

> However, the peace ship was not related to the movement of the
> Woman's Peace Party. The women's plan is to establish a clearing
> house for peace sentiment.[48]

It was fortunate that Miss Addams had not sought to commit the women's group to the enterprise. The organization
would otherwise have shared in the ridicule which was the
chief response of American newspapers to Ford's philan-
thropic effort. Yet Miss Addams did not fear ridicule and
such a fear was no part of her action in keeping the Woman's
Peace Party apart from the Ford enterprise. The truth was
that the peace ship had originated as an individual enterprise,
and its sponsorship by an organization was both improper and
unnecessary.

As an individual Miss Addams continued not only to support Ford's project of a conference of neutrals but to bespeak
the sympathy of her associates in the Woman's Peace Party
for it. At the annual conference of the party in January, which
she attended despite the fact that she was ill, Miss Addams
devoted a considerable part of her address to the defense
of the conference of neutrals which was then being prepared
by the Ford Mission. Remarking upon its nongovernmental
character, she reminded the members of the party that many
governmental activities had started unofficially. In education, in agriculture, and in commerce many things which the
United States government was then doing for society had
been begun, she pointed out, by a group of people who had
no governmental status but who by their success induced the
government to take over the function. Miss Addams noted
that, though there were earnest and enlightened peace groups
in various belligerent countries, they were finding it increasingly difficult to hold meetings or to spread their propaganda.
She then spoke of the assistance which the approaching Conference of Neutrals would give to these now impeded groups:

[48] New York *Evening Telegram*, January 4, 1916; *New York Times*,
January 6, 1916.

It is believed that if there is a neutral spot to which these programs may be sent, in which they may be translated and republished, that it will be much easier to get them into the papers of England and Germany than if they were first issued in those countries. If the suggestions of Englishmen were published in the London papers as issued from a neutral source, they would not so easily be cried down as the unpatriotic act of a group of Englishmen who had dared suggest that England would at present consider any terms of peace. The whole discussion would be taken out of the spirit of controversy so prevalent in a nation at war, and taken into the cooler atmosphere of a neutral country, to a conference in which none could possibly have an axe to grind, and all would try to make an effort to consider the various propositions solely on their merits. That is all I can see which may be hoped for from the conference of neutrals at the present moment—that it may re-establish some sort of international understanding; that the men of Germany may know what Englishmen think and Englishmen may have some way of communicating with like-minded people in Germany, from whom they are cut off; that international public opinion may again have the right of way.

. . . No one expects such a conference to end the war. The war must be ended by the accredited representatives of the governments; but a conference of neutrals may make it impossible that the war should end by the secret diplomacy with which it began; through the conference the people at least may know what the governments are considering, and have an opportunity to make tentative propositions to the different governments. . . . Some of us believe that the informal conference resulting from the Ford expedition may be the nucleus of such a conference of neutrals, that it may perform the valuable social function of bringing open democratic discussion into international affairs.[49]

Miss Addams' hope that ultimately a governmental conference would eventuate was based partly upon some recent developments. One of the most promising was Wilson's annual message of December 1915, calling for a negotiated peace in order to save both sides from either physical or moral catastrophe. Then too Miss Addams had recently received a letter from Miss Macmillan telling her that Lord Crewe, in a recent interview, had shown a more sympathetic attitude toward the mediatory conference. The Dutch Prime Minister, whom she and Dr. Jacobs subsequently told of Lord Crewe's attitude, had also reacted favorably to the prospect of such a meeting.[50] Finally, at the beginning of the current Congressional session, two joint resolutions had been introduced—one by Senator Lane and the other by Representative London—advocat-

---

[49] *Year Book of the Woman's Peace Party, 1916*, pp. 23-24.
[50] Chrystal Macmillan to Jane Addams, December 16, 1915, MS, Jane Addams Peace Collection.

ing that the United States Government call a conference of neutral nations to offer mediation.[51]   The Woman's Peace Party contributed its support to these developments by including in the Congressional program adopted by the annual meeting of January 1916 the following demand: "That action be taken to secure by our government the immediate calling of a Conference of Neutral Nations in the interest of a just and early peace."[52]   On the day after the meeting a delegation of the Party, led by Miss Addams, appeared before the Senate Foreign Relations Committee and the House Committee on Foreign Affairs to support the joint resolutions which accorded with their own views.   Miss Addams declared before the legislators that Holland, Switzerland, Norway, Sweden, and Denmark had given the Hague envoys the assurance that they would participate in a peace conference called by the United States.   Two of these countries, she added, had said that they would themselves call a conference if the United States would participate.   She explained the benefits of such a conference, whether in actually terminating the war, or in establishing a greater international understanding and thus shortening the conflict indirectly.   She also expressed her sense of the value of the Ford Mission, which, even if it should fail, would be an inspiring gesture to the ideal.   The account of her testimony in the *New York Times* gave less emphasis to the foregoing points than to purely incidental but more humanly interesting matters.   Thus it noted Miss Addams' emphatic denial, in response to a question by Representative Cooper, that the women envoys from the Hague Congress had been treated carelessly by the statesmen.   The *Times* also quoted a curious remark by Senator John Sharp Williams to the effect that he was in favor of peace but would not pursue it at the expense of the respect of women.[53]

Nothing came of the hearings, despite Congressional respect for the opinion of women pacifists.   Nor did the prospect for

---

[51] *Congressional Record*, 64th Cong., 1st sess., pp. 32, 228.
[52] *Year Book of the Woman's Peace Party, 1916*, p. 35.
[53] *Hearing before Committee on Foreign Affairs*, 64th Cong., 1st sess., on H. R. 6921 and H. J. R. 32, January 11, 1916, pp. 13-17; *New York Times*, January 12, 1916.

the materialization of a conference of neutrals grow brighter, although the organization continued to advocate it in various pronouncements and recommendations.[54] The attitude of the American government was clearly shown when, on May 11, the American Ambassador in Madrid telegraphed to Secretary Lansing that the King of Spain was anxious to cooperate with President Wilson in offering mediation to the belligerent nations. Secretary Lansing delayed for several months and then finally instructed the Ambassador to inform the Spanish Government that the United States had long been acquainted with the fact that the Allied Governments would not accept from neutral powers any " suggestion looking towards the restoration of peace," that recent information from the capitals of the Allies had indicated that the Entente powers were still opposed to mediation by neutral nations, and that such proposals would " in all probability cause irritation." [55] Yet another member of the presidential family, Joseph Tumulty, on May 16 sent a memorandum to the President urging him to act immediately in the interest of peace and suggesting that the proper procedure would be for the United States simply to announce that it was meeting both sides at The Hague to mediate a settlement. With regard to Tumulty's proposal Walter Millis makes the comment: " One may regret that this idea had not been more cordially received when Jane Addams had been agitating it a year and a half before. . . ." [56] In fact, Wilson at this time did act in the direction of peace, first proposing a conference to Grey and then, in his address of May 27, indicating his readiness to initiate a peace movement.[57] But the Allies were not now in the frame of mind to respond to such gestures. Professor Curti, like Mr. Millis, remarks that when Wilson at length did what Miss Addams had long urged him to do, it was too late.[58]

All the more since their hopes for a governmental confer-

---

[54] Woman's Peace Party, " Proposals Submitted to the Committee on Resolutions of the National Progressive Convention, June, 1916." Mimeographed sheet, Jane Addams Peace Collection.
[55] Quoted from *Foreign Relations, 1916, Suppl.*, pp. 46-47, by Charles Callan Tansill, *America Goes to War*, p. 591.
[56] Millis, p. 308.   [57] Baker, VI, 202-222.   [58] Curti, p. 243.

ence continued to be disappointed, the women pacifists watched with keen interest the development of the Ford Peace Mission after it set itself to productive activity in mediation. On January 24 the Mission transformed itself into a permanent body. The Neutral Conference for Continuous Mediation was set up at Stockholm and a long cherished dream of the women was thus actualized. It is true that the preliminaries had been unfortunate, although Mark Sullivan's judgment that the ridicule of the Peace Ship discredited the whole American peace movement [59] is probably a great overstatement. In any event, Professor Curti seems justified in suggesting that the accomplishments of the later phase of the Ford Mission, the Neutral Conference, constitute a basis for revising the usual depreciation of the Mission.[60]

The personnel of the Neutral Conference consisted of five delegates and five alternates from Denmark, Holland, Norway, Sweden, Switzerland, and the United States. It included in its membership European pacifists of high standing—government officials, scholars, and officers of peace societies. The American delegates chosen were Jane Addams and Dr. Charles F. Aked. Because of her illness Miss Addams was unable to journey to Stockholm, much to her regret.[61] Mme. Schwimmer, partly because of differences with some of the delegates, resigned. A blow from the point of view of public prestige was suffered by the Conference when its backer, Mr. Ford, who had gone with the Peace Ship, departed suddenly and unceremoniously on December 24.

However, the removal of the glare of the limelight seemed to enable the Conference to settle down to the serious study of peace possibilities and to endeavor to direct the attention of both belligerent and neutral governments to the advisability of mediation. First there was issued an appeal addressed "To the Governments and Parliaments of the Neutral Nations Represented at the Second Hague Conference," pleading for an offer of official mediation as a course consonant with the Hague Conventions. This appeal not only received wide

[59] Sullivan, *Our Times*, V, 183.   [60] Curti, p. 245.
[61] Jane Addams to Rosika Schwimmer, *loc. cit.*

attention in the European press but was the occasion of parliamentary debate in three countries and was discussed at a meeting of the prime ministers of the three Scandinavian countries. The appeal was followed by much correspondence and taking of testimony designed to obtain and compare the various national points of view which would have to be harmonized in an attempt at mediation—a study which culminated in another appeal, addressed to "The Governments, Parliaments and Peoples of Belligerent Nations." This was an attempt to call attention to those universal principles and concrete proposals upon which agreement seemed possible and upon which there might be founded a peace satisfying both the legitimate interests of the warring nations and the needs of humanity for advancement. The points which followed were, in general, those which had become popularized among liberals through such organizations as the Union of Democratic Control and the Woman's Peace Party—the right of self-determination, freedom of the seas, parliamentary control of foreign policy, an international organization including a world court, disarmament, guarantee of economic necessities to all peoples, and a world congress to bring about the creation of the new international order.

Miss Addams, who with gratification saw the Conference increase in usefulness and prestige,[62] intended to assume her duties as American delegate as soon as her health permitted. But a recurrence of her illness in April made it seem better to permit Miss Balch, an alternate, to go in her place. In an interview with a New York *Evening Post* reporter, Miss Balch declared:

My main interest in this neutral conference is to do my part toward helping people in one country to know what other people in other countries are thinking. I think that the programme of the Anti-Annexationist party ought to be known and discussed in England. I believe that Germany ought to know of the proposals of broadminded Englishmen. The most helpful thing we can do is to get together all the peace programmes and peace proposals of different countries and make them easily accessible.[63]

Miss Balch's favorable opinion of the Conference was not

[62] Lochner, pp. 141-153.
[63] New York *Evening Post*, April 6, 1916.

dispelled by her participation in its work. In the ensuing months much work was accomplished, not only in the publication of the various peace programs but also in independent investigation of the problems of a constructive peace and in keeping alive the idea of mediation. When Miss Balch returned to the United States in July she still spoke enthusiastically. She had returned in order to organize in the United States cooperation with the Neutral Conference, with special regard to arranging for peace demonstrations which the Conference had invited throughout the world on August 1, anniversary of the beginning of the war. Miss Balch expressed her anticipation of an early peace, and declared that the Conference was playing a modest part in bringing it about.[64]

In July the Neutral Conference was reorganized on the basis of leaving two delegates in each of the five neutral countries, with headquarters at The Hague where the two American members took up their duties. This change permitted the work to be carried on in six different centers instead of one. A still later change was brought about by Ford's desire, communicated to Louis Lochner on his trip to the United States in October, that the Conference turn from publicity and agitation to a concentration of effort on contacts with the governments in behalf of mediation. Subsequently the Conference was changed into an International Commission, divided into departments, with departmental chiefs responsible to the Central Office at The Hague.[65]

The work of the International Commission engaged the interest of the Woman's Peace Party at its December annual meeting. Miss Balch spoke promisingly of it in her address on "Action of Neutrals to Shorten the War." [66] Likewise, Madeleine Z. Doty encouraged the delegates by declaring that the people of France and England, as she was told by responsible people abroad, were "heartily sick of this war" and that

---

[64] "Miss Balch on the Ford Peace Conference," *Survey* (1916), XXXVI, 444.
[65] Lochner, pp. 169-170, 189-190.
[66] "The Second Annual Meeting of the Woman's Peace Party." Mimeographed program, Jane Addams Peace Collection.

the same desire for peace predominated among the people of Germany.[67]

Confirmation of the second part of Miss Doty's statement seemed to be given two days later by the announcement of the German Chancellor that Germany and her allies were ready to enter into peace negotiations. Despite the tactlessness of Germany's manner in the offer, the women pacifists were keyed to a high pitch of expectancy. The New York City branch of the Party showed its zeal by asking Norman Angell to use his influence with the British Government in the direction of a generous reception of Germany's terms without armistice.[68] On December 19 President Wilson sought to aid in the situation by sending a note to the belligerents suggesting that they declare specifically their war aims. The Ford International Commission exploited the possibilities to the fullest by communicating private information to Foreign Offices and by organizing public demonstrations in favor of peace. Miss Addams and her associates viewed the new development with satisfaction, despite the fact that the President did not adopt their program of joint action by neutrals or even make an explicit offer of mediation by the United States. Glad that the President was willing to make any overture in the direction of peace, Miss Addams wrote to him on Christmas day thanking him for taking the step. He answered on the day he received her note, saying:

Thank you very warmly for your word about the note to the belligerent powers. I knew that you would sympathize and am happy to think of your sympathy.[69]

The answers which both sides gave to Wilson's soundings were disappointing. But when, on January 22, Wilson made another valiant effort, his famous " Peace without Victory " address, Miss Addams felt prompted again to commend him. The address contained certain principles that the Woman's Peace Party had long advocated—repudiation of alliances, a concert of nations, abolition of the right of conquest, freedom

---

[67] New York Times, December 10, 1916.
[68] New York Times, December 15, 1916.
[69] Linn, p. 325.

of the seas, provision of direct outlets to the sea by every nation, and limitation of armaments. Miss Addams' letter this
time brought no reply. For, a few days after its receipt, Germany announced the resumption of unrestricted submarine
warfare. The President was engrossed with other matters
than correspondence with pacifists, who, whether they realized
it or not, had seen pass the last chance for American
mediation.

It was not much later that the women witnessed the collapse
of their other hope—the Conference of Neutrals. As its financial supporter saw the United States draw closer to war he saw
also reasons for making an exception to a pacifism which previously had been thoroughgoing. He proposed to offer his
plant to the President for the manufacturing of munitions.
Although the President had told Louis Lochner that nothing
in his work embarrassed him, in February Ford announced
that he would no longer support the Commission after March
1. "Thus," Miss Addams later recorded, "came to an end
all our hopes for a Conference of Neutrals devoted to continuous mediation." [70] Less gentle, Lochner has written: "Henry
Ford had been tried in the balance and found wanting." [71]
The women pacifists had learned that the adage warning
against putting trust in princes applied not merely to statesmen but to impetuously generous industrial magnates as well.

---

[70] Addams, *Peace and Bread*, p. 46.
[71] Lochner, p. 234.

CHAPTER VI

THE MARTIAL SPIRIT AT HOME

In the first few years of its existence the work of the Woman's Peace Party falls chiefly into two phases, both of them attacks upon war but of very different kind. The first phase, which has been reviewed in the preceding three chapters, was the activity designed to bring an end to the European War and to lay the basis for a just and permanent peace. The second phase, as yet but little noted, was defined in the original platform as "organized opposition to militarism in our own country." It was natural that an organization created in protest against the war should at first have given its chief thought to the world conflict which every day involved a fearful sacrifice of human life and carried the world further and further from the ideal of peace. If, for a time, opposition to home evils was considered of secondary importance, it was not only because domestic militarism did not appear immediately menacing, but also because the best cure would have been the ending of the source of infection, the European War. Two factors, however, came into play which caused the domestic situation to seem of much greater immediate importance: increasing realization that the plan for mediation faced tremendous difficulties, and the alarming growth of militarism in the United States. About the time of the second annual meeting of the Party, opposition to America's own militarism began to be the center of the women's interest.

As early as the first few months of the Party's existence, it became evident to the women that there was developing in the United States a movement for preparedness which had dangerous possibilities as a militarist tendency. Indeed, increase in America's military and naval equipment had seemed necessary to some nationalists coincidently with the outbreak of the European War. But the preparedness campaign did not gain great momentum until Germany's establishment of a war zone in February 1915 and Great Britain's simultaneous tightening of her blockade resulted in disputes between the United States and both belligerent parties over war-time incidents of the high seas and commerce. In consequence of these international difficulties Congress in the winter of 1915 considered appropriating $45,000,000 for more battleships. At the same time a large group of nationalists, including Theodore Roosevelt, supported an organization called the American Legion, which proposed to enroll 250,000 volunteers as an army reserve.

An address of Miss Addams before the Massachusetts branch of the Woman's Peace Party in March 1915 shows the alarm with which she and her associates viewed both these manifestations of incipient militarism. It also indicates the chief line of argument which the women were to take in combating the movement for preparedness—the lack of any rational basis for it. " Why spend $45,000,000 for warships," she asked, " when they will only be reduced to the scrap heap after this war is over? " This assumption that the warships would be reduced to the scrap heap became clarified as she proceeded with her argument. She declared: " We cannot foretell what many of the results of the war will be, but it is certain to mean a limitation of armaments." The present, therefore, was " no time to determine a national policy which we are likely to regret." In the same speech Miss Addams characterized the American Legion as not only " unnecessary but shocking." It was unnecessary because " this country was in no danger of being drawn into the war," and wrong because " it was a preparation for war." [1]

Miss Addams could not foresee, to be sure, the sinking of the *Lusitania* in May, which in the view of many ought to have drawn the United States into war. Though many believed that the *Lusitania* incident underscored the wisdom of preparedness, the Woman's Peace Party adhered to its original position. In June Mrs. Lucia Ames Mead, Secretary of the Woman's Peace Party, explained this position. She

---

[1] *Boston Herald*, March 9, 1915.

declared that both she and Miss Addams believed in national defense and adequate defense and that they were not asking for disarmament while other nations were armed. However, she added that they did not consider " armaments " synonymous with " defense " and thus they earnestly urged that there be no increase in military preparations at this time.

Despite such pleas by peace groups the Secretaries of the War and Navy Departments felt that the darkening international situation demanded further military and naval plans, and on October 20 an ambitious naval building program was announced by Secretary Daniels. Alarmed, the Woman's Peace Party wrote to President Wilson a letter calling to his attention " certain views which they have reason to believe are wide-spread, although finding no adequate expression in the press." The letter admitted the necessity of " real preparedness against real dangers," but not that of " a preposterous preparedness against hypothetical dangers." The women argued that such preparedness would " compel powerful nations to imitate us," would " create rivalry, suspicion and taxation in every country," would " inevitably make all other nations fear instead of trust us," and, most important of all, " would tend to disqualify our National Executive from rendering the epochal service which this world crisis offers for the establishment of permanent peace." This service, the hope for which had been expressed in several of Wilson's own messages, was the privilege " not only of helping the war-worn world to a lasting peace, but of aiding toward a gradual and proportional lessening of that vast burden of armament which has crushed to poverty the peoples of the old world." [2] This letter so much appealed to ex-Secretary Bryan that he published it in the *Commoner*.

Up to this time Wilson had seemed the champion of the anti-preparationists. In his annual message of 1914 he had declared that America should not be turned into an armed camp and that he would adhere to this view even if some were nervous and excited. Ironically enough, it was shortly after

---

[2] *The Commoner*, November, 1915. Photostat in Jane Addams Peace Collection.

receiving the letter of the women that he shifted his ground. On November 4 President Wilson made an address showing that he had turned toward the camp of the preparedness movement. He called for the development, within the next three years, of a force of 400,000 citizen soldiers who would be expected to undergo intensive training for a period of each year. Unsatisfactory as this moderate proposal was from the standpoint of the fanatics for preparedness, from the standpoint of the pacifists it was a definite defection from their philosophy.

President Wilson's adoption of a preparedness program was immediately attacked or bewailed by various individuals and groups in the Woman's Peace Party. The branch which protested most aggressively was that of New York City, led by the fearless Crystal Eastman. This branch held several meetings and forums in New York City in the weeks following President Wilson's announcement. It attracted public attention in particular by arranging debates between prominent advocates and opponents of preparedness. As was inevitable, some in the large audience of pacifists did not heed the plea of Miss Eastman for fairness, and their hissing and heckling of advocates Henry Wood and S. S. Menken secured a newspaper notoriety which was not of the welcome variety. At a forum of the Woman's Peace Party on November 15, Miss Eastman made a statement which was critical of her own organization. Saying that it was high time that the pacifists had a program, she proceeded:

So far we have been a party of negation, or at least have offset remote plans for federation against immediate demands for preparedness. Congress convenes December 6. Every Congressman will be bombarded with demands for appropriations to finance a big army and navy. On the first day let the Woman's Peace Party have a bill ready calling for a public investigation of the state of our defenses, with a report in three months. Let that be the first plank in our platform.[3]

This demand for a positive program was very shortly to be responded to by the Woman's Peace Party, and one of the planks was precisely what Miss Eastman had suggested. On

---

[3] *New York Times*, November 16, 1915.

November 19 and 20 there was held a preliminary meeting of delegates to the annual convention of the organization. Of the recommendations made that which received the most stress was a "protest against unprecedented expenditure for war preparations at this session of Congress." Five considerations were adduced in opposition to such expenditure. Three of them were the same as the arguments used in the letter to Wilson: the setting of a bad example to other nations; the weakening of America's influence as mediator; and the imperilment of her opportunity to effect reduction of armaments after the war. Two other arguments brought forth had to do with questions of national self-interest. "The moment of panic," it was pointed out, "is a bad time to decide any matter, and whatever the danger of attack to America, none could be anticipated at the present time when her hypothetical enemies are exhausting their resources elsewhere." And so far as future dangers were concerned, the delegates observed that it was premature at this point to expend enormous amounts of money upon dreadnaughts of the old-fashioned type when it was probable that the study of the naval conduct of the war would greatly modify the type of defense to be used in the future. Advocates of preparedness doubtless gnashed their teeth to see the pacifists arguing against dreadnaughts in terms of naval experts.[4]

It has already been seen that about the end of November 1916 the leaders of the Woman's Peace Party had become discouraged about the calling of an official conference of neutrals to offer mediation in the European War. This continuing discouragement with reference to the European situation increased the disposition of the women to concentrate their efforts upon an evil more within their control—militarism at home. Thus the fight against preparedness was the chief theme of the first annual convention of the Woman's Peace Party, held in Washington, D. C., from January 8 to January 10, 1916. It was in no feeling of complacency that some 150 delegates gathered together after their first year of organiza-

[4] *Year Book of the Woman's Peace Party, 1916*, pp. 56-57.

tional work. The National Secretary, Mrs. Lucia Ames Mead, reflected the general mood when she wrote in her report:

> Our organization begins its second year at a time when American ideals are in jeopardy and democracy is in peril. Militarism and commercialism are in the saddle as probably never before in our history. We are non-voters upholding an unpopular cause at a time when the policy of our country may decide the policy of the world for generations to come.[5]

On the other hand, the organization could consider itself much better girded for the fight than a year ago. From its original membership of 86 the Party had grown till it included now 512 members-at-large and 165 group bodies, of which 33 were local branches and the rest affiliated bodies. With the inclusion of the affiliated bodies, the membership of the Woman's Peace Party at the beginning of 1916 was about 40,000.[6]

An opening business meeting adopted with few changes a constitution which had been presented to the preliminary conference in November. Mention has already been made of the most important change effected by this constitution, the formal designation of the Woman's Peace Party as " The Section of the United States of the International Committee for Permanent Peace." Affiliation with this international body raised the question whether the national group should, like the International Committee, require of members that they subscribe completely to the platform. This question was taken up especially in relation to the suffrage plank, adherence to which was demanded of its members by the international body. Some of the delegates made it clear that a large number of women interested in peace would be excluded from the Party if belief in woman suffrage were made a prerequisite of membership. For this reason it was decided that the constitution, like the preamble adopted at the formation of the organization, should stipulate merely that women desiring membership must " substantially " support the platform.[7]

Substantial acceptance of the platform was doubtless interpreted as sympathy with the purpose of the Party, which, as stated in Article II of the Constitution, was as follows:

---

[5] *Ibid.*, pp. 44-45.
[6] *Ibid.*, p. 48; Addams, *Peace and Bread*, p. 20.
[7] *Year Book of the Woman's Peace Party, 1916*, pp. 6-10.

The object of the Woman's Peace Party shall be to protest against the war system; to substitute law for war; to enlist all women of the United States in arousing the nations to respect the sacredness of human life and to abolish war; to promote methods for the attainment of that peace between nations which is based on justice; and to cooperate with women of other countries who are working towards the same ends.[8]

Noteworthy in the foregoing is the transference of the ideal of respecting the sacredness of human life from the Preamble to the Constitution. Mrs. Villard, proposing this, emphasized that, so far as she knew, the sacredness of human life had been mentioned by no other society than the Woman's Peace Party.[9]

The organizational structure set up by the constitution was not greatly different from that followed since the beginning, and there are only a few features which need engage our attention. Most important of all is the federal character of the organization, which, while giving certain powers to the central agency of the Party, allowed the widest latitude to the local branches and affiliated bodies. The central agency, the National Executive Board, had the following powers: the appointment of the state chairman when a branch in a state was first organized; the giving of general advice and help; the sole authority to issue printed matter in the name of the Woman's Peace Party; the calling of annual and other meetings; the appointment of chairmen of standing committees and the engaging of national organizers; and the representation of the national organization in all emergencies. But, with the exception of the first state chairmen, state and local branches were to elect their own officers and arrange auxiliary or popular membership as they saw fit. In addition to the state and local branches there were to be affiliated independent organizations, holding group membership, on no other condition than that they declare themselves in accord with the object of the Woman's Peace Party. The wide autonomy and independence permitted, which were to be even amplified later, were in considerable measure responsible not only for the endurance of the organization amid differences of opinion but also for its impressive growth.[10]

On the afternoon of the first day of the convention there

---

[8] *Ibid.*, p. 11.   [9] *Ibid.*, pp. 9-10.   [10] *Ibid.*, pp. 11-13.

was held a mass-meeting, presided over by Miss Addams, which was attended by twenty-five hundred. The addresses dealt with the problems and policies which the Party was desirous of calling to public attention at the time. Mrs. Fannie Fern Andrews, discussing " The Education of Youth in the Ideals of Peace," a problem with which she was engaged as secretary of the American School Peace League, urged the teaching of cooperation in the schools and expressed the hope that the spirit of cooperation, thus inculcated from the bottom up, could ultimately be made to control all international relations as it had controlled the recent Pan-American Scientific Congress.[11]   Miss C. E. Mason explained the " Psychology of Peace," saying that it rested upon feelings of kindliness and neighborliness which must be taught in the home as well as in the school.[12]   The most stirring addresses of the afternoon were those made upon the most pressing practical issue of the moment, preparedness.   Crystal Eastman urged that the plank in the party platform advocating limitation of armaments and nationalization of their manufacture be interpreted in a spirit of courage and vigor so as to defeat the efforts of munitions makers to make Congress vote large military appropriations.   She declared that the whole preparedness campaign, in premising that a two-power navy and great army would assure liberty, prosperity and peace, was built upon a lie and that millions in Europe were dying to prove that it was a lie.[13]   Mrs. Mead, analyzing the factors responsible for " The Growth of Militarism," likened militarism to an obsession which affected educated men today in the way that the wide-spread witchcraft delusion affected the Middle Ages. Those relying upon arms were suffering from a delusion because they acted upon purely hypothetical and improbable dangers and ignored the possibility of meeting these dangers more rationally by establishing institutions of international cooperation.[14]   The importance of woman suffrage to the peace movement was elaborated by Laura Clay, who praised the Woman's Peace Party for adding to planks well known to

[11] *Ibid.*, pp. 14-15.
[12] *Ibid.*, pp. 15-16.
[13] *Ibid.*, pp. 16-17.
[14] *Ibid.*, pp. 18-19.

pacifists a demand for the humanization of governments by extension of the vote to the more peaceful sex.[15] After so much display of opposition to current shibboleths the succeeding speakers took pains to emphasize that the women were not pursuing a merely negative policy. Marian Tilden Burritt, grandniece of the famous pacifist Elihu Burritt, pointed out that the word "pacifist" meant peace-maker, and that the making of peace involved nothing less than the reconstruction of society.[16] The final address, by Janet Richards, was a plea for economic pressure and non-intercourse as deterrents from war which would at the same time respect the sacredness of human life and be more effective than any other sanction.[17] In pursuance of this plea a later session of the meeting voted that the party platform should mention, in place of an international police force as the safeguard of peace, "economic pressure and non-intercourse."[18] The women were evidently unimpressed, as are American pacifists today, by the possibility that economic sanctions would quickly lead to war.

The most important accomplishment of the conference was the adoption of a Congressional program, which was to be promoted during the coming year.[19] It was oriented chiefly toward the issue of preparedness, which threatened to be the main interest of the Congress then in session. The first plank demanded that "no increased appropriations for war preparation be voted during the present session." This demand was moderate in merely declaring against increase of appropriations, but in the discussion of the recommendations Mrs. Villard voiced a protest against all recognition of the continuation of war, that is, against all acceptance of arms expenditures.[20] The second plank, foreshadowing the organization's support of the later Nye Investigation, implemented the opposition to increased armaments by proposing an investigation which was expected to show the lack of necessity for them. The women urged upon Congress that it appoint a joint committee to conduct thorough investigations, with public hearings, and report within the next six months upon the following matters:

---

[15] *Ibid.*, p. 20.
[16] *Ibid.*, p. 25.
[17] *Ibid.*, p. 26.
[18] *Ibid.*, p. 32.
[19] *Ibid.*, pp. 35-36.
[20] *Ibid.*, p. 28.

a. The condition of our military and naval defenses with special reference to the expenditure of past appropriations.

b. The probability of aggressive action by other nations against the United States by reason of antagonism with respect to race, trade, national expansion, property-holding in foreign lands, and other causes of war.

c. The possibility of lessening by legislative or diplomatic action the source of friction between this country and other nations.[21]

Of these subjects of investigation the most immediately pressing was the first. With this element of the resolution in mind, Miss Eastman had said in her address at the mass-meeting that Congress should be told to go slow before spending more money. "First investigate," she said, "and find out how the $250,000,000 that we are now spending on national defence is used." [22] It was believed that the facts revealed would not be very stimulative of further expenditures.

Another demand related to the preparedness issue was that calling for "action to provide for the elimination of all private profit from the manufacture of armament." [23] This proposal was a step towards the nationalization of the manufacture of armaments, which had been a plank in the 1915 Program for Constructive Peace. In connection with this part of the Congressional program there was some discussion on the floor about the Party's supporting the Crosser and Cummins bills, which were then before Congress, and which were in line with the women's recommendation.[24]

Realizing that the chief fuel for the preparedness movement came from specific cases of international friction, the women included two suggestions designed to remove the greatest disturbance then existing in the foreign relations of the United States. This was the dispute between the United States and Japan over the exclusion of Japanese from California—a dispute which, it will be remembered, the *New Republic* had recommended for the efforts of the women instead of the termination of the European war. They proposed to solve the issue by the investigative technique used in the Bryan treaties, but in this case without any treaty. The women proposed the following:

---

[21] *Ibid.*, p. 35.   [22] *Ibid.*, p. 17.   [23] *Ibid.*, p. 35.   [24] *Ibid.*, p. 28.

That action be taken to bring about the creation of a joint commission of experts representing Japan, China and the United States, to study the complex and important questions at issue between the Orient and the United States, and to make recommendations to the various governments involved.[25]

Further, in order to prevent any state in the future from causing international friction, the program called for the passage of the law advocated by the American Bar Association, which gave the Federal government control over aliens.

The two remaining planks in the program had reference not to the domestic but to the world situation. One, pertaining to the War, called for a conference of neutrals. The other called for action to convene the Third Hague Conference at the earliest possible moment—a demand which evidently proceeded from the women's desire for the further development of international judicial machinery. In this plank it was further suggested that all delegates from the United States should be civilians representing various important elements in the country, including, if possible, the business, educational, and labor interests, as well as women. Again the women were indulging their predilection for subordinating convention, however old, to what seemed reasonable. One member, however, pointed out the difficulty of having women represent the United States at the Conference before they had even attained the right to vote.[26]

In addition to adopting a Congressional program the meeting passed a number of resolutions, some of which represented interests new for the organization. Thus two resolutions espoused the ideal of Pan-Americanism, which the recent Pan-American Congress and the enthusiasm of Mrs. Andrews for its work had impressed upon the women. One resolution advocated, as an important and timely move in the direction of peace, that Congress " take immediate action toward the united cooperation of the twenty-one republics of America for

---

[25] *Ibid.*, p. 35. On May 24, 1916, Senator La Follette of Wisconsin introduced a Senate joint resolution requesting the President to join in the formation of an international commission to study the questions at issue between the Orient and the United States. *Congressional Record*, 64th Cong., 1st sess., p. 8578.
[26] *Ibid.*, p. 36.

the consideration of all questions relating to the interests of those Republics." The other expressed deep interest in the meeting of the Second Pan-American Scientific Congress and a conviction that the results of the Congress would lay the foundation for more friendly and substantial cooperation on the Western continent, and particularly for the political alliance of the American nations. A resolution of a different type, embodying an apparently novel idea in the tactics of the American peace movement, urged that, inasmuch as the cosmopolitan population of the United States was a source of great strength in the interests of peace, the Woman's Peace Party cooperate in its peace propaganda with all our foreign-born citizens. The remaining resolutions were those thanking Mrs. Pethick-Lawrence for her part in the founding of the organization, endorsing suffrage legislation in the Sixty-fourth Congress as a vital step towards peace, and a series of general pronouncements of protest " against all compromise with the war spirit under any guise whatsoever." [27]

Whatever inspiration and encouragement had come to the assembled pacifists from their communion was well needed for the arduous, up-hill activities of the year to come. In the week following the annual meeting the leaders of the Party, including Miss Addams, Miss Breckinridge, and Mrs. Mead, had the opportunity to urge planks of their Congressional program before House and Senate committees. In the hearing of January 11 before the House Committee on Foreign Affairs, to which allusion was made in connection with Miss Addams' testimony in behalf of a conference of neutrals, Mrs. Mead and Miss Breckinridge made appeals for other features of the women's program. The former laid special emphasis on the need for a world legislature to create new law and on the incompatibility of such world organizations with any international sanctions save economic.[28] Miss Breckinridge urged the committee to recommend that Congress formulate the principle that no citizen seeking concessions among backward

---

[27] *Ibid.*, pp. 36-38.
[28] *Hearings before the Committee on Foreign Affairs*, 64th Cong., 1st sess., on H. R. 6921 and H. J. R. 32, pp. 4-5.

peoples could claim the protection of the military and naval forces of this country.[29] On January 13 Miss Addams presented a lengthy statement before the House Committee on Foreign Affairs with reference to the question of increasing the armed forces of the country. Explaining that she spoke as president of the Woman's Peace Party, she declared that, while she realized that there was a certain absurdity in the appearance of women before that committee in connection with a bill concerning the Army, she also realized that women were affected in time of war as of peace by the national policies of the country. Then, while exercising her usual moderation and tact, she proceeded to state and justify her contention that the demand for a very marked increase of the Navy and Army was a part of war hysteria, caught from Europe and brought on by happenings which had no logical implication for this country. One line of presentation which she adopted was emphasis upon the likelihood of a proportional reduction of armaments as a result of the war which, bringing the nations to bankruptcy, would also convince them of the folly of attempting to settle any international difficulties through warfare. It therefore seemed to the Woman's Peace Party, she declared, that "the United States ought to wait until the war is over before it adopts a new policy, for if there is a chance for pushing the matter of proportional disarmament the United States would be the natural nation to suggest it." The other line of presentation was the argument that the United States was not only in no present danger of being attacked but would not know how best to defend itself until the lessons of the European war had been learned. Miss Addams suggested that the agitation to prepare for a purely hypothetical enemy who might never exist came primarily from men, who were more emotional than women. As a cure for the panic she suggested the appointment of the investigating commission recommended by the Woman's Peace Party.

Some interesting discussion ensued in the course of questioning by members of the committee. An attempt by Representative Quin of Mississippi to have Miss Addams put all

[29] *Ibid.*, pp. 12-13.

blame for the agitation for preparedness upon munitions makers failed to elicit from her any such over-simplified explanation of war. She declared her belief that there were all sorts of motives, including a sincere apprehension that the country was unprepared. Questioned by Representative Kahn on the possibility that war might come as suddenly to the United States as to European countries, Miss Addams emphasized the unique element in our situation—a geographical detachment which would give us time to prepare against any attack. Until we knew who our enemies were, she told Representative Tilson, we could not determine the extent of our military needs. For the present she advocated not going back from our present position—that would be too much to ask of human nature—but at least no increase until the war was over.[30]

Miss Addams' statement before the Military Affairs Committee was considered so effective that thousands of copies were sent out franked by the "Willful Men" in Congress. One of the number, a staunch friend of the pacifists, was the father of Charles A. Lindbergh.[31] Recognition of the value of Miss Addams' testimony came also from William Jennings Bryan, since his resignation as Secretary of State again a private citizen. He wrote to Miss Addams in parts as follows:

I write to thank you for having taken upon yourself the burden of appearing before the committee to protest against the preparedness program. Your very presence was an argument and the manner in which you answered the questions put to you must have impressed the committee.

The reports that come to me all indicate a growing sentiment against preparedness. The papers which formerly spoke of preparedness as a matter of course are now discovering that there are all kinds of reasons why there is going to be difficulty. . . .[32]

Mr. Bryan, however, had not shown great thoroughness in his scanning of American newspapers, many of which found all the difficulties to be in Miss Addams' position. Indeed,

---

[30] *Hearing before the Committee on Military Affairs, House of Representatives,* 64th Cong., 1st sess., January 13, 1916. Reprint by the Woman's Peace Party, Jane Addams Peace Collection.

[31] Addams, *The Second Twenty Years,* p. 134.

[32] W. J. Bryan to Jane Addams, January 22, 1916, MS, Jane Addams Peace Collection.

the numerous shafts of criticism leveled at her began that
experience of disillusionment which caused Miss Addams later
to say: "It seems strange in the light of later experiences
that we so whole-heartedly believed in those days, that if we
could only get our position properly before the public, we
could find an overwhelming response." [33]

The response of the Newark *Morning Star* is epitomized in
its reference to the "childish ideas of the excellent Miss
Addams." [34] The *Chicago Tribune* did not even grant her
candor. Commenting upon Miss Addams' objection to the
waste of money, this paper asserted that "in the name of
morality she made a purely mechanical argument and did so
not because it interests her but because by an appeal, which
weighs little or nothing in her estimation, she might support the courage of congressmen who wish to take money
from the military to waste it elsewhere.[35] The Charleston
News Courier doubted whether Miss Addams had helped
either the cause of unpreparedness or the repute of women for
competence in public affairs.[36] The *Minneapolis . Journal*
sought to put Miss Addams in her place:

Somebody ought to lead Miss Jane Addams back to social service.
As the head of Hull House, Miss Addams has done and is still doing
a great work. As an adviser on adequate national defense to the
Committees on Military Affairs of the Senate and House, she is a joke.
Miss Addams may know a lot about the needs of careless and care-
worn women of Chicago, but what does she know about the condition
of the harbor fortifications of San Francisco or New York? . . .
She may know how long it will take Hull House to get a job for a
woman out of work, but does she know how long it takes to turn
raw recruits into seasoned troops? . . .
Miss Addams has a job which she knows all about. She'd better
stick to it.[37]

Miss Adams, however, had never understood how the job
of a social worker could comprise less than the application of
humanitarianism to all the problems of the social order.
Moreover, militarism, demanding in addition to armaments
military training in the schools, was threatening the welfare

[33] *The Second Twenty Years*, p. 134.
[34] Newark *Morning Star*, January 14, 1916.
[35] *Chicago Tribune*, January 15, 1916.
[36] Charleston *News Courier*, January 15, 1916.
[37] *Minneapolis Journal*, January 17, 1916.

of the special interest of the social worker—the youth of the nation. Thus the Woman's Peace Party undertook to oppose in various ways the movement for militarization of school youth. To refute the argument that military drill was beneficial to boys, it published and circulated a pamphlet entitled "A Protest Against Military Training in the Public Schools." [38] It cited John H. Finley, President of the University of the State of New York and State Commissioner of Education, who declared: "Military drill in schools would imply a perpetuation of international hatreds and brutish warfare." It quoted David Starr Jordan, who emphasized three objections to military training. The first was "that such training is, on the whole highly specialized for a particular profession and that war." The second objection was "that martial spirit or [the] specific bias which this training gives to some degree unfits its possessor to consider justly the affairs in which this nation is concerned" and "tends to exaggerate that perverted form of patriotism expressed in the words 'my country right or wrong.'" The third criticism was "that military drill is in the hands of non-commissioned officers, in general with no fitness for teaching, while its value as exercise is far inferior to that of a well-appointed gymnasium or even of an ordinary athletic field." Still another prominent educational authority quoted was John Dewey, who called rifle training in the public schools "undemocratic, barbaric and scholastically wholly unwise."

At the same time, the various state and local branches fought the preparedness movement in their own commonwealths, offering particular opposition to state legislation calling for compulsory military instruction in the public schools. The activities of the New York City branch of the Woman's Peace Party in this direction were particularly energetic and imaginative. They needed to be. In the winter of 1916 New York was threatened with the passage by the Assembly of five so-called preparedness bills, including the Welsh and Slater bills providing for compulsory physical training of all school children over eight and for military training of all boys be-

---

[38] Jane Addams Peace Collection.

tween the ages of sixteen and nineteen. Such legislative efforts were supported by a group which left nothing undone to bring public opinion to an identification of extreme preparedness and patriotism. Thus on May 13 there was held in New York City a Preparedness Day parade in which a hundred thousand soldiers and civilians took part with the consequence that it lasted almost interminably. Lest the occasion seem to be marked by complete unanimity of opinion the Woman's Peace Party had a representative hold aloft opposite the reviewing stand a bold banner on which were inscribed the dissident words:

> There are only 100,000 of you.
> You are not the only patriots,
> 200,000 farmers, 500,000 mine workers and
> organized labor of America are opposed to what
> you and Wall St. are marching for.
> Are you sure you are right? [39]

A lone banner in a Preparedness Day parade may not have caused any patriot to doubt his rectitude, but in the same month the New York group pursued other means of inducing skepticism. Highly inventive in their methods, the New York women conducted a war-against-war exhibit in Brooklyn and New York which drew thousands of visitors daily. The feature of the exhibit which attracted most attention was a figure of "Uncle Sam as the Jingoes would have him," an Uncle Sam literally armed to the teeth with every type of weapon that could be crowded upon him. After their alleged lese majesty had provoked hostile letters to the newspapers and prompted a Kings County grand jury to a trip of inspection, the women counter-balanced the undignified presentation of Uncle Sam with a different kind. It was an "Uncle Sam as the Pacifists would have him," a benign old gentleman who held out his hand to the world and appealed to it with a scroll bespeaking practices and institutions of international cooperation.[40] On May 15 Governor Whitman signed the preparedness measures. On May 23 the Woman's Peace Party

---

[39] "New York's Parade of Preparedness," *Survey* (1916), XXXVI, 197-198.
[40] *Ibid.*, p. 197.

of New York announced a state-wide movement for the repeal of the legislation, which, it declared, would go far towards stamping out democracy and putting off the day of internationalism which depends upon democracy.[41]

In their fight against the preparedness hysteria the Woman's Peace Party had various allies, notable among which was the American Union against Militarism, ably led by Lillian D. Wald, Paul Kellogg, and others.[42] This effort of pacifists did not avail even to retard the great tide for preparedness which was sweeping over the country. It was the less easy to dissuade its advocates in that they were convinced that they were the true friends of peace. Congress responded to the popular clamor and passed the Administration's measure. By the summer of 1916, when Congress enacted a great increase in the appropriation for the Navy, the victory of the preparedness movement was complete at least in respect to the legislative issues of that session. The only question was how much further the militarist tendencies would go.

The drive for preparedness was not the only policy of the Administration which gave the women concern in 1916. This policy merely foreboded a future war, but at the very time, in one phase of its foreign relations, the Administration was pursuing imperialistic and militaristic policies without declaration of war. This was the field of its Latin-American relations, more particularly the relations with the countries bordering the Caribbean Sea.

The direction taken by the Administration's Latin-American policy in 1916 was the more disappointing to the women pacifists because they had been led to expect great things of President Wilson in this regard. The very calling of the Second Pan-American Scientific Congress by the United States had seemed a pledge of better relations with the southern republics which we had so often treated high-handedly. Signalizing their great interest in Pan-Americanism, several prominent members of the Woman's Peace Party—Mrs. An-

---

[41] *New York Times*, May 24, 1917.
[42] The activity of the American Union against Militarism, closely allied with the Woman's Peace Party in both aims and membership, is described by R. L. Duffus in his recent biography of Lillian Wald.

drews, Mrs. Florence Kelley, Mrs. Post, and Miss Addams—
addressed the Women's Auxiliary Conference of the Congress.
Their hopes rose high, indeed, when at this congress President Wilson put forward a Pan-American program including
not only a mutual guarantee of absolute political independence and territory but also—what seemed even more significant to Miss Addams—the settlement of all disputes by investigation and arbitration. In view of this program, Miss
Addams writes, " we felt that we had a right to consider the
Administration committed until further to the path of arbitration," entered upon with the signature of the Bryan
treaties in 1914. The women did not reckon with the deflec-
tive force of the Monroe Doctrine, concern for which, amid
the disordered Caribbean conditions inviting European intervention, was probably the fundamental cause of what Miss
Addams called " the curious and glaring difference between
the President's statement of foreign policy and the actual bent
of the Administration.[43]

The Woman's Peace Party protested and fought against
every one of the various manifestations of this imperialistic
bent. This much is apparent from the account of Miss
Addams in *Peace and Bread,* though the actual details of
their anti-imperialist battle are for the most part missing
from the available records of the Party. Miss Addams' rather
vague and general account begins with the issue of Haiti,
which had become the unwilling host of American Marines in
July 1915. The marines had set up a military government,
including a strict military censorship. Finally in February
1916, as a result of the military grip upon her, Haiti signed a
treaty with the United States empowering the latter to ad-
minister her customs and finances for twenty years. Such, in
general, was the background of certain stories which reached
the Woman's Peace Party early in 1916. Miss Addams writes
of them as follows:

All sorts of stories were reaching the office of the Woman's Peace
Party, some of them from white men wearing the United States'
uniform, some of them from black men in despair over the treatment

---

[43] *Peace and Bread,* pp. 53-54.

accorded to the island by "armed invaders." We made our protest to Washington, Miss Breckinridge presenting the protest in person after she had made a most careful investigation into all the records to be found in the possession of the government. She received a most evasive reply having to do with a naval base which the United States had established there in preference to allowing France or Germany to do so. In response to our suggestion that the whole matter be referred to the Central American Court we were told that the Court was no longer functioning, and a little later indeed the Carnegie building itself was dismantled, thus putting an end to one of the most promising beginnings of international arbitration.[44]

From a different point of view, the organization was also seriously opposed to the Bryan-Chamorro Treaty of 1916, which gave the United States the exclusive right to build a canal across Nicaragua together with leases of sites for naval bases in return for a payment of $3,000,000 to be spent under American supervision. The women, according to Miss Addams, held this to be "seemingly in contradiction to the President's former stand in regard to Panama Canal tolls and the fortification of the Canal." Thus they asked Washington to explain the situation. Miss Addams recounts that "again the information given in response to the inquiry of the Woman's Peace Party was fragmentary and again responsibility seemed to be divided between several departments of the government." [45] Needless to say, the explanations were not convincing to the women.

In the summer of 1916 the difficulties of the United States with Mexico reached a climax which resulted in the dispatch of the Pershing punitive expedition. The influence of the Woman's Peace Party is evident in the action taken in this issue by the American Union Against Militarism, which was headed by Lillian D. Wald, a member of the Woman's Peace Party, and which included Miss Addams among its founders and continuing members. The Union appealed for an "unofficial commission" of three representative Americans and three representative Mexicans to go to El Paso and prevent the outbreak of war by offering mediation. The plan harked back, of course, to the plan of continuous mediation sponsored by the Woman's Peace Party with reference to the World War. Among those signing the petition to President Wilson

---

[44] *Ibid.*, pp. 54-55.   [45] *Ibid.*, p. 55.

to approve the plan of mediation was Crystal Eastman, head of the New York City branch of the Woman's Peace Party.[46] Mrs. Amos Pinchot, a prominent member of the New York branch of the Party, was one of a delegation of pacifists who pleaded with President Wilson for a peaceful solution of the difficulties. The Party made its voice heard directly through a letter to the *New York Times* written by Mrs. Lucia Ames Mead as National Secretary. Mrs. Mead attacked the interventionist policy pursued by the Administration as fraught with "awful risks to our national character and policies." She declared:

> War once begun, and the public mind influenced with loss of gallant men, we should fight to the bitter end. That end might mean suzerainty from the Rio Grande to Panama, with a suspicious and embittered South America.[47]

Mrs. Mead added that at the same time the triumph of militarism would deflect the United States from its opportunities for international service, with the consequence that "the greatest opportunity for service to humanity which a nation ever had will be gone, never to return." [48] In addition to this public appeal by an officer of the national organization, campaigns against intervention and war were carried on by branches of the Woman's Peace Party, particularly the Massachusetts and New York City groups, which arranged mass-meetings and drew up petitions.[49]

President Wilson had scarcely accepted the mediation of the A. B. C. Powers in his difficulties with Mexico when news came of another imperialistic move by the Administration. In the late summer of 1916 the purchase of the Virgin Islands from Denmark was announced. A plebiscite had been taken in Denmark in regard to the sale, but the people of the Caribbean colony were to be given no voice in respect to the transaction. Miss Addams reports that "when the Woman's Peace Party urged such a plebiscite, we were told that there was no doubt that the Virgin Islands people did wish such a transfer,

---

[46] *New York Times*, June 24, 1916.
[47] *Ibid.*   [48] *Ibid.*
[49] *Report of the International Congress of Women, Zurich, 1919,* p. 402.

but there was no reply to our contention that it would make it all the easier, therefore, to take the vote, and that the situation offered a wonderful opportunity actually to put into practice on a small scale what the President himself would shortly ask Europe to do on a large scale." [50]

When, finally, in November 1916 eighteen hundred United States Marines were sent to the Dominican Republic, the disillusionment of Miss Addams and her supporters with Wilson's Pan-Americanism was complete. With reference to this episode she writes:

Again we made our protest but this time as a matter of form, having little hope of a satisfactory reply although we were always received with much official courtesy. We were quite ready to admit that the government was pursuing a consistent policy in regard to the control of the Caribbean Sea, but we not only felt the danger of using the hunt for naval bases as an excuse to subdue one revolution after another and to set up military government, but also very much dreaded the consequences of such a line of action upon the policy of the United States in its larger international relationships. We said to each other and once when the occasion offered, to the President himself, that to reduce the theory to action was the only way to attract the attention of a world at war; Europe would be convinced of the sincerity of the United States only if the President was himself actually carrying out his announced program in the Caribbean or wherever opportunity offered. Out of the long international struggle had arisen a moral problem the solution of which could only be suggested through some imperative act which would arrest attention as a mere statement could not possibly do. It seemed to us at moments as if the President were imprisoned in his own spacious intellectuality, and had forgotten the overwhelming value of the deed.[51]

However, when in the very midst of these disappointments in regard to President Wilson Miss Addams had been faced with the necessity of choosing whether or not to support him for re-election, she decided to vote for him. This decision was doubtless influenced by the fact that a vote for Hughes, who as well as Wilson appealed for Miss Addams' support, would have meant a vote for one highly critical of whatever pacifist elements had marked Wilson's policies. Miss Addams did feel that on the whole Wilson had been " essentially right in international affairs," that is, right in his policy of neutrality and of support of a league of nations. She believed also that

---

[50] Addams, *Peace and Bread*, pp. 55-56.
[51] *Ibid.*, p. 56.

" the President would finally act, not so much from his own preferences or convictions, but from the impact upon him of public opinion, from the momentum of the pressure for Peace, which we were sure the campaign itself would make clear to him." [52] When, recovering from an illness, Miss Addams became able to undertake a minimum of speaking and writing, " it was all for President Wilson's re-election and for an organization of a League of Nations." [53] Her efforts in Wilson's behalf were recognized signally by an invitation to a White House dinner tendered to a few people who had steadfastly supported the President.

Miss Addams viewed Wilson's victory with satisfaction only slightly mitigated by doubt:

> The results of the campaign had been very gratifying to the members of our group. It seemed at last as if peace were assured and the future safe in the hands of a chief executive who had received an unequivocal mandate from the people " to keep us out of war." We were, to be sure, at moments a little uneasy. . . . It seemed at times as if he were not so eager for a mandate to carry out the will of the people as for an opportunity to lead the people whither in his judgment their best interest lay. Did he place too much stress on leadership? [54]

The disillusioning answer was to be given all too soon.

However, America was still complacently at peace when the women held their second annual meeting, from December 8 to 10, again in Washington, D. C. The gathering was rather small in terms of numbers, but, as an article in the *Survey* pointed out, at this meeting there were the five women whose influence was perhaps the most powerful in the country. They were Jane Addams, Florence Kelly of the National Consumers' League, Julia C. Lathrop of the Children's Bureau, Ella Flagg Young, former superintendent of Chicago schools, and Lillian D. Wald of the Henry Street Settlement. [55]

Miss Addams, in opening the meeting, touched upon the issue which, as at the annual meeting a year ago, was foremost in the women's interest. She pointed out that, although

---

[52] *Ibid.*, p. 57.   [53] *Ibid.*, p. 58.   [54] *Ibid.*, p. 58.
[55] " The Women's Peace Program for 1917," *Survey* (1916), XXXVII, 307.

the members of the Woman's Peace Party were foes of preparedness, they cherished hopes for the nation just as patriotic as those of its advocates. " Because we have the best development of our country at heart," she said, " we work for peace." [56]

However, the cause of peace faced more serious dangers now than a year before. Whereas in the past year the campaign for preparedness concentrated upon increased military expenditures, it now went so far as to agitate for universal military service. Accordingly, as the *Survey* pointed out, the women " emphasized again and again, throughout the conference, in the business routine, at public mass meetings, condemnation of all attempts to menace social, industrial and political liberties by compulsory military service in this country." [57]

This emphasis is evident particularly in the year's Congressional program adopted, to the consideration of which two sessions were devoted. Some elements of the program pertained to bills already passed or introduced. Thus the women called for the repeal of the " draft " clause of the Army Reorganization Bill; the provision of a referendum for the people of the Danish West Indies before completing the purchase of the islands; the endorsement of the Susan B. Anthony Suffrage Amendment; and action under the Hensley clause of the Naval Appropriation Bill of 1916. This clause was in the eyes of the women the one redeeming feature of the bill. Hensley, one of the anti-preparedness minority in Congress in 1915, had inserted in it the request that the President " invite at an appropriate time, not later than the close of the war in Europe, all the great governments of the world to send representatives to a conference which shall be charged with the duty of formulating a plan for a court of arbitration or other tribunal, to which disputed questions between nations shall be referred for adjudication and peaceful settlement, and to consider the question of disarmament." This clause authorized the appointment of nine citizens to

---

[56] *Ibid.*   [57] *Ibid.*

represent the United States at such a conference, called for $200,000 for the carrying out of the proposal, and provided that if the international tribunal was established before the naval construction provided for in the act was contracted for, "such naval expenditure as may be inconsistent with the engagements made in the establishment of such tribunal may be suspended" by order of the President.[58] The plan of Representative Hensley thus met the women's program in respect to both arbitration and disarmament.

Other recommendations in the Congressional program concerned new legislation or national policies which the organization was to support. Most of the measures had been suggested at the annual meeting in the preceding January: the creation of a joint commission representing the United States, Japan, and China to investigate American-Oriental issues, the establishment of federal jurisdiction over alien residents of the United States, and the early calling of the Third Hague Congress. Several additions to the previous Congressional program reflected the opposition to American imperialism which had been occupying the women in the past year. The most important of these was a demand for the formulation of the principle that investments in foreign countries be made at the risk of the investor. This demand, though implied in the 1915 Program for Constructive Peace in its call for elimination of the economic causes of war, had been taken more immediately from the resolutions of the Hague Congress of Women. Still other policies advocated were the establishment and maintenance of "a just and righteous" relationship with our dependencies, and the establishment and maintenance of relationships of comity and good will with the other American commonwealths, including Mexico.[59]

Some of the policies which the women decided to pursue in 1917 were embodied in resolutions. In one resolution the women pledged themselves to work to prevent the passage of

---

[58] "The Hensley Clause and Disarmament," *Survey* (1916), XXXVII, 308.

[59] *The Second Annual Meeting of the Woman's Peace Party.* Program, Jane Addams Peace Collection.

any laws compelling military service of citizens and military training for minors.   Another resolution showed the importance which the pacifists attached to symbols in national life.   They recommended that the next Presidential inaugural ceremony, instead of being a military pageant, should represent the civic, social, educational, industrial, artistic, and religious interests of the country.[60]

The profusion of the domestic issues considered does not mean that Europe and international society in general were forgotten.   Among the subjects treated in addresses at a Sunday afternoon mass meeting were " Action by Neutrals to Shorten the War," " The Effect of this War on the Position of Women in the Belligerent and Neutral Countries," " Dependent Nationalities in Relation to World Peace," and " The War Settlement."   The women concerned themselves with the economic as well as the political needs of the world, devoting one session to the question of " The War in Relation to the High Cost of Living."   The discussion of this dealt particularly with the problem of the food shortage which was taking a heavy toll of life in many of the war-ridden countries. The observations of the women emphasized that, though the bad harvests of 1916 were partly to blame, the primary cause of the increasing dearth of food was the war itself.   The shortage of agricultural labor, the deflection to war purposes of the nitrate essential to fertilizers, the destruction of food-carrying ships by submarines, and the isolation of remote markets—all these accompaniments of war were responsible for extending its suffering to vast civilian populations.[61]

The feature of the December meeting, as Miss Addams points out, was a " Conference of Oppressed or Dependent Nationalities," arranged by Grace Abbott, chairman of the Immigrants' Protective League.   The subject was not novel in the peace movement but certainly the method of presenting it was new.   With their talent for dramatizing issues, the women arranged to have the addresses at the conference made

---

[60] " The Women's Peace Program for 1917," *Survey* (1916), XXXVII, 307.

[61] Addams, *Peace and Bread*, pp. 23-25.

by the American representatives of the oppressed or dependent nationalities—Albanians, Armenians, Belgians, Croa-
tians, Finns, Irish, Letts, Lithuanians, Montenegrins, Poles,
Russian and Roumanian Jews, Ruthenians, Serbians, Slovaks,
and Syrians.   An interesting prospectus of the conference
explained the reasons for having the American representatives
of all these nationalities conduct the discussion of the problem.[62]

The fundamental assumption was that Americans of foreign
origin could interpret the problems of their peoples as they
related to our international policies.   The prospectus pointed
out that the United States was the logical nation to open the
discussion of the rights of oppressed or dependent nationalities
because " we have a citizenship which includes representatives
of these peoples as well as of those powerful nations that have
controlled the destiny of Europe."   Because of our inclusion
of the former element in our citizenship, the question of how
the claims of the various national groups were to be settled
was, it was pointed out, in no sense abstract or remote to us but
a matter of immediate family concern to millions of our fellow
citizens.   Moreover, American public opinion at this time
particularly needed formulation on these questions in view of
the fact that the United States, as the most powerful neutral,
might be able to exert an important influence on the terms of
peace in the direction of a durable peace based on international justice.   In the elimination of the discontent and
suspicion of oppressed races American traditions of government were declared to have peculiar remedial possibilities.
Americans believed in self-government and in the freedom of
every people from oppression.   What was even more important,
they believed that a federal form of government offered the
most satisfactory method of giving local self-government in a
country great in territory or complex in population.   Americans knowing these principles, yet familiar also with the
problems of oppressed and dependent peoples, would be in a

---

[62] *Conference of Oppressed or Dependent Nationalities at Washington, December 10th and 11th.*   Pamphlet, Jane Addams Peace
Collection.

position to tell how the beneficent principles might be applied
to such peoples in the international reorganization which was
to follow the war. The experimental conference, as Miss
Addams has written, " had behind it a very sound theory of
the contribution which American experience might have made
toward a reconciliation of European differences in advance
of the meeting of the Peace Conference." [63]

The theory, indeed, was sound, but like so many theories
of the women it was not given application. Perhaps, human
nature being what it is, it could not have been applied. Miss
Addams was very candid in confessing the shortcomings of
the representatives of the various nationalities. In her reminiscences she wrote that " quite early in the proceedings it was
obvious that each group remembered conditions as they had
existed under the old régime and it was hard for them to hold
any other conception of patriotism than that involved in over-
coming oppression, at least they felt that they could do nothing
constructive until they had gotten rid of alien rule." [64] This
seemed extremely unfortunate to Miss Addams in that she
believed that " had the federal form of government taken
hold of the minds of the American representatives of various
nationalities as strongly as did the desire for self-determination, or had the latter been coupled with an enthusiasm for
federation, many of the difficulties inherent in the Peace
Conference could have been anticipated." [65]

When the meeting adjourned, the women little knew how
quickly events were to develop which would paralyze all their
carefully laid plans. War was not then on the horizon and,
before its lurid streak appeared, there was time to pursue
many objectives which were appropriate to a still normal
America. The first objective to which Miss Addams turned
after the meeting was the Susan B. Anthony Woman Suffrage
amendment. As the Senate Judiciary Committee was holding
hearings upon it in the early part of December, Miss Addams
took advantage of being in Washington to appear before the

---

[63] Addams, *Peace and Bread*, p. 22.
[64] Addams, *The Second Twenty Years*, p. 137.
[65] Addams, *Peace and Bread*, pp. 22-23.

committee on December 12. It doubtless seemed strange to the members of the committee that she should testify before it as representative of the Woman's Peace Party. But Miss Addams explained the connection as follows:

Our Woman's Peace Party is composed of women primarily interested in the question of peace but our organization makes "votes for women" a fundamental issue because we believe that women should have the right to vote on questions of peace and war, or rather to vote for the men who, in this country at least, must ratify all declarations of war and vote for the preparations for it.[66]

Before the events which were to bring such perturbation to opponents of war, there was one development which brought them great encouragement. This was the President's address to the Senate of January 22, 1917, enunciating America's desire for a league of nations and several of the other ideas concerning international organization which later appeared in the Fourteen Points. It has already been mentioned in another connection that Miss Addams wrote a letter to the President expressing her approval of his position. The Woman's Peace Party issued a pamphlet [67] which showed its approval by presenting in parallel columns extracts from the address and the resolutions adopted at the International Congress of Women at The Hague nearly two years earlier. It was the implication of the juxtaposition of the Wilsonian theses and the women's resolutions that the two were in close accord if not identical. Certainly it was true that the Hague Congress had advocated an international federation, general organization of the world for peace, respect for nationality, and the freedom of the seas—all ideals set forth in Wilson's famous address. But whereas Wilson had called merely for recognition of the principle of the consent of the governed, the women had demanded a specific logical implication of this principle—woman suffrage. Whereas Wilson had appealed only for limitation of programs of military preparation, the Hague Congress had advocated universal disarmament

---

[66] *Hearing before the Judiciary Committee*, Senate, 64th Cong., 1st sess., December 12, 1916. Reprint in Jane Addams Peace Collection.

[67] Woman's Peace Party, *An Interesting Comparison*. Pamphlet, Jane Addams Peace Collection.

and the nationalization of the manufacture of arms and ammunition. The most striking difference, one that the " Comparison " ignored, was that between Wilson's implication that military force was needed as a guarantee of world peace and the unwillingness of the women to go beyond social, moral, and economic pressure.

The pamphlet suggested a similar discrepancy between the program of the Peace Party and that of Wilson when it concluded by urging opposition to bills in forty-one state legislatures providing for the compulsory military training of boys in the public schools. From the standpoint of propaganda it was all very well for the women to present such a protest as a response to the gesture of the President in his address. But this line of presentation was exposed to mockery when, a few weeks afterward, Wilson himself led the Preparedness Parade and thus took over, as Jane Addams has remarked, the leadership of the movement started by his opponents.

The women's trust in Wilson's pacifism might not have been misplaced if events beyond the waters had not imposed too great a strain upon his love of peace. On January 31 the German Ambassador made the fate-laden announcement that his government would carry on unrestricted submarine warfare. On the very day the announcement was published in the American press the American Union against Militarism, headed by Lillian D. Wald, also of the Woman's Peace Party, telegraphed to Wilson that the United States should " refuse to allow herself to be dragooned into the war at the very end by acts of desperation committed by any of the belligerents." It urged the President to call on Congress and the press to exercise deliberate and unimpassioned consideration in the light of the interests of mankind, to call on the belligerents to meet and state their terms, and to address to the belligerents a final and personal offer of mediation.[68] The telegram, which was published as an advertisement in the New York press, was signed not only by Miss Wald but by others

[68] *New York Times*, February 2, 1917.

who were also of the Woman's Peace Party—Emily G. Balch, Crystal Eastman, Margaret Lane, and Mary Simkhovitch. The following evening the Union against Militarism and the newly formed American Conference Commission held a mass meeting in Madison Square Garden, addressed by Bryan, which requested the President to act under the Hensley clause of the Naval Appropriation Bill and call a conference of the governments. On the same day the Executive Board of the New York Woman's Peace Party telegraphed to Wilson urging that he forego temporarily the upholding of our rights of the seas in the interest of avoiding war.[69] These were the first efforts in a campaign to keep the United States out of war which henceforth was waged increasingly by the newer and more radical peace societies, in most of which members of the Woman's Peace Party took a prominent part.

The first efforts of these societies were shown quickly to have been fruitless. On February 3 Wilson announced that diplomatic relations with Germany had been severed. There ensued that fever of the war spirit which not only affected the uneducated but, what was more surprising, caused even intellectuals to throw their support to the use of war technique as a solution of the crisis. President Wilson himself was alarmed at the way in which public opinion outran him, and said of the martial spirit of ministers: ". . . I think our ministers are going crazy. . . ."[70] Miss Addams noted what to her was most surprising of all: " The long established peace societies and their orthodox organs quickly fell into line expounding the doctrine that the world's greatest war was to make an end to all wars." [71] Conscious of the President's fearful responsibilities, Miss Addams telegraphed to Wilson on February 4:

Many of us hope that you may find it possible to meet present international situation in league with other neutral nations in Europe and South America, whose interests are involved. Such an alliance

---

[69] *Ibid.*, February 3, 1917.
[70] Baker, VI, 461.   [71] Addams, *Peace and Bread*, p. 61.

might prove to be the beginning of a league standing for international rights and would at least offer a method of approach less likely to involve any one nation in war.[72]

Formerly Miss Addams' appeals for American action in league with other neutral nations had always referred to the plan of a conference for continuous mediation. Her words this time seem to have a different implication—of a league upholding and making representations in behalf of international rights. Miss Addams declared that this approach would be least likely to involve any one nation in war but she did not say, whatever she thought, that it would evolve into a conference to mediate the war. No reply to the telegram was ever received by her. But it is interesting to note that almost at the very time when the pacifist was suggesting the league of neutrals Wilson was actually working towards such an end. A favorable report from the Swiss Ambassador on February 4 encouraged the President to draft his " Bases for Peace" as a foundation for peace. But the unwillingness of the European neutrals, piqued at Wilson's previous refusal to cooperate and now fearful of the consequences of such cooperation, caused the plan to come to nothing.

On February 5 a number of the more thoroughgoing peace societies centered in New York City, including the New York City branch of the Woman's Peace Party, began negotiations for joint action, and by February 7 they had formed the Emergency Peace Federation, a reincarnation of the Emergency Federation of Peace Forces formed at Chicago in 1915. The slogan of the new Federation was " No War without a Referendum." [73] The local branch of the Woman's Peace Party continued energetic work independently as well. It held on February 5 a special executive session at which it was decided to conduct a telephone campaign to urge all its members to write to Congressmen in the interest of avoiding precipitate action and of trying every possible expedient before war, such as refusing passports to Americans travelling in the

---

[72] *Chicago News*, February 5, 1917; *Chicago Examiner*, February 6, 1917.
[73] *New York Times*, February 5 and 7, 1917.

war zone and calling a conference of neutrals.[74] On February
12 a hundred delegates of the Emergency Peace Federation
left for Washington, headed by Mrs. Henry Villard, to lead a
Lincoln's Birthday pacifist demonstration. They urged post-
poning any attempt to force acquiescence in America's claims,
and they proposed that issues be avoided by keeping American
travelers out of danger zones. Miss Addams was unable to go
with the delegation but wired her approval.[75]

As yet, in deference to the rule of democratic procedure, the
Woman's Peace Party had not acted as a national body. It
became necessary for it to take a stand in preparation for a
meeting of some nineteen national peace societies which was
called in New York at the Biltmore Hotel for February 22
and 23. The purpose of the meeting was to adopt a minimum program of the peace societies on which they might conduct joint action in the crisis. On the day preceding the conference of the peace groups, delegates from the state branches
of the Woman's Peace Party met in New York to consider
what program they should urge. The Party pledged itself
" to urge citizens of the United States to refrain from entering the war zone; to remind our government of the successful
settlement of international controversies by arbitration; to
urge, in case of an overt act, the use of its navy as a police
force without declaration of war; to protest against the
United States allying itself with any belligerent; to keep
alive the responsibility of America in helping the warring nations to find a basis for just and stable peace at the earliest
practicable moment; and to oppose compulsory service acts,
military training measures, and the espionage bill." Opposition, especially from the Massachusetts branch, arose in connection with one proposal—the endorsement of an advisory
referendum of the people before a declaration of war. This
meeting marks the earliest consideration by the Party of the
prototype of the Ludlow Amendment. The difference of
opinion was solved in a manner congruous with the democratic spirit of the referendum. It was finally voted to hold a

---

[74] *Ibid.*, February 6, 1917.
[75] *New York Times*, February 12, 1917.

referendum among the members on the question before committing the organization. Of the proposals agreed upon the
only ones that were new were those designed to keep the
United States from entering the European conflict—a danger
that was just beginning to become manifest.[76]

The conference of peace societies that began on February
22 did not live up to the hopes held out for it. The conference did, indeed, quickly adopt certain general principles—
opposition to war, conciliatory and judicial methods of solving disputes, condemnation of the espionage bill, and opposition to conscription and military training in public schools.
But on the question of a referendum on the declaration of
war there arose one of those controversies which anti-pacifists
love to exploit with utmost humor when pacifists, like other
human beings, hold different opinions. Mrs. Mead and Miss
Wald of the Woman's Peace Party took the lead in arguing
for the referendum, while Dr. Kirchwey of the American
Peace Society opposed it. Another bone of contention was
the question whether the conference should vote a resolution
of unconditional confidence in the President's leadership or
limit it to the peace sentiments expressed in his recent address to the Senate. On both these issues the rift of opinion
was between the established peace organizations, like the
American Peace Society, and the younger and more radical
groups conspicuous among which was the Woman's Peace
Party. The latter side won on both issues, committing the
conference to a referendum on war and a conditional vote of
confidence in the President. But so sharp was the division
that the conference, to the openly expressed disgust of Mrs.
Anna Garlin Spencer of the Woman's Peace Party, failed
except in procedural matters to arrive at a full minimum program binding all societies present.[77]

Unaffected by the activities of pacifists and their organizations, the general situation grew steadily worse. On February
26 Wilson asked Congress for the power to arm American

---

[76] *New York Times,* February 22, 1917; "Overruling Veteran Pacifists," *Survey* (1917), XXXVII, 647.
[77] *Ibid.; New York Times,* February 23 and 24, 1917.

ships. Still not without hope, two delegations of pacifists visited the President on February 28. One delegation included Paul Kellogg, editor of the *Survey*, and Lillian D. Wald, acting in behalf of the Union against Militarism. The other, representing the conference of leading peace societies which had been held in New York, consisted of two members of the Woman's Peace Party—Miss Addams and Miss Balch—and three others, including Professor William I. Hull of Swarthmore College, a former pupil of the President, and husband of the recent president of the United States section of the Women's International League for Peace and Freedom. Professor Hull presented a résumé of what other American presidents, notably Washington and Adams, had accomplished through adjudication when the interests of American shipping had been injured by European wars. The President reminded his old student that he was familiar with that history but brushed it aside, as he did also Professor Hull's suggestion that, if the attacks on American shipping were submitted to the Hague Tribunal, adjudication of the issues of the war itself might result. The labor leaders on the committee expressed the hope that war would not be declared without a popular referendum. The representatives of the Woman's Peace Party again pleaded for a conference of neutrals.

The reaction of Wilson to the pacifists has been described by Miss Addams in memorable words:

The President's mood was stern and far from the scholar's detachment as he told us of recent disclosures of German machinations in Mexico and announced the impossibility of any form of adjudication. He still spoke to us, however, as to fellow pacifists to whom he was forced to confess that war had become inevitable. He used one phrase which I had heard Colonel House use so recently that it still stuck firmly in my memory. The phrase was to the effect that, as head of a nation participating in the war, the President of the United States would have a seat at the Peace Table, but that if he remained the representative of a neutral country he could at best only " call through a crack in the door." [78]

Two attitudes of Wilson clearly emerge from this account. The first is his equivocal attitude towards war, which enabled him both to speak to the delegation as fellow pacifists and

---

[78] *Peace and Bread*, p. 64.

still to consider resort to arms. He was, of course, devoted to peace but not in any such absolute way as Miss Addams. As his biographer has noted, Wilson looked upon war as neither good nor wholly evil. To quote his words of 1911, he believed that "there are times in the history of nations when they must take up the crude instruments of bloodshed in order to vindicate spiritual conceptions." [79]   His reason for believing that this was such a time was rather paradoxical. It was the assumption that unless the United States entered the war it could not do anything substantial in behalf of a constructive peace.

Miss Addams has given her reasons for rejecting both theories. In the first place, she had a generalized distrust of force, the reasons for which have become amply manifest in the preceding pages. Of greater interest here is her disagreement with Wilson's belief in the necessity of America's entering the present war. She thought that "the appeal he made was, in substance, that the foreign policy [sic] which we so extravagantly admired could have a chance if he were there to push and defend them, but not otherwise." [80]   This assumption seemed to Miss Addams not only an overrating of the moral leadership which can inhere in any one man but also a deviation from the principle of democracy. Moreover, so far as the opportunity of the President of the United States was concerned, it seemed to Miss Addams to be much greater as a neutral than as the head of a belligerent nation. "The President," she declared, "had a seat at the Peace Table as one among other victors, not as the impartial adjudicator." She asked whether the result would not have been different "if both sides had been present at a conference presided over by a fair minded judge." [81]   Had Wilson stood firmly against participation in the war, Miss Addams thought, he could have had his way with the common people in every country, who then were invigorated by a wind of idealism blowing strongly across all Europe.

Would the belligerent governments, even in the event of a

---

[79] Baker, VI, 491.
[80] *Peace and Bread*, p. 64.   [81] *Ibid.*, p. 66.

stalemate, have submitted, as Miss Addams assumed, to the adjudication of some neutral power, even one whose President had caught the moral imagination of their peoples? Mr. Lansing has implicitly given a negative answer, introducing in his *Memoirs* evidence of the hostility of the Allies, even when they were pressed, to the idea of Colonel House that Wilson should participate in a peace conference as a neutral moderator or umpire to prevent the insistence by one side or the other on unjust terms.[82] If such a rôle was out of the question for the President except as head of a belligerent nation, then the criticism levelled by Miss Addams at the President—that his heart dictated to his head [83]—is equally applicable to her. But, even if it were conceded that Miss Addams excluded the only means which had a fighting chance of success, yet the means which Wilson adopted were undoubtedly open to criticisms, which he himself in a moment of doubt formulated better than anyone. Discussing with Frank Cobb the likelihood that our declaration of war would mean so bad a defeat for Germany that there would be a dictated peace, he went on to say:

> It means . . . an attempt to reconstruct a peace-time civilization with war standards, and at the end of the war there will be no bystanders with sufficient power to influence the terms. There won't be any peace standards left to work with. . . ." [84]

This hesitant, self-critical side of Wilson did not show itself to Miss Addams, and she and her fellow pacifists left the interview of February 28 greatly discouraged even if not hopeless. Her sense of the imminence of war was shown by her haste to make some final public gesture in behalf of international comity while there was still time. She cabled a message to the German branch of the International Committee of Women. The message, which was published in American newspapers after the German women gave it out, was as follows:

> Many American women combine with the members of the International Committee for Durable Permanent Peace to send their

---

[82] Robert Lansing, *War Memoirs*, p. 175.
[83] Addams, *Peace and Bread*, p. 61.
[84] Quoted by Baker, p. 490, from *Cobb of The World*, pp. 268-269.

German sisters hearty greetings. We hope war has not become unavoidable yet.[85]

This was to be the last formal communication between the American and the German pacifists before the declaration of war.

Whatever hopes the American pacifists still entertained for the avoidance of war were somewhat heightened by the President's Inaugural Address. Therein, Miss Addams noted, he continued to stress the reconstruction of the world after the war as the aim of American endeavor. She writes with reference to his avowal of this aim: " Certainly his pacifist friends had every right to believe that he meant to attain this by newer and finer methods than those possible in warfare, but it is only fair to say that his words were open to both constructions." [86]   Another thing which cheered the pacifists in the generally drear days of March was the news of the Russian Revolution. This transformation, which seemed patently connected with a revulsion of Russian peasants from further fighting, was hailed by Miss Addams from the standpoint of pacifism as well as of democracy. She believed that the revolution signified " the spontaneous effort of the first Russian revolutionists to break through the belief that any spiritual good can be established through the agency of large masses of men fighting other large masses." [87]   Shortly she was to deplore the insistence of the Allied Governments that the Russian soldier, desirous of returning to his land, be compelled to continue to fight.

Any optimism aroused by the Inaugural Address was dispelled on March 12 when the President ordered the arming of American merchantmen. About the middle of March American public opinion, as Ray Stannard Baker notes,[88] believed that war was inevitable. And it was about this time, though doubtless from sincere convictions as well as from submission to the manifest destiny of events, that two prominent members of the Woman's Peace Party renounced pacifism. One of

---

[85] *New York Times*, March 3, 1917.
[86] *Peace and Bread*, p. 62.
[87] *Ibid.*, p. 103.   [88] Baker, VI, 500.

these was Mrs. Carrie Chapman Catt, who had played such an important rôle in the formation of the party, and who at the time was honorary vice-chairman of the New York City branch. Mrs. Catt, speaking as president of the national suffrage organization, offered to President Wilson the services of the suffragists in case the United States went to war. In consequence the New York Woman's Peace Party did not re-elect Mrs. Catt to her office, and Mrs. Margaret Lane explained that the New York City branch of the Woman's Peace Party did not feel that Mrs. Catt's new position in regard to war permitted her to figure any longer as an officer of the group.[89] This episode led to Mrs. Catt's later resignation from the Woman's Peace Party. For the organization the break with Mrs. Catt was a matter of some sacrifice since it placed in jeopardy the support of all those suffragists within the group who accepted Mrs. Catt's leadership. Another prominent member who found it impossible to agree with its unyielding position in the crisis was the well-known Socialist and philanthropist, Rose Pastor Stokes. Mrs. Stokes presented her resignation from the New York City branch of the Woman's Peace Party on March 17. In a public statement she asserted her conviction that if the United States entered the war it would be "for the perfecting of human unity and human freedom." She declared—what was fast becoming a cliché among patriotic intellectuals—that she loved peace but was not a pacifist.[90]

There is something both curious and pathetic in the struggles of the true pacifists to the very end against an overwhelming tide of events. The Woman's Peace Party was among the peace groups which never recanted or compromised, but, probably for practical reasons, it permitted the final efforts to be made by the peace organization especially formed for that purpose—the Emergency Peace Federation. This group, to which a number of the leaders of the Woman's Peace Party belonged, put forth proposals which reflect the influence of the women's organization. On March 31 it published in vari-

---

[89] *New York Times*, March 13, 1917.
[90] *Ibid.*, March 18, 1917.

ous newspapers an advertisement which, under the caption
"War is not Necessary," proposed several substitutes for war.
These included a conference of neutral nations to promulgate
and urge the Declaration of London as the law of maritime
war, encouragement of mediation of the submarine dispute
by neutrals, a joint high commission of German and American legislators to meet on neutral soil, a peace appeal by the
President to all belligerents, and an advisory referendum on
war.[91] So many women appeared as leaders of the Emergency Peace Federation that the Women's Preparedness Committee of the Civic Federation, feeling it necessary to clear
their sex, denounced "the hysterical cry of the feminine
pacifists to arouse the timidity in American women" as an
insult to American womanhood.[92] Undeterred, fifty women,
including Miss Balch of the Woman's Peace Party, left on
April 2 for Washington as members of a delegation of the
Federation. The Hague Congress of Women was brought into
the picture when representatives of the Federation distributed
among the women waiting at the station the "Hague Peace
Flower," a tulip. Miss Addams, though going separately, also
went to Washington at the beginning of April to urge a
referendum on war.

Prevented by the police from holding a peace parade, the
pacifists did hold a meeting, demonstrate before the Capital,
and argue with Congressmen. Their efforts were made light
of by the papers and the Congressmen were said to have had
no use for them—what was undoubtedly true in the case of
the pugnaciously inhospitable Senator Lodge.[93] But according to a letter of Miss Balch, read into the *Record* by Representative Sherwood, the fact that stood out to the pacifists was
that "so many Congressmen are ready to vote against their
own judgment, against their conscience, and against what
they have reason to believe to be the will of their con-
stituents." [94]

But at any rate there was one member of Congress who, in

[91] *Ibid.*, March 31, 1917.
[92] *Ibid.*, April 1, 1917.
[93] *Ibid.*, April 3, 1917.
[94] *Cong. Rec.*, 65th Cong., 1st sess., p. 338.

the eyes of the women, fulfilled preeminently the demands of integrity and courage. This was Representative Jeannette Rankin of Montana, the only woman member of Congress, who had been deluged with mail from her fellow-suffragists appealing to her to vote in a way that would do the women of America proud. The only difficulty was that Miss Rankin was a pacifist, a member of the Woman's Peace Party,[95] and had unconventional ideas about the vote which would redound to the glory of American women. Her long hesitation, her emotional agitation, and her final declaration, "I want to stand by my country—but I cannot vote for war," formed a dramatic story which was featured in the newspaper accounts of the declaration of war.[96] This was the first time in American history that a woman participated in a Congressional referendum on war. To the Woman's Peace Party her negative was, if not a consolation for failure to prevent war, a gesture of idealism charged with the highest symbolic value.

---

[95] *Report of the International Congress of Women, Zurich, 1919,* p. 463.
[96] *New York Times,* April 7, 1917.

CHAPTER VII

PACIFISTS IN WAR TIME

According to a rather gloating press account,[1] the representatives of the Woman's Peace Party in the capital spent most of April 6 planning what to do next after the declaration of war which they had unsuccessfully opposed. In fact, the Woman's Peace Party faced the most difficult task of adjustment which had yet come to it. Its disappointments called first for changes in philosophy—a realization of the great odds against even the most ardent pacifist efforts and the recapturing of hope that these might ultimately be overcome. The greatest readjustment necessary, however, was in regard to the immediate program of the Woman's Peace Party. Hitherto the organization had been free to fight for whatever it believed in and in this respect it occupied a position of distinct advantage over its affiliates in warring countries. Now that the United States too was at war, the members of the Woman's Peace Party had to consider what changes in activity, if not also in avowed credo, were imposed upon them by the new situation.

Their activities directly after the declaration of war are not revealed by the Party records. However, according to the *New York Times*, representatives of both the Woman's Peace Party and the Emergency Peace Federation indicated that they were deriving consolation from Wilson's statement that the war was only with German autocracy. Furthermore, they were reported to have professed a desire to work steadfastly for a peace that presupposed a revolution, peaceful or otherwise, in Germany and the establishment there of a democratic form of government. The pacifists expressed the belief that there was every probability that such a development would lead ultimately if not immediately to cessation of the practices about which the United States had complained.[2]

Shortly afterward another article in the *New York Times*

---

[1] *New York Times*, April 7, 1917.
[2] *Ibid.*

discussed the activities of the New York City branch of the Woman's Peace Party. A "secret call to a secret meeting" was said to have been issued by its Executive Secretary soon after the declaration of war. According to the writer, this secret call came to light because one of its recipients, becoming remorseful over her participation in pacifist activities, showed it to unsympathetic eyes. The meeting was called in order that members might determine the policy of the organization. One immediate action, however, was suggested by the letter itself. This was that as many members of the party as possible write a word of appreciation to Miss Jeannette Rankin for her "fine and courageous act" in voting against the declaration of war despite the argument of many suffragists that it would be more expedient for the lone woman member of Congress to vote with the majority. The writer in the *Times,* while admitting that the letter of Mrs. Lane was not "a particularly incendiary or seditious document," evinced distinct antagonism. This hostility was reflected in the very caption of the article, "Really Are Foes of Peace." It stated that what the Party had decided to do was veiled in dark mystery to the uninitiate, but that "it will doubtless be their little best to interfere with and delay the measures by which, as all people of sanity see, the war can be soonest ended, and peace restored." [3]

It was not long before the Woman's Peace Party removed any mystery as to its plans. A few weeks after the declaration of war, it published a statement entitled "A Program during War Time." This statement was far from being a recantation but at the same time it made it clear that the women had no intention of seditious obstructionism or lack of patriotism. It began by stating their general attitude toward the country's war:

Under the shadow of the war which we hoped our country might not be called upon to enter, members of the Woman's Peace Party do not need to affirm or reaffirm their patriotism and the devotion of their lives to our country's higher life. The Internationalism to which the Woman's Peace Party is pledged came to fulfil the highest national life and not to destroy it.

---

[3] *Ibid.,* April 17, 1917.

13

After this statement that the new and higher law was inclusive of the old, the statement proceeded to specify the kinds of patriotic work in which its members could cooperate with all citizens. The first was that of " promoting the spirit of good will and mutual comprehension between persons of varying points of view." This task involved particularly, it was implied, the discouragement of a spirit of ill will or violence toward pacifists and minority groups such as war had engendered in the past. The second activity recommended was the amelioration of social needs which would be complicated or overlooked through the deflection to the war of the energy and interest formerly devoted to them. It was suggested that effort would be needed to prevent any increase in suffering, poverty, and crime, as well as to give intelligent sympathy and help to immigrants. Finally, the pronouncement called for work to bring about a league of nations to substitute law for war. Without a just war settlement and a definite advance toward world organization, the women declared, peace would " prepare the way to a new war " and millions would have suffered and died in vain.

Together with the work for remoter objectives there were set forth certain immediate tasks of the Woman's Peace Party, chiefly involving opposition to contemporary militarist tendencies. There was an appeal for opposition to the espionage bill which had just been reintroduced into Congress after passage in the Senate of the last Congress. It was held that the safeguarding of military and naval information, which was the purpose of the bill, could be secured without endangering our fundamental liberties of free speech, free press, and free assemblage. " We should instantly urge," the pamphlet stated, " our Senators and Representatives in Congress to secure in the bill an explicit statement that its provisions apply only to naval and military matters, and not to a discussion of general questions, nor to propaganda directed toward securing change of laws or of governmental action and policies." In the second place, the measure to establish conscription was opposed as unnecessary. It was pointed out that the President already had the power to draft to full war strength the regular army and the National Guard, that our country was in no danger of invasion, and that Australia and Canada had not yet adopted the policy of sending conscripts beyond the sea. In the third stand the organization was able to maintain that it was supporting the President; this stand was opposition to compulsory military training as a permanent policy, consideration of which Wilson had in fact discouraged. Finally, it was urged that the members continue to oppose military training for school children and press in state legislatures the alternative of required physical training. This recommendation was declared to have the backing, with extraordinary unanimity, of both military and educational experts.

The program concluded with a fervid appeal for respect of minorities and the courage of minorities:

> The constitution of the United States offers a sacred guarantee of the rights of minority opinion. It often happens that the minority of today is the majority of tomorrow. Let us who are outvoted be neither abashed nor discouraged. Let us hold fast the truth as God gives us to see the truth. Let us never allow ourselves for one moment to feel discredited in working to promote the reign of Peace on Earth among Men of Good Will.[4]

At the outset, the chief task before the minority group of pacifists was to attempt to prevent Congress from passing certain measures which, though allegedly essential to the conduct of the war, were dangerous to individual liberties. Even before the war-time program of the Woman's Peace Party was published, Miss Addams had returned to Washington from Chicago to oppose the passage of the conscription bill. She appeared before the Military Affairs Committee to urge that the measure be not passed without the sanction of the country. Miss Addams' contacts with immigrants at Hull House had reinforced her opposition to this bill by making her aware of the peculiar burden which it would impose upon many of our naturalized citizens. She had come to know how many of them had left Europe in order to escape from compulsory military service; moreover, she felt a per-

---

[4] *A Program During War Time.* Publication of the Woman's Peace Party, Jane Addams Peace Collection.

sonal responsibility through having encouraged so many aliens to become American citizens. To Miss Addams, as to the immigrants, it seemed that "war and its conscriptions were something which belonged to the unhappy Europe they had left behind." [5]

When it became evident to Miss Addams that, despite its apparent repugnance to American tradition, the conscription law would pass, she thought that at least it might be possible to obtain the same measure of consideration for the conscientious objector that prevailed in England, which gave its tribunals power to grant absolute exemption from military service. Miss Addams was one of a committee which called upon Secretary of War Baker to urge him to recommend such a provision for the conscientious objector in the conscription measure then under consideration. She describes the interview as follows:

The Secretary was ready to talk to our committee, each member of which could claim either acquaintance or friendship with him in the years before the war. He seemed so sympathetic and understanding that possibly we made too much of his somewhat cryptic utterance that "there would be no conscientious objector problem in the United States," and we left his office more reassured perhaps than we had any right to be.[6]

In a very few weeks it became evident that the conscientious objector was not to have his burden legally mitigated in any way. He was to be punished under military law on the same basis as any other soldier who refused to carry out an order given to him. Miss Addams visited Mr. Baker twice again on the matter, once with a committee and once alone. However, it became quite evident that he had taken the position that the conscientious objector could not be treated as a political prisoner since there was no such thing as a political offense in a democracy. For the sake of a specious conformity with democracy the holder of a minority opinion had to be treated as a criminal!

As president of the Woman's Peace Party Miss Addams also raised her voice in Washington against another war measure—

---

[5] Addams, *Peace and Bread*, p. 120.
[6] *Ibid.*, p. 121.

one which affected the party more directly than the conscription bill. This was the drastic espionage bill, which heavily penalized all persons who interfered in any way, deliberately or otherwise, with the conduct of the war. The women objected particularly to the vague section which prohibited the making of speeches or the publishing of articles that might cause or be feared to cause disaffection in the military services. Might this provision render seditious the discussions of an organization devoted to the development of internationalist war aims? Miss Addams appeared before the Senate Judiciary Committee to call attention to the danger of the bill in this and other respects. In her statement at the hearing she first gave a description of the objective of the women's group:

I am president of the Woman's Peace Party of America. We believe that the present international situation will have to find some international solution; that one alliance fighting another alliance will never settle it. If, holding that belief, we should express our views, if we feel that the only real moral outcome is to utilize the tremendous composition of the peoples of the United States to get some sort of international point of view, can we go forth and say that? Can we say that this war will be fought in vain unless there is some apparatus to recognize this question? Now, we believe that the creation of some sort of international mind would be a great contribution to the development of the world. Can we say that, in spite of the fighting—and we do not wish to talk against war during the time of war—in the end these questions must be settled upon some other than the nationalistic point of view?

Miss Addams went on to point out the dangers which the espionage bill presented to her own organization as advocate of an international ideal:

We have in our international peace organization representatives from all countries except Japan. We correspond with one another. That correspondence is not to abuse each other—we have a clause prescribing that we shall not discuss the war—but we do discuss international programmes. Is such a thing permissible or will it be construed " to cause disaffection " in our military forces, as the language of the bill reads? Certainly we are lawabiding citizens, although as pacifists we are sometimes called names. Nevertheless it would be difficult to understand that we could not in this country preach our international point of view.[7]

One of the members of the committee asked Miss Addams

[7] *New York Evening Post*, April 12, 1917.

if she would agitate against compulsory military service after it had become a law. She answered frankly:

> I'm constantly agitating against laws that are in existence, such as laws that permit the sale of liquor in dance halls. I do not know exactly what discussion would arise.

From these words it was evident that Miss Addams proposed to continue during the war the Party's campaign for an international program to be carried out at the close of hostilities. This intention was attested even more clearly when, a few weeks later before the City Club in Chicago, Miss Addams gave an address on " Patriotism and Pacifists in War Time." Miss Addams on this occasion described the general character of the proposed post-war reorganization of international society:

> We pacifists, so far from passively wishing nothing to be done, contend on the contrary that this world crisis should be utilized for the creation of an international government able to make the necessary political and economic changes when they are due; we feel that it is unspeakably stupid that the nations should have failed to create an international organization through which each one, without danger to itself, might recognize and even encourage the impulse toward growth in other nations.

> Pacifists believe that in the Europe of 1914 certain tendencies were steadily pushing towards large changes, which in the end made war, because the system of peace had no way of effecting those changes without war, no adequate international organization which could cope with the situation. The conception of peace founded upon the balance of power or the undisturbed *status quo* was so negative that frustrated national impulses and suppressed vital forces led to war, because no method of orderly expression had been devised.

> .   .   .   .

> The very breakdown exhibited by the present war reinforces the pacifists' contention that there is need of an international charter— a Magna Charta indeed—of international rights, to be issued by the nations great and small, with large provisions for economic freedom.

Thus Miss Addams proposed as did Wilson to make a virtue of necessity—to use an otherwise deplorable war as an opportunity for realizing the league of nations advocated by the Hague Congress of Women. Patriotism itself could be reconciled with such a purpose. Denying the charge of lack of devotion to country, Miss Addams pointed out that she wished to impose on the international organization a federal constitution similar to the constitution of the United States and a supreme court similar to the national Supreme Court. Further, she declared that the United States had a peculiar duty in the field of international relations in view of the fact that " our very composition would make it easier for us than for any other nation to establish an international organization founded upon understanding and good will, did we but possess the requisite courage and intelligence to utilize it." One source of strength in the international venture was the very presence in our national composition of a multitude of emigrants from the Central Powers, with whom, as with all other nations of the earth, we needed to be bound by ties of blood if this great venture was to succeed. Miss Addams concluded with a climax of boldness. Arguing that pacifism was not cowardice, she declared that

the pacifist is making a venture into a new international ethics. He is afforded an opportunity to cultivate a fine valor . . . for new ethics are unpopular ethics. . . . The pacifist must serve his country by forcing definitions if possible. If it seems to him that the multitude of German subjects who have settled and developed certain parts of the United States had every right to be considered as an important factor in the situation before war was declared, he should say so. He should insist that the United States declare its refusal to regard the deliberate starvation of the women and children of any nation as a proper war measure. Since war was declared, some of us have had a feeling that we are shirking moral service.[8]

The address, which was repeated at a number of meetings, stirred a terrible wave of resentment against Miss Addams, the culmination of a tide that had been gathering with ever-increasing force. Even before the actual declaration of war and the delivery of the address, Mary Kingsbury Simkhovitch, president of the National Federation of Settlements and formerly a member of the Woman's Peace Party, had announced that " it has been very painful to many of us who hold Miss Addams in deep affection and wholly respect her, to find that we cannot think or act in unison with her." [9] But when she learned that it had been difficult to secure a chairman to preside over the Chicago City Club gathering, Miss Addams began to realize what she was to suffer for her con-

---

[8] *Chicago Post*, April 30, 1917; Linn, p. 331.
[9] Linn, p. 330.

victions.[10]　On June 10, when she repeated the address at the First Congregational Church at Evanston, Illinois, there occurred an incident which was even more distressingly illuminating.　A terrible silence followed her remarks and then Orrin C. Carter, Chief Justice of the Illinois Supreme Court, rose to his feet.

" I have been a life-long friend of Miss Addams," he said, " I have agreed with her on most questions in the past—"

" That sounds as if you were going to break with me," interrupted Miss Addams, laughing.

" I am going to break," the Justice retorted.　" I think that anything that may tend to cast doubt on the justice of our cause in the present war is very unfortunate.　No pacifist measures, in my opinion, should be taken until the war is over."

" I am not sure that such a paper as I have just read is altogether advisable in a time like the present," Miss Addams said, " but if there is any question on that score it should be referred to the committee that invited me here to speak." [11]

Over night the incident became of national importance and Miss Addams a target for general attack.　Commenting on her assertion that pacifism was not cowardice, the *New York Herald* said:

It may not be cowardice for an American to oppose a war in which the United States is engaged, but it is something infinitely more despicable.　It is bordering on treason, and if Miss Addams does not have the intelligence to appreciate the fact that her maunderings over " the feelings of the German born American citizens " give aid and comfort to the enemy then the position she has occupied in the public life of this country has been wrongly bestowed.

It is too late for pacifists to be permitted to hinder the successful prosecution of the war by resurrecting the issues that were buried when the kaiser's submarines commenced the war months ago.　If Miss Addams and her professional peace-loving associates want a speedy end of the war let them emigrate to their dear Germany and there convert the originators of the conflict, the gentle barbarians of Louvain, of Rheims, of the Lusitania, in whose " feelings " they have an interest that transcends that which they have in the fate of the murdered men, women and children in the train of the Teutonic army and navy.　America is fighting because she was forced to fight or become a nation of Jane Addamses, and the sooner the Chicago pacifist lets that fact infiltrate into her brain the sooner will she understand why this nation is going to fight for a righteous peace.[12]

---

[10] Addams, *Peace and Bread*, p. 111.
[11] *New York Times*, June 11, 1917.
[12] Quoted by the *Hartford Times*, June 13, 1917.

The Louisville *Courier-Journal* was more personal in its vituperation. It labeled Miss Addams "silly Sallie," pronounced her to be "of limited mentality, somewhat over-educated," and insinuated that in lieu of Christianity she espoused "the Gospel of Free Love." [13] A biting editorial in the *Cleveland News* interpreted the reaction against Miss Addams as the natural tendency of war not only to develop new American leaders but to bring into discredit those once held in esteem. The paper was sufficiently careful of its women readers, however, to say that the performance of Miss Addams and Miss Rankin was not to be cited as a fair sample of woman's intelligence. "To accept," it concluded, "a couple of foolish virgins as accurately typifying the attitude of a whole sex toward war would be to do hideous injustice to thousands of noble women who, in this as in other wars, were quick to perceive what it was all about and to lend their aid with splendid discrimination and devotion." [14] Afraid that she would not see these pleasant editorials, many people forwarded them to Miss Addams with letters which were scarcely any warmer than the enclosures.

The leader of the Woman's Peace Party did not make or maintain her decision to remain a pacifist without a struggle. She felt not only a terrifying sense of isolation but also an uncertainty as to whether an isolated position could be the correct one. Some time later she wrote that "the force of the majority was so overwhelming that it seemed not only impossible to hold one's own against it, but at moments absolutely unnatural, and one secretly yearned to participate in ' the folly of all mankind.'" This impulse was strengthened by Miss Addams' acceptance of the democratic dogma, which, teaching that popular impulses possess in their general tendency a valuable capacity for evolutionary development, caused her to wonder whether the individual or a very small group had the right to stand against millions of his fellow countrymen. "Is there not," she asked herself, "a great value in mass judgment and in instinctive mass enthusiasm, and even

---

[13] Quoted by the *Louisville Herald*, June 17, 1917.
[14] *Cleveland News*, June 12, 1917.

if one were right a thousand times over in conviction, was he not absolutely wrong in abstaining from this communion with his fellows?" Finally, Miss Addams wondered whether she was not surrendering all possibility of future influence for the sake of a doctrinaire fanaticism.[15] But, as she declares at the end of this record of torturing doubt, she finally decided that "ability to hold out against mass suggestion, to honestly differ from the convictions and enthusiasms of one's best friends did in moments of crisis come to depend upon the categorical belief that a man's primary allegiance is to his vision of the truth and that he is under obligation to affirm it."[16]

In some respects, however, Miss Addams found it possible to reconcile her pacifist conscience with the acquiescence and positive contribution expected by the country of all citizens in time of war. She did not attempt to dissuade any, even conscientious objectors, from submitting to the draft; the serious consequences which awaited non-conformists pressed too painfully upon her imagination. Hull House, in fact, even helped many immigrants to meet the formalities of the conscription law. In May 1917 Miss Addams appealed to the members of the Woman's Peace Party to join in the civilian relief work for the war.[17] She declared that as president of the organization she was eager to make clear that pacifists should do everything possible to relieve the sufferings that resulted from war, just as in times of peace many reformers tried to relieve the sufferings resulting from industrial disorganization. For this public stand Miss Addams received from the *Indianapolis Star* a commendation which contrasted markedly with the great body of editorial comment concerning her utterances on internationalism. The midwestern paper declared that the peace people were "Americans first" and that in their nation's emergency they would not stand aloof but rather prove their loyalty by engaging in such services as they could.[18]

Miss Addams adopted as her most congenial service in

---

[15] *Peace and Bread*, pp. 140-143.
[16] *Ibid.*, p. 151.
[17] *Ibid.*, pp. 118-119.   [18] *Indianapolis Star*, May 15, 1917.

war the undertaking of lecture tours in the service of the Department of Food Administration, whose Quaker director, Herbert Hoover, had said of his work that it was a matter of human survival rather than merely of war. For this contribution the *Chicago Evening Post* called her a " good sport," making clear, however, that it utterly disagreed with her views on war.[19] Though Miss Addams was praised on the assumption that in this work she was temporarily suppressing her pacifism, she was, in reality, finding a special expression for it. The conservation of food was related in her mind to that " instinct of bread labor " which, in commenting upon the peasant traditions and aims that had led to the Russian Revolution, she had characterized as " the very antithesis of war." Furthermore, Miss Addams in her pleas for food conservation was able to present this objective as an integral element in that peaceful international organization of society to which she looked forward. Thus in her addresses she pointed out that the assumption by the warring governments of control over the food supply represented a stage in the rational replacement of the old order whereby the world's food supply was in the hands of commercial interests, considering private profit rather than social needs. She also emphasized that a number of the nations had been drawing closer together since the beginning of the war because of their common interest in the food problem. The common hunger of the nations, impelling them to cooperation in the control of food supply, was said by Miss Addams to render inevitable " a new internationalism," which would never consent to any nation being cut off from its food supply in times of peace and would thus insist upon an international regulation of national production and of means of commercial intercourse.[20]

While appearing before the public chiefly as a lecturer in behalf of food conservation, Miss Addams did not, in the course of the war, come to forget her own obligations to the Woman's Peace Party or permit this organization to languish in its activities. From the spring to the fall of 1917 the

---

[19] Quoted by the *Pittsburgh Leader*, November 27, 1917.
[20] *Peace and Bread*, Ch. V.

women did not, indeed, take any public stand in the name of the national organization but confined their activities to the now unobtrusive work of the individual branches. However, as the time for the annual meeting of the Party drew near, the Executive Board met for the first time since the declaration of war. The meeting took place in October 1917 and was held in a country house in the suburbs of Philadelphia. The officers, who came from New York, Boston, St. Louis, Chicago, and Philadelphia, appeared in the rôle of guests at a house party in order that their hostess might not suffer from public opinion.

This meeting resulted in a public statement of the Board, issued on October 25, 1917. The pronouncement began by noting that, though the Party had continued to pursue its function of increasing internationalism among the women of all nations, it had "avoided all criticism of our Government as to the declaration of war, and all activities that could be considered as obstructive in respect to the conduct of the war, and this not as a counsel of prudence, but as a matter of principle." The activities in which it had engaged were declared to be of the greatest diversity because of the independence of the state and local branches of the National Board of Officers and of each other. Some of the branches had stressed the work of mitigating the sufferings of the war for both soldiers and civilians; others had sought to lessen the threat which the war raised for civil liberties and conscientious objectors; still others had specialized on study classes and lecture courses in order to learn and teach the principles of international justice that must underlie all effective peace settlements. The statement recalled the platforms and activities of the past through which the Party had established its right to offer in the present a constructive program. It stressed the elements of similarity between the Hague platform and President Wilson's recent presentations of international issues. In one respect the original Hague platform was said to have been modified by America's entrance into the war. It was now necessary to substitute for the originally espoused Neutral Conference an "Inter-Allied Conference," a project given great stress in the document but which is reserved for discussion at a later point of the present study.

Perhaps the most notable words of the Executive Board are those which set forth the attitude that the members of the party were resolved to maintain toward the trials besetting pacifists in war time:

> We gladly note all the incitements to noble and unselfish action of which these troubled times bear fruit. Any suspicion or resentment manifested toward any "pacifist" group meets with no "reprisals" from us. Our business is to help mitigate all the horrors of war by consistently refusing to make any sacrifice of human fellowship and good will. We throw back no verbal brick-bats; on the contrary, we set ourselves to sympathetic understanding of those from whom we differ, and to grateful recognition of their contributions to that common fund of ethical idealism and of wise mastery of political problems upon which the reconstruction of the world depends.[21]

The literature of pacifism scarcely contains any formulations in which tolerance and patience are more appealingly expressed. Yet these words bespeaking such great self-restraint were followed by a verbal gesture that was bold indeed for the time—a message of affectionate sympathy for the women of the twenty nations associated with the American women in the International Committee, nations including Germany and Austria.

On December 3 the New York City branch also displayed the same measure of fortitude when, meeting to celebrate the achievement of woman suffrage in the state, it passed a resolution demanding of the President that he respond in his Congressional message to Lord Lansdowne's peace letter. He was called upon to declare the American people in favor of the restatement of Allied war aims and eager for any peace that gives "promise of freedom for all nations based on disarmament and a democratic world federation." [22]

The Woman's Peace Party was not timorous about the holding of its annual conference. The gathering took place in Philadelphia on December 6 and 7, and the women had the

---

[21] *Statement of the Executive Board of the Woman's Peace Party, October 25, 1917.* Pamphlet, Jane Addams Peace Collection.

[22] *New York Times*, December 4, 1917.

use of the Twelfth Street Meeting House which the Orthodox Friends placed at their disposal. In deference to the insistence of the Friends no newspaper representatives were permitted to be present; still the meetings were reported by members in some detail in several Philadelphia papers. The conference was attended by seventy-odd women delegates. It became known at the sessions that the organization still had two hundred branches and affiliated groups—only one branch had gone out of existence since the United States had declared war—and a total of twenty thousand members. If this fact seemed to indicate the persistence of pacifism among women, there was one episode which showed quite clearly the changed repute of pacifism in the eyes of the government. While no officers of Philadelphia put in an appearance, there was one plain-clothesman who rushed up and demanded entrance just as the last session was closing. He had his cap far down over his ears like a burglar. A gentle Quakeress standing at the entrance told him that no one but delegates was allowed to enter. The man then identified himself as an agent of the Department of Justice, saying that he had received a wire from Washington to listen to Jane Addams' address. Although told that the meeting was about over, he felt it necessary to look in. Then finding that everything looked harmless—the women were at the moment engaged in silent prayer—he decided that no one was plotting to overthrow the government and left reassured.[23]

Nothing said at the sessions had in fact been very dangerous or radical. Considerable discussion was given to the proposal of one group that the organization use the word " Justice " in its name instead of the opprobrious " Peace." The resolution, in favor of which even Miss Addams conceded that she was sick of the name " pacifist," was voted down by a majority. In expressing the opposition to a change from the " Peace " to the " Justice " Party, Mrs. D. Frank Kitts declared that, despite a number of members who were afraid to voice their sentiments, the majority were united in maintaining a pacifist attitude and a large number were

---

[23] *Public Ledger*, December 8, 1917.

ready to acknowledge a desire for immediate world peace and
the cessation of hostilities. However that may be, Constance
Drexel reported in the *Public Ledger* that it could not be too
strongly emphasized that the women present " were not trying to meddle in the present situation, nor did they discuss
the subject of immediate war." [24]   In the preamble to the
resolutions presented by the Executive Board the members of
the Woman's Peace Party were referred to as " loyal citizens
of a belligerent nation." The women refrained from sending
the customary greetings to the International Committee,
which included individuals of enemy countries; moreover, in
the preamble was the remark that with the entrance of the
United States into the World War the organization was " less
able to serve that International Committee and to be in
friendly communication with all its members." Further, in
an interview given in connection with the conference, Miss
Addams not only expressed her confidence in Wilson's internationalism but said that, although the Party desired peace
as soon as possible, it was not acting to bring it about.[25]

The tasks most stressed in the preamble and resolutions
adopted at the meeting were the support of " all the efforts
making throughout the world for the substitution of law for
war in the adjustment of human relationships," and the contribution of " such national service as may help toward the
establishment of world-wide democracy as a condition of
permanent peace."   One resolution adopted as a means to
these objectives committed the Woman's Peace Party to promoting in every possible way " a public demand that an
agreement for a League of Nations shall be made the basis
of the war settlement," and also petitioned the Government
" to urge upon the Allied governments an explicit agreement
to this end that all nations on the earth may know that they
will be assured mutual protection and economic equality upon
the complete establishment of such a League."   The women
implicitly identified this project of a league of nations with
President Wilson's program by expressing the gratitude of

the organization for his enunciation of " the great principles and ideals of Internationalism on which our Woman's Peace Party is founded."

With the demand for the league was conjoined a proposal to which the President had not committed himself. It had been first touched upon in the October statement of the Executive Board and there attributed to the previous suggestions of Norman Angell, Dr. Charles W. Eliot, and others. It was resolved that the Woman's Peace Party initiate a nation-wide campaign for the creation of public sentiment for an " Inter-Allied Conference." The purpose of this conference, which was to be called at the earliest possible date, was to formulate and announce the political and economic aims of the Allied governments. The conference, the resolution stated, was to take the form of " a Parliament to be composed, not only of representatives of the Governments, but also of the elected representatives of the peoples, whose welfare is involved in the decisions of the conference." Furthermore, it was proposed that this form of conference be adopted at the final Peace Conference. The plan of having elected representatives of the people at both the Inter-Allied Conference and the final Peace Conference was justified by reference to the principle of democracy, which had been ignored in previous war settlements but was held to be the sole valid method for settling a war fought to make the world safe for democracy.

Aside from a resolution opposing all Congressional action for universal compulsory military service, the remainder of the resolutions adopted were concerned with organizational questions. The important decision was made that in the future every state or local branch of the Party should function as " an autonomous body in so far as name, policy, propaganda, publications, and activities of any sort in accord with the constitution and platform are concerned," although the branches and the National Board were to give each other reports on all actions and were to maintain intimate relationship as far as practicable. This extreme decentralization involved, on the one hand, the principle that the National Board be hereafter held responsible only for its own publications and activities, and, on the other hand, the principle that the activity of a branch should not commit either the National Board or any other branch. The change in the structure of the party was explained by the following considerations: that the party was unified in its general objective of a democratic world organization for a durable peace but not in respect to immediate duties and activities; that the National Board, charged with maintaining relationship with the International Committee, should be able always to act promptly and efficiently in its aid; and that in view of the new responsibilities placed by the entrance of the United States into the war, each branch required full freedom of action.[26]

Another organizational question was raised by the proposal of the radical New York City branch that the national group follow it in its decision to concentrate upon support of those candidates for federal and state offices who agreed with the principles of the society. No action was taken upon this proposal, which seemed to the majority to deflect the organization from educational activity to politics. On one point there was unanimity among the delegates. This was the necessity of Miss Addams' remaining in the chairmanship. Sick when she came to the meeting, Miss Addams wished to retire, but a chorus of "No" protested the statement of her preference and Miss Addams was reelected president.

Not long after this meeting the faith which the delegates had shown in the purposes of the President was confirmed and enhanced by one of his most important war-time pronouncements. On January 8, 1918, President Wilson delivered his message on the Fourteen Points, and the members of the Woman's Peace Party now felt definitely that their hopes for a new international order bade fair to be realized. The gratification of the women was expressed in a statement issued by the Executive Board of the New York City branch on January 13. "We are glad," the pronouncement declared, "to see in the forefront of these times the fundamental bases

---

[26] *Resolutions Adopted by the Woman's Peace Party . . . at the Third Annual Meeting.* Pamphlet, Jane Addams Peace Collection.

of the new world-order—democratic diplomacy, freedom of the seas, equality of trade conditions, the greatest possible reduction of armaments, prime regard in colonial matters for the welfare of the population themselves, cooperation with the new Russia, and, finally, the formation of a general association of nations." The Board invited the sections of the International Committee in twenty-one other countries to study the message as " the most profound and brilliant formulation in the progress of international reorganization as yet put forward by any responsible statesman." However, it was not forgotten that the program of the Woman's Peace Party forbade the leaving of the peace settlement to responsible statesmen alone. The announcement was made that a questionnaire had been issued to a selected list of students who had been asked to give their ideas as to the best method for the nomination and appointment of a democratic representation of the varied interests of the countries at the peace conference.[27]

On February 3, 1918, the New York City branch came forth with projects which also reflected the increasing interest of the women in the prospective peace settlement. A resolution called for the appointment to the peace conference not of professional diplomats, but of men and women representing the ideals of their countries. Jane Addams was, of course, suggested as one delegate. To strengthen the influence of pacifists among women's organizations it was proposed to establish a peace committee in every woman's club in New York City. The resolution to this effect was also designed as a defiant answer to the Federation of Women's Clubs, which at its last convention had resolved that its branches take action against pacifists in their midst. Other resolutions of the New York City branch expressed sympathy for the aims of the President, petitioned the government to accede to Russia's request to be given a share in the peace negotiations in progress, and demanded the immediate passage of the Federal Suffrage Amendment.[28] The New York City branch

[27] *New York Times*, January 13, 1918.
[28] *New York Times*, February 3, 1918.

also published and promoted a book on various proposals for the peace terms after the war—*Approaches to the Great Settlement,* edited by Emily Greene Balch, with an introduction by Norman Angell.

The remainder of the war period was spent largely in support of the President's program for a league of nations and a new international order. In this work Mrs. Lucia Ames Mead, National Secretary, took a particularly active part. Through the Massachusetts branch Mrs. Mead secured wide distribution of a pamphlet written by her, entitled " Organize the World through a League of Nations." By means of questions and answers it sought to create " an informed public opinion " concerning the need for world organization and the principles of structure and function which would make the league of nations an effective instrumentality for world peace. Mrs. Mead considered the essential foundations of the league to be a world court, a permanent council of conciliation, and a world conference, meeting regularly for the creation of new international law and the making of new arrangements for justice under changing circumstances. It is interesting to note that in this pamphlet there is not the uncompromising rejection of military force which characterizes the pronouncements of the Woman's Peace Party generally. Mrs. Mead declared that the league of nations would use, in addition to a propaganda of education, " economic force, and the armies and navies of the nations of the League acting under collective control." She added, however, that " as soon as possible . . . after the war, national armies and navies should by mutual agreement be reduced and transformed into a genuine international police force whose sole function will be to maintain law and order." Another noteworthy feature of her exposition was the candid admission that the nations in the league would lose a portion of their sovereignty by yielding control in matters of international concern.[29] Such an admission was very unusual among proponents of the league.

---

[29] *Organize the World through a League of Nations.* Leaflet published by the League to Enforce Peace, Jane Addams Peace Collection.

In another publication Mrs. Mead elaborated in considerable detail the plan of the Woman's Peace Party for popular representation at the peace conference. She proposed that the lower and more popular houses of the parliaments of all the countries should appoint committees to arrange for the presentation by all important functional organizations of nominees to the conference, from which the lower houses were to elect delegates. These experts in international affairs and representatives of the various interests of society were to be equal in number to the official delegates.[30] The great interest of the Woman's Peace Party in the securing of representation of the people at the peace conference reflects the distrust that the women pacifists and many others at the time felt in regard to professional diplomats and the traditional methods of secret diplomacy.[31]

The sympathy of the women with Wilson's international program made it easier for them to hold in abeyance or moderate some of the pacifist policies which were contrary to the exigencies of America's war policies. An illustration of this restraint is afforded by the activities of the Legislative Committee in 1918. Formerly it had been rich in projects embarrassing Congress by either opposition to legislation of militarist tendency or promotion of rather radical steps towards peace and international cooperation. But at the meetings of this committee in 1918 the subject which chiefly occupied it was the possibility of having insignia provided by the Government for food managers and other persons highly necessary to the production of food. Interviews were had with the Secretary of War and the Assistant Secretary relative to this matter and some progress was reported, though nothing definite had been accomplished when the Armistice made further work unnecessary. Military training was also considered to the extent that the committee examined bills and made preparation for work if it should later be deemed

---

[30] Lucia Ames Mead, "Representation of the People at the Peace Settlement," reprinted from the *Advocate of Peace* by the *Internationaal*, III, No. 4, 141-142. Jane Addams Peace Collection.
[31] On this same point see below, p. 217.

advisable to take a hand in the opposition. However, no action was taken "lest prejudice should be excited by suspicion of undue pacifism in the sentiments of the Committee." [32]

An example of the way in which local branches, which carried on most of the activity of this period, integrated their work with the problems of war is afforded by the *Suggestions for Work in War Time* published by the Chicago branch. The services suggested for members were along the lines of conservation of food and increase of food supplies, opposition to attempts to injure child welfare by lowering educational standards or breaking down child labor laws, Red Cross Relief Work, defense of labor standards, protection of immigrants, and prevention of compulsory military service and military training in the schools as a permanent policy. Topics suggested for discussion were raising the conscription age of soldiers, better pay for soldiers, the defense of constitutional rights of free speech and free assemblage, paying the cost of the war from the resources of the present generation rather than by drawing upon the resources of future generations, and democratic control of war policies. The principles affirmed by the Chicago branch were the establishment of a society of nations and "an early statement by our Government to the American people setting forth the objects of the war which we are waging and the terms upon which we will terminate our participation in it." [31]

In general, members of the party responded to the early appeal of Miss Addams to participate in humanitarian war work. Members of the Massachusetts branch were particularly active along this line, even operating a desiccation plant for vegetables. Several leaders, like Miss Addams herself, lectured on the food question. The National Secretary, Mrs. Mead, gave addresses on such subjects as "The New Pre-

[32] Report of the Legislative Committee of the Woman's Peace Party to the Annual Meeting in Philadelphia, November 3-4, 1919, MS, Jane Addams Peace Collection.
[31] *Suggestions for Work in War Time Submitted by the Chicago Branch of the Woman's Peace Party.* Pamphlet, Jane Addams Peace Collection.

paredness," "After the War, What?" "Civic Efficiency in Wartime "—subjects which were far from the prevailing theme of nationalism and yet, with tact, could be handled without arousing opposition.[32]   Miss Balch, as has been noted, edited a book dealing with programs of international reconstruction, *Some Approaches to the Great Settlement*.   Mrs. Fannie Fern Andrews lent her literary efforts to the Government, participating as representative of the American Military Department of Education at Hotel Crillon and preparing a book of history and citizenship for soldiers.

Its cooperation with some phases of government activity, its relative moderation, and the prestige of its leaders combined to save the Woman's Peace Party from the extreme persecution or the annoyance which was suffered by many unpopular minority groups during the war.   As far as the Government itself was concerned, Miss Addams remained persona grata throughout the war, and Secretary of War Baker once emphasized his objection to "suspect lists" of pacifists by declaring that Miss Addams would lend dignity and greatness to any list in which her name appeared.[33]   However, on one occasion Secret Service agents entered the headquarters of the Woman's Peace Party in search of material.   The visit was not hostile so much to this organization, however, as to the Fellowship of Reconciliation, an international group of religious pacifists with the American section of which Miss Addams had associated herself early in the war.   The suspicions of the Secret Service men seem to have been aroused mainly by the pacifist implication of the words "Fellowship" and "Reconciliation."   "The only defense," Miss Addams writes, "which in the least appealed to the newspaper men was made by one of themselves to the effect that the word reconciliation was very like in sound and purport to the word conciliation and that Nicholas Murray Butler was chairman of an organization to promote international arbitration and conciliation, and that every one knew he was for the war!"[34]

---

[32] Addams, *Peace and Bread*, p. 130.
[33] Linn, pp. 329-330.
[34] Addams, *Peace and Bread*, p. 128.

In addition to this governmental visitation, which had no
consequences, the national office of the Party had to endure
no little annoyance from purely private quarters. Miss
Addams describes some of its tribulations in the following
account of war-time experiences:

> Throughout the war the national office of the Woman's Peace Party
> was kept open in a downtown office building in Chicago. We did
> not remove any of our records, being conscious that we had nothing
> to hide, and our list of members with their addresses was to be
> found in a conspicuous card catalogue case. It was often far from
> pleasant to enter the office. If a bit of mail protruded from the
> door it was frequently spat upon, and although we rented our
> quarters in a first class office building on Michigan boulevard facing
> the lake, the door was often befouled in hideous ways.[35]

Some of the branches also had their difficulties, especially the
New York City branch, which was more radical than the rest.
Not long before the war it began the publication of a magazine, *Four Lights*, which after the declaration of war dis-
pleased the federal authorities on several occasions. The work
of the branch also offended many civilian patriots. One of the
bitterest criticisms leveled at it came from a woman. The
National Commandant of the National League for Woman's
Service assailed the New York City branch of the Woman's
Peace Party for its appeals in behalf of internationalist attitudes and policies. She asked furiously whether their work
was pacifism or treason. " It certainly is a disgrace to American womanhood," she declared.[36]

Remaining faithful to pacifism in war time was, at the
best, not a cheerful experience. But finally there came the
event for which the women had never ceased to hope—the
signing of the Armistice. It had been looked forward to not
only as the end of slaughter but also, and even more, as the
beginning of a new world order. Thus the women waited
with all suspense for the answering of a great question—
would the aftermath of war be a true peace?

---

[35] *Ibid.*, pp. 127-128.
[36] *New York Times,* August 14, 1917.

CHAPTER VIII

WOMEN AND THE PEACE TREATIES

The Armistice had scarcely been signed when a dramatic event brought Miss Addams and the Woman's Peace Party back into a national limelight from which they had long been crowded out by events of the war. This event ensued from the harshness of the Armistice terms, which scarcely foreshadowed such magnanimity in the peace settlement as the women pacifists desired. On November 15 American newspapers carried as a front-page headline the wireless appeal of German women to two American women that they induce their government to intercede in behalf of milder conditions of armistice. One of these American women, addressed by Gertrud Baer and Alice Salomon, was the wife of President Wilson. The other was Jane Addams, the recipient of a message from Anita Augspurg. Frau Augspurg, speaking in the name of German women, urged Miss Addams and her American sisters to influence their government to ameliorate the truce conditions in respect to terms of demobilization, blockade, and delivery of trains and locomotives. In the absence of such relief German women foresaw, it was said, " entire famishment and mutiny for their country." [1]

Because of governmental restrictions this message, which was picked up by a government wireless station, was never delivered and became known to Miss Addams only through its publication in the press. The day after its publication she was asked to comment upon it. She did not care to do more than identify the three women who had wired to Mrs. Wilson and herself. All were known to her as prominent in the feminist and welfare movements of their country. Anita Augspurg, she revealed, was a German delegate to the women's Hague Congress of 1915, and there the two had met.[2] The fact that Miss Addams had presided over the congress was the real reason why the cable was sent to her, although an

[1] *New York Times*, November 15, 1918.
[2] *Ibid.*, November 16, 1918.

216

interminable chain of speculation seized upon everything else. In a later interview Miss Addams reported that the State Department had advised her not to answer the message.[3] How greatly it must have moved her may be inferred from her strongly expressed concern over the suffering of the German people during her trip of 1919 into Germany. It was an irony that, shortly after finding herself helpless in the face of this moving appeal from a land of starvation, she was asked to address the League for Political Education in New York on the subject, "The World's Food and World Politics."[4]

Yet the harsh terms of the armistice might well have seemed but the last episode in a grim chapter that was closed. The thoughts of the women had immediately turned to the future—a future which they hoped to be different from the past for men, women, and children of both the victorious nations and the defeated. By a plan which had been adopted at the Hague Congress of 1915, the International Committee of Women for Permanent Peace was to hold its next meeting at the same time and in the same place as the peace conference of the governments. The women felt that diplomats, who in every country were " seldom representative of modern social thought and the least responsive to changing ideas,"[5] could not be expected to take account of interests which like those of women had hitherto been inarticulate, except as such interests should be urged upon them. International groups other than the women pacifists held conferences simultaneously with the Peace Conference and for the same reasons, but none seems to have planned that procedure so far in advance. It is interesting to note the way in which the women's congress of 1915 planned every detail so that, despite the fact that both time and place of the official conference were then unknown, their own congress could quickly start in motion and take shape without dependence upon congested wires, but merely through every national section's acting on its own initiative in accordance with the predetermined arrangements.

---

[3] *Kansas City Star*, November 29, 1918.
[4] *New York Times*, December 1, 1918.
[5] Addams, *Peace and Bread*, pp. 152-153.

From each country, as soon as the time and place of the official conference were known, a committee of five was without any summons to set out for the designated city, while twenty delegates and ten alternatives were to arrive there in the fifth week of the official conference.

Everything depended, of course, upon whether the International Committee of Women for Permanent Peace could maintain its existence through the perilous years of war. That it succeeded in doing so was due not merely to the Woman's Peace Party, the United States Section of the International Committee, and to Miss Addams, president of both organizations, but to the initiative and steadfastness of women in many lands. The Jane Addams Peace Collection contains letters to Miss Addams telling of police raids and other inquisitions directed against the women pacifists of belligerent countries, of remarkable communications between women of many lands under the most difficult conditions, of attempts to promote the work of the committee in all corners of the earth.[6] The center of the international organization was Amsterdam. The Dutch vice-president, Dr. Aletta H. Jacobs, was the most active official. The headquarters published a magazine, the *Internationaal,* which served as a clearing-house of information and a medium of communication. Miss Addams, partly because of her long illness and partly because of her distance from the European sections, left most of the work to Dr. Jacobs. However, she never ceased to maintain touch with the central office, transmitted financial contributions to the European headquarters from the American section, and in November 1916 sent a circular letter to the National Committees of Five reminding them of the plans for the congress after the war. By January 1917 Miss Addams noted with gratification that Committees of Women for Permanent Peace had been established in twenty-seven countries, including China and Japan.[7] After the entrance of the United States into the war the contact of Miss Addams with the other members of the Committee be-

---

[6] Chrystal Macmillan to Jane Addams, December 17, 1915, MS, Jane Addams Peace Collection.

[7] Jane Addams to the United States branches, January 10, 1917, MS, Jane Addams Peace Collection.

came perforce less close and communication with the central
office less frequent. However, as soon as the Armistice was
announced Miss Addams and Dr. Jacobs entered into regular
correspondence with reference to the international congress
which now came definitely into view.[8]

The announcement that the Peace Conference would be held
at Paris upset all the previously laid plans of the women since
obviously the women delegates from the Central Powers could
not go to France. Instead, it was proposed at first to hold the
congress at The Hague. Soon after the Armistice Miss
Addams went to see Secretary of State Lansing in regard to
the attendance of the American delegates. She gained the
impression from him that, although the actual decision was
primarily up to the passport section, there was no real obstacle
in the way of the women's attendance. Miss Addams also
visited Secretary of War Baker, who, she said, listened to her
proposal in a " friendly fashion." Thus encouraged in official
quarters, Miss Addams at the end of the month made public
announcement of the plans for the congress, tentatively setting
its time as February and its place of meeting as The Hague.[9]

The announcement of the women's congress was generally
reported in the newspapers. The *New York Times* devoted to
the plan a lengthy editorial with an arresting caption, " Are
Women People? " The editorial argued that the only effect
of the gathering would be to do a good deal of injury to the
interests of feminists, who had fought for woman suffrage
upon a ground directly opposite to the premise of the pacifist
congress. The premise of the suffragists had been that women
were people, that is, shared the fundamental interests, aspirations, and duties common to human beings regardless of sex.
On the other hand, the pacifists held the " socialist " theory
of a world divided into hostile classes: " Women are not people; they are a class, a group, something apart, with class interests which require a congress of their own for definition; a
class which apparently hates and distrusts men, regarding
them as another class which can be met only in momentary

---

[8] *Internationaal*, III, No. 4, 131.
[9] *Kansas City Star*, November 29, 1918.

attraction by way of interlude in fundamental and eternal hostility." Just why women should have expressed this hostility by seeking to abolish the warfare in which men killed and were killed was not made clear. However, the rest of the editorial made it fairly clear that the true grounds of the writer's animus against the women pacifists were their views not in regard to sex but in regard to war and nationalism. He mentioned with evident disapproval their protest against the war in 1915, while Germany was still undefeated, and their present intention of receiving the German delegates as sisters. He concluded: " The millions of women who have worked and suffered to help win the war for democracy will hardly relish the revival of sex-antagonism by women who insisted that the war was wrong." [10]

It is interesting that one of the leaders of the woman suffrage movement opposed the congress for precisely the reason which the *New York Times* urged against it. Miss Mary Garrett Hay, chairman of the Woman Suffrage Party of New York City, made the following comment: " I don't believe in women forming separate organizations for any cause; it's always better to work with the men." She also declared that she did not see what a woman's convention could do about the matter of peace when it was in the hands of an official conference. And Mrs. Harriet Stanton Blatch, a suffragist who had originally been identified with the Woman's Peace Party, declared that Miss Addams' opposition to America's entrance into the war would detract from general confidence in her views now.[11]

For the time being, however, the women pacifists were not interested in the prestige of their congress as much as in the building of a public sentiment which would strengthen the hand of President Wilson in working for the adoption of his program at Paris. With this task in view the Executive Board of the Woman's Peace Party issued on December 10, 1918, a declaration of the main principles for which the group had stood since its organization. These principles were de-

---

[10] *New York Times*, November 30, 1918.
[11] *New York Tribune*, December 1, 1918.

clared to be in "perfect accord" with President Wilson's Fourteen Points of January 1918 and with ideas more recently proclaimed by him.

The first principle of the women, literally in accord with Wilson's program, was the establishment of a league of nations as "the indispensable instrumentality for securing international justice and its by-product, a peace that shall endure." The women proposed that the chief agency of the league be "a Council of Nations—a permanent international conference open to all nations—to meet every two or three years to reconstruct international law and to apply the principles agreed to by the League of Nations." These principles were to be endorsed at the Peace Conference itself in the form of "a Declaration of Rights and Principles which shall be the basis of a new world order to promote justice, security and cooperative effort for the progress and welfare of humanity." In addition to the Council of Nations—which corresponds to the present League Assembly—the Peace Conference was to establish other agencies of international government. One was a "World Court of Justice" which, supplementing the Tribunal of Arbitration, was to deal with all justiciable disputes between nations. Still another agency, the most novel feature in the women's plan, was the "Executive Commission," which was to act as council of inquiry and conciliation in nonjusticiable disputes, as temporary guardian of undeveloped peoples and those needing assistance and protection, and as regulator and guardian of international waterways, commerce, sanitation, etc. The chief ends to be served by all these agencies were: "the drastic reduction of rival armies and navies and the nationalization of the manufacture of armaments; the use of concerted economic pressure as the chief sanction for the enforcement of international law; the removal of the economic causes of war; democratic control of foreign policies; the abolishment of secret covenants; international control of seas and of international waterways; no transference of territory without consent of its inhabitants; and a universal system of ethics in schools prepared by an international commission."

The statement of principles did not limit itself to issues of international organization. It included the demand that national governments be further humanized by the extension of suffrage to women, and it expressed opposition to compulsory military training for all youth. The contemporary problem presented by revolutionary Russia was met by a declaration of hearty sympathy with President Wilson's plea that fair treatment and self-determination be accorded this nation. In conclusion the hope was expressed that American patriots might realize the opportunity which our government faced, one which none ever had before or perhaps would have again. "The fate of the world's future," it was said, "hangs in a delicately adjusted balance." [12]

Unfortunately, at this time a numerous class of American patriots was much more interested in assailing pacifists like Miss Addams than in fulfilling America's mission to the world. Not long after the issuance of the Executive Board's statement, Miss Addams became the object of a public attack which made her recent appeal to the magnanimity of American patriots seem an irony.

On January 24, 1919, dispatches from Washington gave an account of the proceedings before the Overman Sub-Committee of the Judiciary Committee of the Senate. One Archibald Stevenson, a member of the propaganda section of the New York Bureau of the Military Intelligence Service, presented the committee with a list of one hundred names of men and women who allegedly "had not helped to win the war." The accuracy of the list may be appraised in the light of the fact that all but sixty-two names were eliminated in an executive session of the committee. [13] The list was headed by Jane Addams, who thus received a curious recognition in return for her arduous work in behalf of the Department of Food Conservation. Included also were three other leaders of the Woman's Peace Party—Lillian D. Wald, Emily Greene Balch,

---

[12] *Statement of the Executive Board of the National Woman's Peace Party . . . Issued December 10th, 1918.* Leaflet, Jane Addams Peace Collection.

[13] *New York Times,* January 25, 1919; Chicago *Herald Examiner,* January 25, 1919.

and Sophonisba Breckinridge. The women were in good company, for others indicted by Mr. Stevenson were David Starr Jordan, Norman Thomas, Oswald Garrison Villard, Harry F. Ward, Charles A. Beard, and Rufus Jones.[14]

Miss Addams took the incident as an opportunity for a public declaration of pacifist faith. She said in part in a press interview:

> I am a pacifist but I have been loyal to my country. . . . I did not see the Stevenson list and do not know how I got on it, but I cannot change my convictions. I have been against wars for many years. I believe there may be formed other methods of adjusting relations between nations, and I believe they will be speedily found at the Paris Conference.[15]

Secretary of War Baker repudiated the researches of Mr. Stevenson and was particularly incensed at his inclusion of the name of Miss Addams, whom he regarded as high-minded and patriotic.[16] Nevertheless Stevenson, backed by the Union League Club of New York, persuaded the New York Assembly of the necessity of appointing the inquisitorial Lusk Committee. For several years the martial spirit, having no longer the Germans as targets, was to expend itself upon " Reds " and pacifists, who were scarcely distinguished. For Miss Addams the Stevenson report marked the beginning of a period of unpopularity that exceeded in animus even the criticism of her pacifism during the war.

Miss Addams, however, was fully engrossed in the first months of 1919 with a project that touched her more deeply than her own fate and, in its high promise, could well anaesthetize her to the pain of any personal discomfitures. This was the making of final preparations for the congress of the International Committee of Women for Permanent Peace. The Hague had proved to be impracticable as a meeting-place, and the cabling incident to the consideration of a new meeting-place, together with numerous difficulties in regard to passports, had entailed much delay.[17] Thus it was not until April 1919 that the American delegates set sail for Paris. The

[14] *New York Tribune*, January 25, 1919.
[15] *Brooklyn Times*, January 25, 1919.
[16] Linn, pp. 329-330.   [17] *Internationaal*, III, No. 4, 1.

delegation consisted of twenty-five women—the five members of the permanent national committee and twenty ordinary delegates. The Committee of Five, arranged for in 1915, was composed of Lucia Ames Mead, Florence Kelley, Alice Thacher Post, Jeanette Rankin, and Lillian D. Wald. Among the delegates were Jane Addams, Emily Greene Balch, Madeleine Z. Doty, Constance Drexel, Dr. Alice Hamilton, and Lucy Biddle Lewis. The members of the delegation were, in the aggregate, as intellectually and professionally distinguished a group as could have been gathered from a " Who's Who " of American women.

Arriving in Paris in the Easter season, the American delegates encountered at once certain disappointments. They found that the English passports had been delayed and that the French delegates had been refused their passports by a government unsympathetic to international pacifist congresses. Numerous meetings of the delegates then in Paris were necessary before the congress was finally arranged for May 12 at Zurich. During the fortnight of delay in France the Americans had conferences with their French colleagues, interviews with various officials of both the Peace Conference and the Food Administration, and a five-days' visit to the devastated regions in which their repugnance to war was reenforced by grim object-lessons.[18]

On May 6 the American members of the Executive Committee of the international organization settled down in Zurich to the work of preparing the agenda of the congress. Since the Executive Committee included women from the Central Powers, the American women had the rather stirring experience of seeing the " alien enemy " face to face. An Austrian woman, in blooming health when she had met Miss Addams at the Hague Congress, appeared before the American delegates so emaciated and marked by hunger that she was scarcely recognizable.[19] Yet all extraneous differences disap-

---

[18] Addams, *Peace and Bread*, p. 154.
[19] The women from the Central Powers had to live in such poor quarters that Miss Addams felt impelled to give up her own rooms at one of the best hotels and move to more modest accommodations. *Buffalo Enquirer*, May 20, 1919.

peared as this dying woman showed the persistence of her old spirit and thought, telling Miss Addams that greater than the suffering of Austrian women from starvation had been the enforced intellectual sordidness from which she now found release in resuming acquaintance with her old comrades. The members of the. Committee, Miss Addams later wrote, all felt in relation to each other a curious fellowship as they not only recounted similar war experiences but also found that resolutions on the same subject, coming in from one country after another, were so similar in intent that it was a hard task to decide which resolution most clearly expressed that which was common to them all.[20]

Finally came the day for the opening of the congress—the strange international tryst which had been made four years ago and had not been voided by what seemed an eternity of nationalist hostility. About a hundred and fifty women arrived from sixteen countries—Austria, Argentina, Australia, Denmark, France, Germany, Great Britain, Holland, Hungary, Ireland, Italy, Norway, Roumania, Sweden, Switzerland, and the United States. One of the delegates later wrote for the *New York Times Magazine* an account of the experiences of various delegations in coming or attempting to come to the congress. The experiences so interestingly reflect the abnormal conditions of the time as to justify quotation at length:

. . . Each of the twenty-six English women received their passports after promising "to indulge in no Socialist propaganda." France refused passports to her women, but three finally arrived after combining personal business in Switzerland with the conference. One Italian delegate was allowed to come " to study the costumes of *tout le monde.*" Belgium had no delegate, for her threat to expatriate any woman attending proved so effective that only Mlle. La Fontaine sat as a silent onlooker.

For weeks the Munich women, too, were refused passports, but for quite a different reason. "There is no such country as Switzerland," said the Communist Government which held the power after Kurt Eisner's assassination. But the Communists' creed, recognizing no national boundaries, was not to be swayed by telegraphed evidence. So the women waited until the counter-revolution took place and passports were in vogue again. Twenty-seven women finally arrived from Germany, four from Austria, and two from Hungary.

.   .   .   .

[20] Addams, *Peace and Bread*, p. 157.

15

It was necessary for the Scandinavian women to cross through Germany. It was an eight instead of the usual three day journey, and the delegates took their luncheons with them—also their dinners and breakfasts. Sometimes they cooked their meals over their little spirit lamps on station platforms while waiting for trains which ran without time tables.[21]

The writer went on to describe the social status of the women who had come together under such difficult circumstances. They were not women of great wealth or social status, nor, with one or two exceptions, were they workingwomen. Although Jane Addams termed them " just an ordinary group of citizens," they were a little out of the ordinary in that they were typically " doers." Most of them were professional women—doctors, lawyers, teachers, professors, social and civic workers, and writers. Their careers had been linked with the suffrage movement and with all kinds of welfare work for both women and children, and many had held public office in their communities. Politically there was almost a preponderance of socialists, and the ranks included even some communists from Germany and Hungary. This fact reflected the radicalization of opinion wrought by the war, for at the Hague Congress the socialists were decidedly in the minority.

The woman to whom fell the difficult task of presiding over this diverse group and guiding them to common ground was Jane Addams, chairman of the International Committee of Women since the meeting of 1915. In her opening address she observed that the plan of the Hague Congress to meet again at the same time as the Peace Conference was being fulfilled in a most extraordinary sense. For the meeting of the women was taking place in the very week when the representatives of the Central Powers were adding their presence to the membership of the Paris Conference, thus giving the official conference its formal beginning. Miss Addams reviewed the trials of the women during the war years, the efforts of some of them to prevent bloodshed in post-war revolutions, and their pleasure at finding so much like-mindedness when they finally met again to frame the resolutions of the congress. She expressed her sense of the momentousness of

---

[21] *New York Times Magazine Section*, June 22, 1919, p. 11.

the task, and declared her certainty that the women would approach it " free from animosity or sense of estrangement, as . . . the women have been too close to the clarifying spirit of reality to indulge in any sentimentality or unconsidered statements." [22]

The address of welcome was given by Clara Ragaz, head of the Swiss delegation, who had served on the Neutral Conference Commission for Continuous Mediation set up by Henry Ford in Stockholm in 1916. Her address was notable for the sanity and moderation of its presentation of the meeting's purpose. " No one among us," she said, " will suppose that this Congress or any other congress could be in a position to bring very great influence to bear on the formidable events which are taking place or are in preparation around us." It would also, she declared, be foolish to suppose that those gathered pretended to be all of the same mind, or proposed to appear before the world with a hard and fast program and to offer it as a solution of the problem. But despite differences of thought as to the causes of the war, and varieties of opinion as to the details of the solution, the women would not be prevented " from recognizing a common share of the responsibility in its deepest sense and in its deepest causes, nor from assembling here in the consciousness of our common responsibility in order to seek a common solution and a common deliverance through our united efforts." [23] Miss Addams in response called upon the congress to rise and stand in memory of those who had lost their lives in the war. This symbolic expression of the transcendence of recent enmities was much noted in the accounts of the congress.

The work of the women is to be viewed chiefly in the resolutions adopted by the congress in its six days of session. Resolutions had been prepared by various committees which met in the days preceding the congress. However, these resolutions were debated and in some respects amended; those which finally emerged represented the decision of the entire

[22] *Report of the International Congress of Women, Zurich, May 12 to 17, 1919,* p. 3.
[23] *Ibid.,* pp. 15-16.

congress by majority vote. The first resolution touched upon the famine and blockade from which so many of the delegates were suffering personally. After expressing their view that the prevalent famine and pestilence in Europe were " a disgrace to civilization," the women called upon the governments assembled at the Peace Conference "immediately to develop the inter-allied organizations formed for purposes of war into an international organization for purposes of peace, so that the resources of the world—food, raw materials, finance, transport—shall be made available for the relief of the people of all countries from famine and pestilence." To this end the congress urged that immediate action be taken to raise the blockade, and, if there was insufficiency of food or transport, to prohibit the unnecessary use of transport from one country to another and to ration the people of every country.[24] The resolution in full was telegraphed to President Wilson. The President promptly telegraphed a reply:

> Your message appeals both to my head and to my heart, and I hope most sincerely that ways may be found, though the present outlook is extremely unpromising, because of infinite practical difficulties.[25]

The public reception of this telegram, Miss Addams wrote, was "one of the most striking moments of the Congress." For, on Miss Addams' announcement of the reception of the message, there fell a hush on the great audience which indicated the recognition that " out of the confusion and misery of Europe one authoritative voice was about to be heard." Upon the reading of the telegram " there arose from the audience a sigh of religious resignation, as if a good man were doing his best and in the end must succeed." [26]

But the congress was far from believing that the President had succeeded as yet. This view was shown by its critical resolutions regarding the peace treaty, an advance copy of which was received while the congress was in session. The congress was the first public body to protest against the terms of the peace. It is interesting that the strongest words against these terms in its discussions were spoken by an English dele-

---

[24] *Ibid.*, pp. 241-242.   [25] *Ibid.*, p. 162.
[26] Addams, *Peace and Bread*, pp. 161-162.

gate, Mrs. Pethick-Lawrence, who also urged the congress to hold a protest meeting. The women from the Central Powers did not enter into this part of the discussion. The resolution of protest, introduced by another Englishwoman and seconded by an American, was directed not against the League of Nations but against the terms imposed on the defeated nations. It spoke in truly prophetic terms:

This International Congress of Women expresses its deep regret that the terms of peace proposed at Versailles should so seriously violate the principles upon which alone a just and lasting peace can be secured, and which the democracies of the world had come to accept.

By guaranteeing the fruits of the secret treaties to the conquerors, the terms of peace tacitly sanction secret diplomacy, deny the principles of self-determination, recognize the right of the victors to the spoils of war, and create all over Europe discords and animosities, which can only lead to future wars.

By the demand for the disarmament of one set of belligerents only, the principle of justice is violated and the rule of force continued.

By the financial and economic proposals a hundred million people of this generation in the heart of Europe are condemned to poverty, disease and despair which must result in the spread of hatred and anarchy within each nation.

With a deep sense of responsibility this Congress strongly urges the Allied and Associated Governments to accept such amendments of the Terms, as shall bring the Peace into harmony with those principles first enumerated by President Wilson upon the faithful carrying out of which the honor of the Allied peoples depends.[27]

While the peace terms met unanimous condemnation, the Covenant of the League presented a problem upon which agreement was not so easy. The women were torn between an impulse of gratification at the realization of their chief dream and, on the other hand, their disappointment at finding such serious faults in the actualization. Two sections of the Political Committee presented reports of which that submitted by the section composed of two American women was the more favorable. A third committee, whose resolution was adopted, reconciled the two views by approving the League in principle without committing the congress in regard to the existing Covenant. The resolution was, in part, as follows:

---

[27] *Report of the International Congress of Women, Zurich*, pp. 242-243.

This Congress holds that the peaceful progress of the world can only be assured when the common interests of humanity are recognized in the establishment of a League of Nations which shall represent the will of the peoples and promote international cooperation. It therefore records its satisfaction that the idea of a League of Nations, regarded as impracticable by the majority of people at the time of the Congress of Women at The Hague in 1915, has become so widely accepted; that, incorporated in the armistice terms of November 11, 1918, it was agreed to, both by the Allied and Associated Powers and by Germany. But the Congress regrets that the Covenant of the League, now submitted by the Allied and Associated Powers, in many respects does not accord with the fourteen points laid down as the basis for present negotiations, contains provisions that will stultify its growth, and omits others, which are essential to world-peace.[28]

The resolution then specified the essential principles which had been omitted from the Covenant. Some of them pertained to a more democratic organization of the League: the admission of any state willing to perform the duties of membership, an increase of the executive to at least eleven nations, the right of nationalities and dependencies within any government to present directly to the League their desires as to self-government, and easier amendment of the constitution. Other principles were those considered essential to peace: immediate reduction of armaments on the same terms for all member-states and abolition of conscription in all states joining the League. Still others envisaged the attainment of greater justice in international relations: adherence to the principle of self-determination in territorial adjustments and matters of nationality, free access to raw materials for all nations on equal terms, and abrogation of regional understandings, including the Monroe Doctrine, in so far as they were inconsistent with the Covenant of the League.[29]

In addition to these proposed changes regarded as essential, there were set forth certain principles which it was desired that the League should incorporate as soon as the nations composing it agreed to the adoption. These principles include the most radical of the suggestions offered: total disarmament (land, sea, air), universal free trade, a plan of world economy, national ratification of treaties only by an elected legislative body, abrogation of all treaties not registered with

---

[28] *Ibid.*, p. 243.   [29] *Ibid.*, p. 244.

the League, and complete freedom of communication and travel. Other principles pertained to the action or organization of the League: the enforcement of the decisions of the League by other means than military pressure or food-blockade, a more democratic election of the executive power of the League, and assignment of mandates over backward peoples in their interests. Still other proposals had to do with national policies: abolition of the protection of the investments of the capitalists of one country in the resources of another, guarantee of the rights of civil and political minorities, abolition of child labor, abolition of governmental censorship, and establishment of full equal suffrage and full equality of women with men politically, socially, and economically. To implement the last proposal the Peace Conference was urged to insert in the Peace Treaty a " Women's Charter," a set of ideas of equal rights. The women also passed resolutions which asked that at least one representative from each country to the Labor Conference should be a woman, and that a clause be inserted in the Peace Treaty giving women the same voting rights in plebiscites as men. Finally, the women urged the cessation of both military and economic attacks upon Austria and Hungary and likewise the proclamation of an amnesty for political prisoners, including conscientious objectors to military service.[30]

The foregoing resolutions were to be presented to the Peace Conference in the hope that the Covenant of the League and the various objectionable policies might be changed by public opposition. Other resolutions were submitted to the national sections as bases for future work. These included more detailed objectives with regard to the Covenant of the League, action to be proposed to the League when it was established, a program in matters affecting the status of women, an international council on education for world organization and international ethics and citizenship, and measures in behalf of peace and liberty. Most striking of the provisions under the last category was that urging the national sections to work for an international agreement of women to strike against war of

---

[30] *Ibid.*, pp. 245-249.

all kinds by refusing their support of war in money, work, or propaganda.[31]

If the extensiveness and moral absolutism of this program provoke a smile from the worldly-wise, it must, on the other hand, be remembered that the time was one when high hopes and daring plans were in the air, when not merely Wilson but also his more conservative associates at the Peace Conference were espousing a new organization of world society that in some respects was not much less a deviation from past international conventions than the ideas of the pacifist women. The most unconventional projects of the women simply carried the principles of Wilson to their logical conclusion, a process which Wilson was often careful not to employ. Moreover, some of the planks which seemed wild at the time, such as the withdrawal of protection from investments in foreign countries, have since become part of the foreign policy of this country. Finally, it must be considered that the women themselves were as conscious of the impracticability of many of their demands as anyone else, and, like the authors of the Declaration of Independence, were simply formulating a set of ideals which were to serve to future aspiration as lodestars.

That the women were well aware of the long stretch of effort still required is indicated by nothing so much as their organizational arrangements. They did not disband their international organization, but, adopting a constitution, formed themselves into a permanent body under the name of " The Women's International League for Peace and Freedom." The constitution declared the object of the League to be the organization of support for the resolutions passed at the two international congresses and the support of " movements to further peace, internationalism and the freedom of women." The League was to consist of national sections, and representation by one national section was open to every nation, free or subject, to every self-governing dominion, and to every minority in a country which claimed the status of a separate nationality. Outside of being obligated to support the object of the League, each national section enjoyed au-

---

[31] *Ibid.*, pp. 255-262.

tonomy. Organs of the international body were the president, an executive committee consisting of nine persons (both to be elected at the international congresses), and a consultative committee consisting of two persons from each national section who had the right to attend meetings of the executive committee but not to vote. The office of the organization was to be in the place where the headquarters of the League of Nations were to be located—a provision which indicates the close affinity which, despite criticisms, was felt with the League. Jane Addams was elected president of the organization and Emily G. Balch was chosen to be its secretary-treasurer. The selection was not merely a tribute to the two women but also a sign of the importance attached to the rôle which the United States was then playing in the reconstruction of international society.

Whereas the League of Nations created through Wilson's efforts retained traces of the enmity of war in temporarily excluding Germany, the women's organization established at Zurich exhibited a complete transcendence of the recent nationalist cleavages. The Women's International League for Peace and Freedom not merely included sections from the Central Powers but had as its vice-president a German woman, Lida Gustava Heymann. The unwillingness of the Zurich congress to recognize any interruption of the spiritual solidarity of women was shown even more strikingly by an episode outside its formal acts. When the French delegate Jeanne Mélin unexpectedly arrived during the course of the congress, Lida Gustava Heymann came forward to greet her and gave this woman from the devastated region a great bunch of roses. She then said:

A German woman gives her hand to a French woman, and says in the name of the German Delegation, that we hope that we women can build a bridge from Germany to France and from France to Germany, and that in the future we may be able to make good the wrongdoing of men.[82]

Mlle. Mélin, after accepting the greeting, replied with an address which voiced the protest of women against the wrong-

---

[82] *Ibid.*, pp. 154-155.

doing in which statesmen of her own country were participating at Versailles. The American Emily Balch improvised the concluding gesture in this rather dramatic episode. After Mlle. Mélin's address Miss Balch stood and, raising her hand, invited all present to join her in pledging themselves to do everything in their power towards the ending of war and the coming of peace. The entire audience did so.[33]

The disparity between their internationalist ideal and the hatreds which still burned in the world at large could not but have weighed heavily upon the women, even as their League came into birth. Thus it was natural that Miss Addams should try to raise, within sane and moderate limits, their hopes. In an address at a public meeting she reminded them of the influence which the Hague resolutions had exercised, even suggesting that they may have played some part in bringing about Wilson's formulation of the Fourteen Points.[34] At the closing banquet, given by the Swiss section, Miss Addams adjured the women against too great discouragement over the peace treaty, reminded them that the very meeting of women in genuine friendship and understanding after a world war was a thing of greatest promise, and called for faith in the ideal which had animated them. Seeking to impress the potency of this ideal of moral energy, she related an incident which revealed memorably the essence of her faith in pacifism. It was a story which she had heard from Herbert Hoover while taking dinner with him during her recent stay in Paris:

He told me a very touching tale of all the difficult things he had had to do during the war and since the war. None had been more difficult than the requirement to pass through a starving country with trainloads of food, and enter another country which was also hungry. For instance, at one of the docks to which a shipload of food came, the men who had to unload it were hungry and their wives and children were hungry, and their work was to take it into an enemy country. One man said, "We could not do it," and it was found necessary to appeal to their goodwill and use moral suasion. Then they did it. When that great test was put upon them, to go hungry that their enemies might be fed, nothing but a moral appeal could meet the situation. We shall have to believe in

<hr>

[33] *Ibid.*, p. 156.

[34] Miss Addams in this connection gave the previously described report of Wilson's words of praise to her when he returned the Hague resolutions papers. *Ibid.*, p. 196.

spiritual power. We shall have to learn to use moral energy, to put
a new sort of force into the world and believe that it is a vital thing—
the only thing, in this moment of sorrow and death and destruction,
that will heal the world and bring it back into a normal condition.[35]

In this spirit the women set their gaze upon the future, but
the reaction of contemporary public opinion to this work was
obviously of great moment in relation to their immediate
tasks.   What notice and evaluation had articulate opinion in
the United States given to this congress, led by an American
woman?   It may be said in the first place that many news
items appeared about it, despite the fact that attention at the
time was focused upon the official Peace Conference.   The
New York Times not only reported regularly the day-by-day
activities of the congress but also devoted a long story in the
magazine section to its work as a whole.[36]   In the news accounts particular notice was taken of the resolutions condemning the food blockade and the Versailles Treaty.   These
resolutions were also brought to the attention of the American
public indirectly through the account of a conspicuous reference to them at the meeting of the American Unitarian Association in May.   At this meeting, which was considering what
stand to take toward the Versailles Treaty, the Reverend
Henry W. Pinkham of Winthrop, much to the disgust of Mr.
Taft who was presiding, attempted to have the gathering pass
the same resolutions as had been voted by the women at
Zurich.   He declared that " these noble resolutions, as adopted
by those noble women, are based upon the spirit ' if thy enemy
hunger feed him; if he thirst, give him drink.' "   His praise
was, to be sure, unavailing.[37]

Some evaluations of the Zurich congress which appeared in
the American press were not very serious.   The *New York
Times* published a rather gay editorial on the resolution of
the women to render no support to any future war—a pledge
which reminded it of the women's war strike described in
Lysistrata.   One of the most amusing appraisals was that of
an elderly American business man who had wandered into the

[35] *Ibid.,* p. 237.
[36] *New York Times,* May 14, 15, 16, and 18, 1919.
[37] *New York Times,* May 21, 1919.

gathering of women. Asked what he thought about it, he responded:

Well, I think you have every kind of woman here that you could find. Some of them are real good looking and some are real earnest looking. I have counted six with short hair. But what I would like to see is men and women getting together on these things—not one group of men sitting off at Versailles and one group of women at Zurich. They ought to get together on the peace terms and the league of nations.[88]

Of the serious attempts to appraise the work of the women we may select two samples—one unfavorable and the other favorable. The critical editorial of the *Chicago Evening Post* did not object to women's sitting apart from men but rather to their taking a position which was " not truly representative of the world's womanhood in the matters they are attempting to advise the world upon." It declared that whereas most women had realized the issues of justice involved in the war, women like Miss Addams and Miss Rankin had failed in this respect. They had been unable to discover in the welter of blood the struggle of ideals to survive, of moral values to triumph. The editorial continued:

This blindness from the beginning unfits them now to pass judgment on the great closing act in the drama. . . . Their sympathy lacks the direction of intelligent understanding. . . . In its eagerness to be kind even to criminals, it overlooks the necessity of doing justice to the victims of crime and of protecting them from a repetition of the injuries that have been inflicted upon them.[89]

On the other hand, the *Nation* regarded the memorial of the women to the Peace Conference as an " honest and straightforward " reminder of the vast gap between the international justice promised by the Fourteen Points and the selfish, imperialistic character of the actual settlement. The editorial declared:

The memorial does particularly well to insist strongly upon the fact which the conferees so dearly wish might be forgotten, that the peace terms " guarantee the fruits of secret treaties to the conquerors." It is greatly to the credit of these women's perspicacity that they discern so clearly and state so accurately the true position of the

---

[88] *Chicago News*, May 19, 1919.
[89] *Chicago Evening Post*, May 20, 1919. A similar view was expressed by the *New York Times*, May 18, 1919.

secret treaties in the international settlement; and we hope they will continue in and out of season to be outspoken about it hereafter.[40]

The women, in fact, were determined to be outspoken at the Peace Conference itself. The congress had appointed a committee to take one section of the resolutions to the Conference, which, theoretically at least, might still be induced to modify its position. The delegation chosen consisted of Jane Addams as president, Charlotte Despard and Chrystal Macmillan of Great Britain, Gabrielle Duchêne of France, Rosa Genoni of Italy, and Clara Ragaz of Switzerland. Miss Addams writes as follows of the efforts of the women in behalf of the resolutions:

> Two of the English members discussed them with Lord Robert Cecil, I saw Colonel House several times, our committee through the efforts of an Italian member was received by Signor Orlando and we also had a hearing at the Quai d'Orsay with the French minister of foreign affairs, and with the delegates from other countries. In Paris at that time the representatives of the smaller nations were already expressing their disappointment in the League but its proponents were elated over its adoption and hopeful for the future. They all received our resolutions politely and sometimes discussed them at length, but only a few of the journalists and " experts " were enthusiastic about them.[41]

Further information is given by a contemporary newspaper account. One American delegate to the Peace Conference told the committee that women would participate in the various plebiscites provided for by the peace treaty. George Nicoll Barnes of the British delegation informed them that nothing prevented women from insisting that their governments allow a woman to be appointed to membership on the Commission on International Labor Legislation, while Lord Robert Cecil assured them women could be elected to the highest offices in the League of Nations.[42]

But these sops of information did not blind them to the essential disappointment received at Paris. After this disappointment Miss Addams felt that " only the feeding of the hungry seemed to offer the tonic of beneficent activity." Unfortunately the Nansen plan of entering Russia to feed the

---

[40] " The International Congress of Women," *Nation* (1919), CVIII, 819.

[41] *Peace and Bread*, p. 164.   [42] *New York Times*, June 8, 1919.

women and children had been indefinitely postponed, and the blockade continued against Hungary as well as Russia. However, the possibility of beneficent activity was offered to Miss Addams by an invitation from the American Friends Service Committee to go into Germany, as member of a committee which was to distribute " Gifts of Love " in the form of food, clothing, and other necessities. The suffering which Miss Addams saw in that country, especially among children, confirmed the impressions which had animated the resolution of the International Congress on famine and blockade. It also strengthened her revulsion from nationalism, the cause of this suffering, and her attachment to such an internationalism as might, through the newly created League of Nations, have " considered this multitude of starving children as its concrete problem." [43]

Finally, in August, Miss Addams and the other American women arrived home, " inevitably disappointed in the newly formed League, but eager to see what would happen when ' the United States came in ! ' " [44]   During the absence of the delegation a rift of opinion had already manifested itself among the members of the Woman's Peace Party with regard to the League. Some had cooperated with the League to Enforce Peace in support of the establishment of a League of Nations. Miss Addams herself had joined the League to Enforce Peace in the winter of 1919, despite an earlier hesitation to adopt a program which emphasized military sanctions. Other members of the Woman's Peace Party, especially those of the Philadelphia branch with its many Quaker members, had been unable to accept the Covenant worked out at Paris. " The difference of opinion," Miss Addams wrote, " was limited always as to the existing League and never for a moment did anyone doubt the need for continued effort to bring about an adequate international organization." [45]

The problem of the League of Nations and other problems of the post-war world were more complex than those which the Woman's Peace Party had faced heretofore. The moral

---

[43] Addams, *Peace and Bread*, pp. 166-173.
[44] *Ibid.*, p. 177.   [45] *Ibid.*, pp. 197-198.

ends pertinent to their solution could not be condensed into
any single value, even one as broad as peace. And the means
required for their solution were a matter less of criticism of
existing political instrumentalities than of the positive and
constructive task of determining and working for new instrumentalities of both political and social character. It was
doubtless with these considerations in mind that the Executive Board of the Woman's Peace Party decided in the fall of
1919 that the party, facing a new chapter, required a change
in name, constitution, and program.

For submission to the annual meeting to be held on November 3 and 4, the Executive Board drew up a recommendation which foreshadowed both the end of the Woman's
Peace Party and the beginning of a new and broader organization. The statement opened by recalling the original purpose of the party—" to protest in the name of Womanhood
against the cruelty and waste of war, and to give united help
toward translating the mother instinct of life-saving into
social terms of the common good." It noted that its original
program of principles had been affirmed in substance by all
the leading statesmen of the world, since they had come to see
that civilization demanded that this war should end war and
that the cause of war must be eliminated by the organization
of the world in an effective League of Nations. The statement then pointed out another fact which reinvigorated the
women in their purposes. It was that, although America's
entrance into the war had divided the membership in individual approach to immediate duty, the end of the war·al-
lowed them to become wholly reunited, not only in regard to
ultimate convictions but also in every-day service.

In view of these facts the Board of National Officers first
urged upon the membership changes in name, in organization
of the official Board, in form of group membership, and in
organic affiliation with the Women's International League for
Peace and Freedom. Second, the Board called attention to a
new task, arising from a crisis-situation in the life of the
countries devastated or crippled by the World War. " We are
confronted at this hour with a common life so depleted by

famine, disease, weakness and discouragement," the Board declared, " that we perceive that all the forces of conservation must be freely used, and at once, if the fabric of that common life is to bear the weight of human progress." It therefore urged upon the membership " an immediate Fight-the-Famine propaganda and an heroic effort to help save suffering humanity."

The attention of the organization was thus to be claimed by the problems involved in food supply and its distribution, the problems of economic adjustments, of cooperative consumers' associations, and of legal restraint of profiteering, together with measures of effective appeal for simplicity and thrift in personal living in the interest of generous sharing. Such work, for which the society was specially fitted by its internationalism and broad sympathies, was to be taken up not as a substitute for its already accepted work but as an added service to humanity.[46]

The meeting to which this recommendation was addressed was the last in the history of the Woman's Peace Party as such. For the group which met in Philadelphia in the traditionally hospitable Friends Meeting House adopted the changes proposed by the Board. Accepting the resolutions of the Zurich Congress in their principles, the Woman's Peace Party signalized its new affiliation with the organization created by that congress by a change in name. It became the Section for the United States of the Women's International League for Peace and Freedom (abbreviated as W. I. L. P. F.). Such is still the name of the influential women's pacifist organization which traces its origin to the Woman's Peace Party. The addition of the word " freedom " to the name signified the belief that peace is evil without freedom and that freedom cannot be achieved or maintained without peace.[47] The meeting also adopted a new constitution together with a new form of organization. Those elected to lead the organized group

[46] Statement recommended by the Board of Officers of the Woman's Peace Party to the Annual Meeting, November 3rd and 4th, 1919, MS, Jane Addams Peace Collection.
[47] Emily Greene Balch, *Why Peace and Freedom?* Leaflet of the Women's International League for Peace and Freedom.

were, in the main, those who had been in the movement from
the start. Miss Addams, believing that the presidency of the
international body should be separated from that of the national, would accept only the title of honorary chairman of
the latter body. Mrs. Anna Garlin Spencer became chairman;
Mrs. Lucy Biddle Lewis, vice-chairman; Mrs. Eleanor Daggett
Karsten, executive secretary; and Mrs. Hannah Clothier Hull,
later the president of the national organization, was elected
treasurer.[48]

As the *Survey* pointed out, the new program of the women
emphasized " preventive policies and activities which make it
an agency for constructive social reform." [49]   The wide range
of these policies and activities is indicated by the standing
committees, which were to concern themselves with the world
famine, Oriental relations, international relations on this continent, education—with a sub-committee on physical training
without military drill—labor, free trade, the League of Nations, and national and state legislation. Effort was first to
be given to the relief of world famine. An appeal was made
for more funds—much had been given already by the Woman's Peace Party—to be contributed to the starving and dis-
eased of Europe and the Near East.

Yet the program also emphasized the traditional activity of
the women—the uniting of women in an international effort
to prevent war. Mrs. Anna Garlin Spencer restated the convictions upon which this program of separate pacifist action
by women was based:

So far in the history of the world, women have had small chance
to declare their convictions in regard to war as a method of settling
international disputes, while always called upon to sacrifice themselves and their children to the utmost when men chose to start a
war. It seems to many women necessary to band together, for a while
at least, in order to get strength from mutual association to make
vocal the desire of human beings of the mother-sex for the substitution of law for war and for the focussing of effort upon human salvage
rather than human destruction.[50]

---

[48] Women's International League for Peace and Freedom, *Reports:
Zurich 1919—Vienna 1921*, p. 57.
[49] " Constructive Pacifism," *Survey* (1920), XLIII, 387.
[50] *Ibid.*

16

Writing of the work of this meeting, Miss Addams speaks of the "indomitable faith of the women gathered there who, after nearly five years of anxiety and of hope deferred, still solemnly agreed to renew the struggle against the war system and to work for a wider comity of nations." [51]

Their faith indeed needed to be strong to withstand the many and great disappointments which had been suffered— disappointments which might make the history of the organization seem a record of continuous failure. The women had failed in relation to the World War, their consternation at which had primarily motivated their organization: they had not persuaded the neutral governments to call a conference for continuous mediation and later they had witnessed the shipwreck of their alternative plan, the accomplishment of mediation through an unofficial conference. The pacifists had failed in relation to the peace of their own country: they had not induced its government to refrain from entering upon the path of hectic preparedness and they had not prevented it from joining the conflict and thus extending and prolonging its slaughter. They had not succeeded at the end of hostilities in prevailing upon the makers of peace to establish what seemed to pacifists a permanent and just peace: the Treaty of Versailles appeared to them in all too many respects to perpetuate the evils of the older order, and their objections to it had of course not persuaded the statesmen at Versailles to amend their plans. More even than the past, the spectacle of the present might have depressed their hopes at their last meeting as the Woman's Peace Party. In their own land there burned ominously fires of selfish nationalism and isolationism which cast a cloud over the aspirations of internationalist pacifism and their own organization.

Yet, in reviewing their efforts, the women might well have refused to acknowledge that they had been mistaken in their objectives or tactics, though they could not but admit that they had been unable to dissuade others from choosing wrong ends and means. Moreover, this inability could not have been foreseen. While the adverse forces to be overcome had been

---

[51] *Peace and Bread*, pp. 178-179.

much stronger and their own influence much weaker than the women had anticipated,[52] there was no point at which their optimism could have been called a fool's hopefulness. In the whole period in which they strove, the factors determining the world's destiny were so fluid and novel that the moulding of this destiny appeared unusually inviting to human effort; and it was, in fact, only by a few hairs' breadth that the visions of a minority did not become realities through acceptance by a majority.

Moreover, in estimating the accomplishment of reform movements one must be very wary of absolute judgments of success or failure. Failure to reach a distant goal is often accompanied by considerable progress towards it—progress which may be important even when it is only the preparation of public opinion for renewal of efforts. Thus the Woman's Peace Party could place on the credit side a number of substantial even though only partial achievements. Among these the following in particular stand out: the preservation, through its efforts in conjunction with the International Committee of Women for a Permanent Peace and the Ford Neutral Conference, of a sentiment for peace which affected considerably at least the Scandinavian neutral countries and perhaps helped to keep some of them from entering the war;[53] the preparation of a state of public opinion in the United States which, even if it did not prevent the United States from entering the war, at least facilitated Wilson's effort to dedicate this entrance to the cause of a better world; and the presentation of a specific program for this international order which may have influenced President Wilson in formulating, and in any event influenced broad sections of American public opinion in supporting, a League of Nations which despite its many defects is a milestone on humanity's long ascent towards an enlightened international order. To be sure, the forces and

---

[52] Miss Emily G. Balch writes to the author on the issue raised by the above lines: "I think that throughout you imagine that we expected more than we did expect and overrated our own power more than we really did."

[53] This is the claim of Louis Lochner in his account of the Ford Neutral Conference.

groups which assisted in these achievements were many and no one of them should claim an undue share of the credit for itself. Yet there is danger of underestimating the influence which was exerted upon both individual statesmen and public opinion by so dramatic a spectacle as that of the aggressive efforts of an organization which comprised many of the leading women of this country and which worked with peace leaders in other countries.

Still further, the success of any movement must be judged in large part in relation to a broad temporal span, with reference not merely to what was accomplished by the participants in this movement but also to the accomplishments of those who built or may yet build upon their work. The Woman's Peace Party, as the parent of the United States Section of the Women's International League for Peace and Freedom, brought into being an organization which was destined to carry on the ideals of the Party with a greater measure of apparent success than came to the parent group. Whereas her leadership of the Woman's Peace Party brought Jane Addams little but sacrifice, it was in the course of her participation in the work of the Women's International League for Peace and Freedom that in 1930 she received a belated recognition of her service to peace—the Nobel Peace Prize. Though the history of the Women's International League lies beyond the boundary of our theme, it is necessary to an appreciation of the effects of the Woman's Peace Party to bear in mind some of the important features of this subsequent history. The so-called W. I. L., though suffering in certain periods from chauvinistic and anti-pacifist condemnation as great as that visited upon the Woman's Peace Party, has steadily grown in membership and in scope of activities and influence. Today it is one of the major factors in an imposing American peace movement. It is influential in part because it has taken over that constructiveness in ideology and energy in method which was first notably exhibited among American peace societies by the Woman's Peace Party. In the two decades since its birth, the W. I. L. has vigorously pressed its conception of the ways to peace and freedom in every important issue of America's international and domestic life. With its emphasis shifting in accordance with the changing problems of this country and the world, it has fought for a wide range of causes including such broad objectives as the removal of militaristic and exploitative elements from America's foreign and domestic policies and the reorganization of international society in the interest of peace embracing both freedom and justice.

At least within the sphere of American legislative and diplomatic history the W. I. L. has witnessed the attainment of numerous objectives long on its program. Among these are recognition of the U. S. S. R., withdrawal of marines from Haiti and Nicaragua, freedom for the Philippines, renunciation of the policy of military intervention, repeal of the Platt Amendment, passage of the Nye-Vandenberg Resolution which resulted in the investigation of the munitions industry, and passage of neutrality legislation incorporating in major though not all particulars the proposals of the W. I. L. In recent years the efforts of the organization have been directed particularly on keeping America out of war and thus upon the two last-mentioned measures. Its important influence in the promotion of the Nye investigation and neutrality legislation has been generally recognized, and the skillful methods of its Executive Secretary, Dorothy Detzer, have made the art of lobbying seem particularly adapted to the qualities of the feminine mind and personality.

Despite past success both in legislation and in the development of a widespread American peace sentiment, the present legislative program of the W. I. L. has a range which indicates how much work it sees before it still. This program emphasizes measures establishing still further insulation of this country from war: extension of present mandatory neutrality legislation to include embargoes on the shipment of raw materials essential for war purposes; support of the Nye-Fish bill restraining the shipment of munitions to foreign countries; greater democratic control over foreign relations, including a war referendum; and the recall of American military and naval forces from China. Other elements in the program fall under the ideal of freedom: opposition to legislation adverse to civil liberties, to the Sheppard-May Industrial Mobilization Bill, to compulsory military training in civilian educational institutions; support of the Wagner-Gavagan Anti-Lynching Bill, of legislation removing the present exclusion of pacifists from naturalization, of legislation extending and liberalizing the immigrant quota system.[54]   The continuity of this program with that of the Woman's Peace Party is obvious in respect not only to general principles but also to many specific measures.

This continuity with tradition is perhaps not as manifest as regards the attitude of the W. I. L. towards the issue of America's positive rôle in international society.   The aversion of the W. I. L. to war has caused it to oppose not only America's participation in wars for collective security but even measures of international collaboration tending in that direction; thus the organization has at times been in the ironical position of opposing the advocates of international collaboration and of cooperating in effect with isolationists and rabid nationalists.   Yet this fact does not mean that the group has forsaken the ideals of internationalism and world organization which the Woman's Peace Party championed.   It signifies rather that it has adhered to the tenet of the Woman's Peace Party that war cannot be the means to peace or any other good.   The present program of the W. I. L. contains professions and proposals which vouch for its preservation of the international ideal of the parent organization in fact as well as in name.   Thus it continues to support American membership in the League of Nations with exemption from military obligations and revision of the League Covenant to conform with the spirit and letter of the Paris Pact.   Further, the program calls for participation of the United States in an international conference to try to reach a world settlement of economic and political issues; for the extension of help to the victims of persecution in dictatorial countries; and for various far-reaching measures of economic internationalism.[55]

---

[54] *Program of Women's International League for Peace and Freedom, 1939.*

[55] Women's International League for Peace and Freedom, *Program and Policies as Authorized by Annual Meeting, U. S. Section, 1937.*

If in some aspects the epilogue to the history of the Woman's Peace Party indicates the ultimate fruit borne by its efforts, in other aspects the subsequent tale is far from bright. Just as the end of the Woman's Peace Party was surrounded by the wreck of many hopes, so today there is much to try the faith of the women who have gone on in the path of that group. In the first place, even the pacifism of America is marred by the lack of that generous interest in other nations and of that willingness for international cooperation which both the Woman's Peace Party and the W. I. L. have sought to ally with pacifism. And, when the progress of pacifism is estimated in terms of conditions outside the United States, one must acknowledge that the peace movement has fallen upon a dark present and a darker outlook. Fascism and National Socialism, the antitheses of peace and freedom, have grown in power until they may challenge on equal terms the democratic nations, bring the world to the verge of a war more fearful than that of 1914, and threaten a seizure of world hegemony in some thrust of force which the sacrifice of Czechoslovakia will only have postponed. Even those nations which for the moment have shrunk from war are actuated by no distrust of force as a principle but only by the belief that for the time being war is not to their interest or is impracticable.

Not the least discouraging feature of the present scene for the pacifist is the increasing appeal to people of good will, in both Europe and America, of the belief that in the present international setting pacifism is not merely without logical foundation but is calculated more than anything else to play into the hands of dictators by paralyzing all opposition to their ambitions. Pacifism in its absolute form meets increasing repudiation from those who command respect through their specialization in problems of morals and political philosophy. The great majority of the contemporary critics of pacifism bring to bear objections which, though long familiar to critics of political ideas, seem to have particular force in the light of the present international situation. One of their most important criticisms is that absolute pacifism makes of a mere

desirable condition—the desirability of peace is of course no
more questionable than that of sunshine—something prefer-
able to the momentous moral ideals and values which, these
men hold, can at times only be preserved or enhanced by war.
Another criticism is no less important and it is perhaps even
more telling because it admits, for the sake of argument, the
pacifist's premise.   It holds that, even granting that peace is
something of great intrinsic moment, the rejection of war on
principle makes impossible the realization of peace.   Human
nature being what it is, capable in its less ethical and intelligent specimens of inordinate egotism and of ruthless
methods in gratifying this egotism, only force applied by the
decent and law-abiding can keep the world in its maximum
state of peacefulness.   This principle, anti-pacifists argue, is
recognized in the ethics of national life by the maintenance of
a police force to suppress criminals; it must be recognized in
the ethics of international life by the maintenance of armies
to defend the individual nation and international society
against law-breaking nations.

It is true, of course, that in the social relations within the
nation the use of force is denied to the individual and is
monopolized by the government.   But, as Professor Lovejoy
has pointed out,[56] when one transfers the principles of what
he calls inter-social ethics to the sphere of international ethics,
one fails to realize that the conditions of international life
are essentially different.   In the international life there is no
authority superior to individual nations in the same way that
the government which performs the function of the municipal
police force in preserving order is superior to citizens.   And
for this reason it appears essential that nations be armed to
discourage aggression against them and to wage defensive war
when such aggression occurs.

It is very difficult not to feel the force of such criticisms of
absolute pacifism when considering the questions at issue
abstractly.   And, even when following the history of women
as admirable in their character and intelligence as were the

---

[56] Arthur O. Lovejoy, " Ethics and International Relations," *Bulletin of the Washington University Association*, April 23, 1904, p. 57.

members of the Woman's Peace Party, even when paying full attention to their abundant and eloquent arguments, it may be difficult not to feel that they are chargeable with a certain philosophical one-sidedness and lack of realism, due to the distortion of their thinking by their emotions. But, on the other hand, it also seems true that the issue is one so difficult that one cannot be sure what is right or even expedient. What seems most probable is that truth in this instance, as in most others, is a matter of relativity and of the synthesis of elements of the arguments on both sides. The force of the critique of absolute pacifism is greatly weakened, in any event, by certain contributions to its ideology which have been made by the best recent thought in pacifism, so much of which finds in the ideas of the Woman's Peace Party a noteworthy presentation. It is perhaps just in those times when pacifism is least popular, when once again there is an over-confident cry for a war to end war, that consideration of the best case for this philosophy is most profitable.

The doing of justice to these ideas has required a long historical account, but it may be worth while at the end to place in focus certain doctrines which in particular constitute forceful even if not decisive answers to the criticisms that have been outlined. In the first place, the philosophy of Jane Addams and her associates makes it abundantly clear that peace cannot justly be distinguished from other values as being devoid of moral significance. Pacifism to these women was itself a moral philosophy. It was based by them upon the moral duty to respect the sacredness of human life, a duty which they regarded as paramount to all others. Furthermore, they held that respect for human life is at the same time respect for all the moral qualities and potentialities of human nature, and that consequently it is impossible to claim respect for moral values in general except upon the soil of respect for human life. In accordance with this viewpoint, the pacifist women associated the pursuit of peace with the pursuit of all ends essential to a moral and desirable international and national order. One of the most striking of these was that true internationalism in both sentiment and experience which they expressed by a solidarity with like-minded women of all countries.

In the second place, the ideas of the Woman's Peace Party diminish considerably the plausibility of the paradox that war may be the only means of attaining peace. The women insisted that war even for the sake of peace arouses passions and attitudes which are antagonistic to peace, and it would seem that the failure of the World War to bring peace or any other good is a confirmation of their position in this respect. The position of the women was not merely negative but presented an alternative to war: it was the proposal that aggressors be restrained by economic and moral sanctions. More important and fundamental was their emphasis upon making aggression less likely through the elimination of specific and remediable evils in the international and national order. The appearance of sinister menaces to peace in the world today is doubtless traceable in the last analysis to the fact that the peace makers of 1919 did not, as the Woman's Peace Party urged, build a world order that was safe for peace. And today, even if it be true that the ruthless ambitions of dictators can be stopped now only by force, the most advanced thinking on international relations regards as of crucial importance the principle espoused by the women that the failure to provide means of peaceful change in accordance with changing national needs can lead only to international disaster.

Finally, the pacifist women called to attention the fact that the fight for peace, dependent fundamentally upon the demand of the masses to whom governments are responsive, has at its disposal a hitherto untapped but tremendous and perhaps decisive source of added support. This is the support of the sex which by habit, interests, and ideals is least committed to war and most disposed to peace. When the Woman's Peace Party strove for peace, women in the great democratic countries had not even attained the franchise and thus could not exercise direct political pressure. Since then they have been admitted to political equality in the two most powerful democratic countries of the world, England and the United States. Should women, now participating in political power in these and other countries, actually become organized for peace to anything like the degree which the Woman's Peace Party envisaged, a new factor will have been introduced into the determination of international policies which may well have the most momentous promise for the ideal which men have not had a sufficiently informed good will to accomplish— peace on earth.

BIBLIOGRAPHY

MANUSCRIPTS

Jane Addams Peace Collection, Friends Historical Library, Swarthmore College.

GOVERNMENT PUBLICATIONS

United States Congress, *Congressional Record*, 1914-1920.
——, *Hearing before the Committee on Foreign Affairs*, 64th Cong., 1st sess., on H. R. 6921 and H. J. R. 32.

PAMPHLETS AND REPORTS

Official Pamphlets and Reports of the Woman's Peace Party.
(Most are undated.)

A Program during War Time.
A Protest against Military Training in the Public Schools, 1916.
Addams, Jane, *The Revolt Against War.*
Addresses Given at the Organization Conference of the Woman's Peace Party, Washington, D. C., January 10, 1915.
Balch, Emily G., *Why Peace and Freedom?*
Conference of Oppressed or Dependent Nationalities at Washington, December 10th and 11th, 1916.
Hearing before the Judiciary Committee, Senate, 64th Cong., 1st sess., December 12, 1916. Reprint by the Woman's Peace Party.
Hearing before the Committee on Military Affairs, House of Representatives, 64th Congress, 1st sess., January 13, 1916. Reprint by the Woman's Peace Party.
Manifesto, Issued by Envoys of the International Congress of Women at The Hague to the Governments of Europe and the President of the United States, October 16, 1915.
Preamble and Platform Adopted at Washington, January 10, 1915.
Program for Constructive Peace, January 10, 1915.
Program of The Second Annual Meeting of the Woman's Peace Party.
Program of the Women's International League for Peace and Freedom, 1939.
Report of the International Congress of Women, The Hague, 1915.
Report of the International Congress of Women, Zurich, 1919.
Reports: Zurich 1919-Vienna 1921. Women's International League for Peace and Freedom.
Resolutions Adopted by the Woman's Peace Party . . . at the Third Annual Meeting.
Statement of the Executive Board of the National Woman's Peace Party . . . Issued December 10, 1918.
Statement of the Executive Board of the Woman's Peace Party, October 25, 1917.
Suggestions for Work in War Time Submitted by the Chicago Branch of the Woman's Peace Party.
Wales, Julia Grace, *International Plan for Continuous Mediation Without Armistice* (Condensed Statement), 1915.

254 BIBLIOGRAPHY [556

Women's International League for Peace and Freedom. Program and Policies as Authorized by Annual Meeting, U. S. Section, 1937.

Pamphlets and Reports Issued by Other Organizations.

International Committee for World Peace Prize to Rosika Schwimmer, *Rosika Schwimmer, World Patriot,* 1936.

Mead, Edwin D., "Julia Ward Howe's Peace Crusade," *World Peace Foundation Pamphlet Series,* IV, October, 1914.

Organize the World Though a League of Nations. Leaflet published by the League to Enforce Peace.

The foregoing publications are in the Friends Historical Library, Swarthmore College.

AUTOBIOGRAPHIES AND MEMOIRS

Addams, Jane, *Peace and Bread in Time of War,* New York, 1922.

——, *The Second Twenty-years at Hull-House, September, 1909 to September, 1929, with a Record of a Growing World Consciousness,* New York, 1930.

Addams, Jane, Balch, Emily G., Hamilton, Alice, *Women at The Hague,* New York, 1915.

Courtney, K. D., *Extracts from a Diary during the War* (printed for private circulation), 1927. Copy at Friends Historical Library, Swarthmore College.

Gerard, James W., *My Four Years in Germany,* New York, 1917.

Lansing, Robert, *War Memoirs of Robert Lansing, Secretary of State,* Indianapolis, New York, 1935.

Lloyd George, David, *War Memoirs of David Lloyd George,* 2 vols., Boston, 1933-1937.

Lochner, Louis P., *Henry Ford—America's Don Quixote,* New York, 1925.

Pethick-Lawrence, Emmeline, *My Part in a Changing World,* London, 1938.

Seymour, Charles, ed., *The Intimate Papers of Colonel House Arranged by Charles Seymour,* 4 vols., Boston, 1926-1928.

Wald, Lillian D., *Windows on Henry Street,* Boston, 1934.

SPECIAL WORKS AND BIOGRAPHIES

Addams, Jane, *A New Conscience and an Ancient Evil,* New York, 1912.

——, *Newer Ideals of Peace,* New York, 1911.

Baker, Ray Stannard, *Woodrow Wilson, Life and Letters,* 7 vols., Garden City, 1927-1939.

Bourne, Randolph S., *Towards an Enduring Peace; a Symposium of Peace Proposals and Programs, 1914-1916,* New York, 1916.

Curti, Merle Eugene, *Peace or War: the American Struggle, 1636-1936,* New York, 1936.

Duffus, R. L., *Lillian Wald, Neighbor and Crusader,* New York, 1938.

Gilman, Charlotte Perkins, *The Man-Made World; or, Our Androcentric Culture,* New York, 1911.

Hendrick, Burton J., *The Life and Letters of Walter H. Page,* 2 vols., New York, 1922-1925.

International Peace Year-Book, ed. Carl Heath, London, 1915.

Linn, James Weber, *Jane Addams, a Biography*, New York, London, 1935.

Millis, Walter, *Road to War; America, 1914-1917*, New York, 1935.

Moritzen, Julius, *The Peace Movement of America*, New York and London, 1912.

Proceedings of the Third American Peace Congress, Baltimore, 1911.

Sullivan, Mark, *Our Times, the United States, 1900-1925*, 6 vols., New York, 1927-1935.

Tansill, C. C., *America Goes to War*, Boston, 1938.

PERIODICALS

Addams, Jane, " Is the Peace Movement a Failure? " *Ladies Home Journal* (November, 1914), p. 5.

Balch, Emily G., " The International Congress of Women at The Hague," *Home Progress* (1915), V, 110-113.

Chamberlain, Mary, " Women at The Hague," *Survey* (1915), XXXIV, 219-222.

Christian Work, " The Observer " (July 31, 1915), p. 139.

Davis, Elmer, " Henry Ford's Adventure with the Lunatic Fringe," *New York Times Book Review* (October, 1925).

Independent, " Women for Peace " (1915), LXXXI, 120.

Internationaal, III, no. 4.

Literary Digest, " Is the Women's Peace Movement ' Silly and Base ' ? " (1915), L, 1022-1023.

——, " Was the Women's Peace Congress a Failure? " (1915), L, 1139-1140.

Lovejoy, Arthur O., " Ethics and International Relations," *Bulletin of the Washington University Association* (April 23, 1904), p. 57.

Mead, Lucia Ames, " Representation of the People at the Peace Settlement," reprinted from the *Advocate of Peace* by the *Internationaal*, III, No. 4, 141-142.

Nasmyth, George W., " Constructive Mediation: an Interpretation of the Ten Foremost Proposals," *Survey* (1915), XXXIII, 616-620.

Nation, " The International Congress of Women " (1919), CVIII, 819.

New Republic, " The Sum of all Villainies " (1915), II, 36-37.

Outlook, " Women and War " (1915), CIX, 676-677.

——, " Women and Peace " (1915), CX, 49-50.

Pethick-Lawrence, Emmeline, " Motherhood and War," *Harper's Weekly* (1914), LIX, 542.

——, " Union of Women for Constructive Peace," *Survey* (1914), XXXIII, 230.

Survey, " A Woman's Party Full Pledged for Action " (1915), XXXIII, 433-434.

——, " Constructive Pacifism " (1920), XLIII, 387.

——, " For a Peace Conference of Neutral Nations " (1915), XXXIII, 597-98.

——, " Jane Addams Back " (1915), XXXIV, 327.

——, " Miss Balch on the Ford Peace Conference " (1916), XXXVI, 444.

——, " National Efforts Crystallizing for Peace " (1915), XXXIII, 393-394.

——, " New York's Parade of Preparedness " (1916), XXXVI, 197-198.

——, " The Hensley Clause and Disarmament " (1916), XXXVII, 308.

——, "The Women's Peace Program for 1917" (1916), XXXVII, 307.
——, "War and Social Reconstruction" (1915), XXXIII, 603.

NEWSPAPERS

Baltimore *Evening Sun*   *Chicago Evening Post*
Chicago Daily News   *Gazette de Holland*
New York Times

Miss Addams subscribed to the services of clipping bureaus. Many newspaper clippings about the Woman's Peace Party are thus to be found in the Jane Addams Peace Collection.

INDEX

Abbott, Grace, 70, 86, 176.

Addams, Jane: sources of pacifism, 17; attitude toward annexation of Philippines, 18; speaks at Boston Peace Congress, 18; speaker at National Peace Congress, 18; *Newer Ideals of Peace*, 18-20; speaks on peace at Carnegie Hall, 21; reaction to outbreak of World War, 21-22; joins Union Against Militarism, 23-24; interest in woman suffrage, 24-27; chairman of Chicago Emergency Federation of Peace Forces, 35; on platform committee of Woman's Peace Party conference (Jan. 1914), 38; elected national chairman of Woman's Peace Party, 51; presides over National Emergency Peace Conference, 57; chairman of National Peace Federation, 58; invited to preside over International Congress of Women (The Hague, 1915), 68; represents Woman's Peace Party at Hague Congress, 69; words closing Congress, 89; placed on committee visiting belligerent countries, 92; interviews Cort van der Linden, 94; talks with Asquith and Grey, 96; interview with von Jagow, 96; talks with von Bethmann-Hollweg, 96-97; visits Stürgkh, 97-98; audience with Burián, 98; talks with Tisza, 98-99; interviews Motta, 99; speaks to Hoffmann, 99; interviews Salandra and Sonnino, 100; conference with Gasparri, 100; audience with the Pope, 100; speaks with Delcassé, 100-101; interviews Viviani, 101; journeys to Havre, 101; receives letter from Grey, 102; sees Crewe, Cecil, Lloyd George, 102; audience with Archbishop of Canterbury and Bishop of Winchester, 102; impressions of Hague missions, 102; Grey's reaction, 109; arrives home from Hague Congress, 110; address at Carnegie Hall, 111-114; speaks in Chicago on Hague Congress, 114; signs manifesto regarding neutral conference, 119; interview with House, 122; favors unofficial delegates, 128-129; talks with Ford about mediatory commission, 132; opposes chartering of ship, 133; objects to Ford slogan, 135; maintains decision to sail, 136-138; illness prevents going, 138-139; advises International Committee in regard to Ford enterprise, 140-141; public statement in regard to Peace Ship, 142; addresses Woman's Peace Party on Ford Mission, 142-143; appears before Congressional committees, 144; chosen delegate to Neutral Conference, 146; thanks Wilson for note to belligerents, 149; address on militarism, 152; testifies before Congressional committees (Jan. 1916), 162-165; addresses Women's Auxiliary, Pan-American Congress, 169; presidential election of 1916, 172-173; testifies at suffrage amendment hearing, 178-179; urges league of neutrals, 181-182; wires approval of Emergency Peace Federation demonstration, 183; speaks with Wilson (Feb. 28, 1917), 185-187; view of Wilson's Inaugural Address, 188; urges referendum on war, 190; opposes conscription, 195-196; interviews with Newton D. Baker, 196; address at Chicago City Club, 198-199; criticized by Justice Carter, 200; aware of isolation, 199-202; appeals

War: abolition of, 41, 42; economic causes of, 41, 45, 48, 75, 87, 162-163, 175, 221, 230, 246.
Ward, Harry F., 223.
Ward, Lester F., 25.
Washington, Booker T., 113.
Washington Peace Association, 38.
Welsh Bill, 166-167.
White, Mrs. John Jay, 51.
Wilhelmina, Queen of The Netherlands, 74.
Williams, Senator John Sharp, 144.
Wilson, Woodrow: receives Mme. Schwimmer, 30; comments on Hague Congress, 89; receives Hague resolutions, 114, 115; asks Lansing about plan for continuous mediation, 116; reply to Lansing, 116; receives Emily G. Balch, 117; talks to Dr. Jacobs, 118-119; reaction to interview with Dr. Jordan and Louis Lochner, 121-122; receives Mme. Schwimmer and Mrs. Snowden, 125-126; reaction to unofficial conference of neutrals, 129; speaks with Ford, 132-133; annual message (Dec. 1915), 143; seeks to initiate move for peace, 145; note to belligerents (Dec. 19, 1915), 149; preparedness, 153-154; Pan-Americanism, 169; Nicaraguan canal, 170; Mexican policy, 170; election of 1916, 172-173; "Peace without victory," 149-150, 179; "Bases for Peace," 182; reaction to pacifist delegation (Feb. 28, 1917), 185-186; sets forth the Fourteen Points, 209-210; reply to Zurich Congress resolution on famine and blockade, 228.
Woman suffrage, 24-27, 31-32, 33, 36, 41, 43, 45, 48, 68, 82, 83, 86, 88, 156, 158-159, 162, 174, 179, 205, 210, 219, 220, 222, 231.
Woman's Cooperative Guild, 80.
Woman's Lawyers Association, 69.
Woman's Peace Party: charter members, 39-40; preamble and platform, 40-44; "Program for Constructive Peace," 44-50; officers (1915), 50-51, 55; presents "Five Souls," 58-59; produces *Trojan Women*, 59-60; membership (1915), 62; campaign for peace plan, 119; organizes demonstration in behalf of neutral conference, 124-125; referred to by Ford, 133-134; meeting addressed by Ford, 134; not affiliated with Peace Ship, 133, 142; supports neutral conference, 143-144; interest in Ford International Commission, 148-149; and preparedness, 153-155; becomes U. S. Section of International Committee, 89, 156; 1916 Constitution, 156-157; membership (1916), 156; annual meeting (Jan. 1916), 155-162; opposition to military drill in schools, 166-167; protests against imperialism in Haiti, 169-170; opposition to Bryan-Chamorro Treaty, 170; and Wilson's Mexican policy, 170-171; urges plebiscite in Virgin Islands, 171-172; protests against occupation of Dominican Republic, 172; election of 1916, 173; annual meeting (Dec. 1916), 173-178; representatives testify at suffrage amendment hearing, 178-179; program presented to meeting of peace societies (Feb. 1917); "A Program During War Time," 193-195; opposition to Espionage Bill, 197-198; "Statement of the Executive Board" (Oct. 25, 1917), 204-205; membership (1917), 206; annual meeting (Dec. 1917), 205-209; reaction to the Fourteen Points, 209-210; works for popular representation at the peace conference, 212; work of Legislative Committee in 1918, 212-213; work of local branches during war, 204, 213-214; wartime difficulties, 215; attitude toward League of Nations, 238; Fight-the-Famine Movement, 239-240; becomes Section

THE JOHNS HOPKINS UNIVERSITY

STUDIES IN

HISTORICAL AND POLITICAL SCIENCE

✓ ✓ ✓

A subscription for the regular annual series (about 600 pages) is $5.00. Single numbers may be purchased at special prices. A complete list of the series is given on pages vii-xiv.

The Origins of the Foreign Policy of Woodrow Wilson

By Harley Notter

The author has had the exceptional opportunity of seeing the papers of both President Wilson and Colonel House, and to a large extent, the papers of Robert Lansing. The Bryan papers have also been studied. For the first time, in addition, this book has drawn upon the now completed publications of the Senate Committee on Investigation of the Munitions Industry. The result is that the interpretations of the author are based upon his use of the most important collections of manuscript materials in the United States, as well as upon the contemporary writings and governmental documents of the neutrality period and upon the extensive monographs, biographies, letters and memoirs which have appeared since the War. From these sources the author has reached a radically altered interpretation of Wilson's attitude toward the groups of belligerents shortly after the beginning of the War. He has shown the fallacy of the widely-held view that Wilson was negotiating for intervention by the House-Grey memorandum of 1916, explained Wilson's change in attitude toward the Allies in May, 1916, and reëvaluated the relationship between the President and Colonel House. He has revised the impression that the Russian Revolution exerted a strong influence on either the decision for war with Germany or the character of the issue of making " the world safe for democracy." He has examined the economic policy of the United States for its effects upon neutrality, and has given the most complete answer so far presented to the question of why Wilson decided, on March 20-21, 1917, to go to war.

vii + 695 pages, $4.50

THE JOHNS HOPKINS PRESS · BALTIMORE

iii

RECENT PUBLICATIONS IN ECONOMICS

TENCH COXE: A STUDY IN AMERICAN ECONOMIC DEVELOPMENT.
By HAROLD HUTCHESON.   *239 pages, $2.25.*

American economic writers of the early nineteenth century wrote in
favor of a balanced national economy, especially emphasizing the ad-
vantages to be had from the growth of manufacturing enterprise. Of
these writers, Tench Coxe and Alexander Hamilton are to be ranked
as precursors.

While the contributions of Hamilton as a statesman and financier
have been adequately examined, those of Tench Coxe, who at a critical
period was Hamilton's assistant, have not. This study is an effort to
fill the gap. All available sources of information have been used to set
forth Coxe's life and thought, with attention to the men and events of
his time. His interest in constitutional reform as revealed in his work
for adoption of the Federal Constitution is recounted. Exponent of a
national government, Coxe also favored the creation of a balanced
national economy. The economic impact of the Napoleonic struggle
upon America reinforced his views in this respect. He wished for a
proportioned development of our productive capacity. More specifically,
he advocated an American cotton' culture and manufacture; and this
at a time when little attention was being paid to either.

BRITISH CORPORATION FINANCE, 1775-1850: A STUDY OF
PREFERENCE SHARES. By GEORGE HERBERTON EVANS, JR.
                                               216 pages, $2.25.

" Mr. Evans joins those who have continued the work of W. R. Scott
on British joint-stock companies with a study which shows his industry
with the spade and his skill in piecing fragmentary findings together.
The result is a valuable contribution to the narrow field of business
history and to the wider one of economic development. . . . The book
is full of good things. Chapter II, on the promotion of the early
corporations, ought to be made compulsory reading for those who find
the early nineteenth century so easy to describe in terms of Industrialism, High Capitalism, and other such labels."

—*American Historical Review,* October, 1937.

THE DELAWARE CORPORATION. By RUSSELL CARPENTER
LARCOM.   *210 pages, $2.25.*

Through a discussion of the development of corporation law in a
" liberal " state, the author provides a basis for an intelligent appraisal
of the American system of state incorporation.

THE JOHNS HOPKINS PRESS · BALTIMORE

ALBERT SHAW LECTURES ON
DIPLOMATIC HISTORY

UNDER THE AUSPICES OF THE WALTER HINES PAGE
SCHOOL OF INTERNATIONAL RELATIONS

Duodecimo, cloth

THE JOHNS HOPKINS PRESS · BALTIMORE

v

A REPRINT OF ECONOMIC TRACTS

EDITED BY JACOB H. HOLLANDER

First Series

1. **Three Letters on " The Price of Gold."** By DAVID RICARDO. London, 1809. $1.00.
2. **An Inquiry into the Nature and Progress of Rent.** By T. R. MALTHUS. London, 1815. $1.00.
3. **Essay on the Application of Capital to Land.** By EDWARD WEST. London, 1815. $1.00.
4. **A Refutation of the Wage-Fund Theory.** By FRANCIS D. LONGE. London, 1866. $1.00.

Second Series

1. **Discourse of Trade.** By NICHOLAS BARBON. London, 1690. $1.00.
2. **Several Assertions Proved.** By JOHN ASGILL. London, 1696. 50 cents.
3. **Discourses upon Trade.** By DUDLEY NORTH. London, 1691. $1.00.
4. **Englands Interest and Improvement.** By SAMUEL FORTREY. Cambridge, 1663. $1.00.

Third Series

1. **The Querist, containing several queries proposed to the consideration of the public.** Parts I, II, III. By GEORGE BERKLEY. Dublin, 1735-37. $1.00.
2. **An Essay on the Governing Causes of the Natural Rate of Interest; wherein the sentiments of Sir William Petty and Mr. Locke, on that head, are considered.** By JOSEPH MASSIE. London, 1750. 50 cents.
3. **Money answers all Things: or an essay to make money sufficiently plentiful amongst all ranks of people, and increase our foreign and domestick trade.** By JACOB VANDERLINT. London, 1734. $1.00.
4. **An Essay on Ways and Means for Raising Money for the support of the present war, without increasing the public debts.** By FRANCIS FAUQUIER. London, 1756. 50 cents.

Fourth Series

1. **Letters of John Ramsay McCulloch to David Ricardo, 1818-1823.** $1.00.
2. **Observations on the Effects of the Corn Laws and of a Rise or Fall in the Price of Corn on the Agriculture and General Wealth of the Country.** By T. R. MALTHUS. London, 1814. $1.00.
3. **Observations on the circumstances which Influence the Condition of the Labouring Classes of Society.** By JOHN BARTON. London, 1817. $1.00.
4. **Two Letters on the Measures of Value Contributed to the Traveller (London) in December 1822.** By JOHN STUART MILL. $1.00.

Fifth Series

(In preparation; subscription, $4.00)

1. **Two Tracts by Gregory King:**
   (a). **Natural and Political Observations and Conclusions upon the State and Condition of England.** 1696.
   (b). **Of the Naval Trade of England A° 1688 and the National Profit then arising thereby.** 1697. MS.
   Edited with an Introduction by GEORGE E. BARNETT. $1.50.
2. **Natural and Political Observations Mentioned in a following Index and made upon the Bills of Mortality.** By JOHN GRAUNT. London, 1676. With an introduction by WALTER F. WILLCOX. $1.25.
3(a). **A Memorial Concerning the Coyn of England.** 1695. MS.
   (b). **A Memoriall Concerning Creditt.** 1696. MS.
   By CHARLES DAVENANT. Introduction and notes by Jacob H. Hollander.
4. **Estimate of the Degrees of Mortality of Mankind. 1692.** By EDMUND HALLEY. Introduction and notes by Lowell J. Reed.

THE JOHNS HOPKINS PRESS · BALTIMORE

THE JOHNS HOPKINS UNIVERSITY STUDIES IN
HISTORICAL AND POLITICAL SCIENCE

* Not sold separately.

vii

SEVENTH SERIES.—1889.

(Complete volume out of print.)

I. Arnold Toynbee. By F. C. MONTAGUE. 50 cents.
II-III. Municipal Government in San Francisco. By BERNARD MOSES. 50 cents.
IV. Municipal History of New Orleans. By WM. W. HOWE. 25 cents.
*V-VI. English Culture in Virginia. By WILLIAM P. TRENT.
VII-VIII-IX. The River Towns of Connecticut. By CHARLES M. ANDREWS. $1.00.
*X-XI-XII. Federal Government in Canada. By JOHN G. BOURINOT.

EIGHTH SERIES.—1889.

(Complete volume out of print.)

I-II. The Beginnings of American Nationality. By A. W. SMALL. $1.00.
III. Local Government in Wisconsin. By D. E. SPENCER. 25 cents.
*IV. Spanish Colonization in the Southwest. By F. W. BLACKMAR.
V-VI. The Study of History in Germany and France. By P. FREDERICQ. $1.00.
VII-IX. Progress of the Colored People of Maryland. By J. R. BRACKETT. $1.00.
*X. The Study of History in Belgium and Holland. By P. FREDERICQ.
XI-XII. Seminary Notes on Historical Literature. By H. B. ADAMS and others. 50 cents.

NINTH SERIES.—1891.

(Volume sold only with complete set.)

*I-II. Government of the United States. By W. W. WILLOUGHBY and W. F. WILLOUGHBY.
III-IV. University Education in Maryland. By B. C. STEINER.—The Johns Hopkins University (1876-1891). By D. C. GILMAN. 50 cents.
*V-VI. Municipal Unity in the Lombard Communes. By W. K. WILLIAMS.
VII-VIII. Public Lands of the Roman Republic. By A. STEPHENSON. 75 cents.
*IX. Constitutional Development of Japan. By T. IYENAGA.
*X. A History of Liberia. By J. H. T. McPHERSON.
XI-XII. The Indian Trade in Wisconsin. By F. J. TURNER. 50 cents.

TENTH SERIES.—1892.—$4.00.

*I. The Bishop Hill Colony. By MICHAEL A. MIKKELSEN.
II-III. Church and State in New England. By PAUL E. LAUER. 50 cents.
IV. Church and State in Maryland. By GEORGE PETRIE. 50 cents.
V-VI. Religious Development of North Carolina. By S. B. WEEKS. 50 cents.
*VII. Maryland's Attitude in the Struggle for Canada. By J. W. BLACK.
VIII-IX. The Quakers in Pennsylvania. By A. C. APPLEGARTH. 75 cents.
X-XI. Columbus and His Discovery of America. By H. B. ADAMS and H. WOOD. 50 cents.
XII. Causes of the American Revolution. By J. A. WOODBURN. 50 cents.

ELEVENTH SERIES.—1893.—$4.00.

I. The Social Condition of Labor. By E. R. L. GOULD. 50 cents.
II. The World's Representative Assemblies of To-day. By E. K. ALDEN. 50 cents.
III-IV. The Negro in the District of Columbia. By EDWARD INGLE. $1.00.
*V-VI. Church and State in North Carolina. By STEPHEN B. WEEKS.
VII-VIII. The Condition of the Western Farmer, etc. By A. F. BENTLEY. $1.00.
IX-X. History of Slavery in Connecticut. By BERNARD C. STEINER. 75 cents.
XI-XII. Local Government in the South. By E. W. BEMIS and others. $1.00.

TWELFTH SERIES.—1894.—$4.00.

I-II. The Cincinnati Southern Railway. By J. H. HOLLANDER. $1.00.
III. Constitutional Beginnings of North Carolina. By J. S. BASSETT. 50 cents.
IV. Struggle of Dissenters for Toleration in Virginia. By H. R. McILWAINE. 50 cents.
*V-VI-VII. The Carolina Pirates and Colonial Commerce. By S. C. HUGHSON.
VIII-IX. Representation and Suffrage in Massachusetts. By G. H. HAYNES. 50 cents.
X. English Institutions and the American Indian. By J. A. JAMES. 25 cents.
XI-XII. International Beginnings of the Congo Free State. By J. S. REEVES. 50 cents.

THIRTEENTH SERIES.—1895.—$4.00.

I-II. Government of the Colony of South Carolina. By E. L. WHITNEY. 75 cents.
III-IV. Early Relations of Maryland and Virginia. By J. H. LATANÉ. 50 cents.
V. The Rise of the Bicameral System in America. By T. F. MORAN. 50 cents.
*VI-VII. White Servitude in the Colony of Virginia. By J. C. BALLAGH.
VIII. The Genesis of California's First Constitution. By R. D. HUNT. 50 cents.
IX. Benjamin Franklin as an Economist. By W. A. WETZEL. 50 cents.
X. The Provisional Government of Maryland. By J. A. SILVER. 50 cents.
XI-XII. Government and Religion of the Virginia Indians. By S. R. HENDREN. 50 cents.

FOURTEENTH SERIES.—1896.—$4.00.

I. Constitutional History of Hawaii. By HENRY E. CHAMBERS. 25 cents.
II. City Government of Baltimore. By THADDEUS P. THOMAS. 25 cents.
III. Colonial Origins of New England Senates. By F. L. RILEY. 50 cents.
IV-V. Servitude in the Colony of North Carolina. By J. S. BASSETT. 50 cents.
VI-VII. Representation in Virginia. By J. A. C. CHANDLER. 50 cents.

viii

VIII.   History of Taxation in Connecticut (1636-1776).   By F. R. JONES.   50 cents.
IX–X.   A Study of Slavery in New Jersey.   By HENRY S. COOLEY.   50 cents.
XI–XII.   Causes of the Maryland Revolution of 1689.   By F. E. SPARKS.   50 cents.

FIFTEENTH SERIES.—1897.—$4.00.

I–II.   The Tobacco Industry in Virginia since 1860.   By B. W. ARNOLD.   50 cents.
III–V.   Street Railway System of Philadelphia.   By F. W. SPEIRS.   75 cents.
VI.   Daniel Raymond.   By C. P. NEILL.   50 cents.
VII–VIII.   Economic History of B. & O. R. R.   By M. REIZENSTEIN.   50 cents.
IX.   The South American Trade of Baltimore.   By F. R. RUTTER.   50 cents.
X–XI.   State Tax Commissions in the United States.   By J. W. CHAPMAN.   50 cents.
XII.   Tendencies in American Economic Thought.   By S. SHERWOOD.   25 cents.

SIXTEENTH SERIES.—1898.—$4.00.

I–IV.   The Neutrality of the American Lakes, etc.   By J. M. CALLAHAN. $1.25.
V.   West Florida.   By H. E. CHAMBERS.   25 cents.
VI.   Anti-Slavery Leaders of North Carolina.   By J. S. BASSETT.   50 cents.
VII–IX.   Life and Administration of Sir Robert Eden.   By B. C. STEINER. $1.00.
X–XI.   The Transition of North Carolina from a Colony.   By E. W. SIKES.   50 cents.
XII.   Jared Sparks and Alexis De Tocqueville.   By H. B. ADAMS.   25 cents.

SEVENTEENTH SERIES.—1899.—$4.00.

I–II–III.   History of State Banking in Maryland.   By A. C. BRYAN. $1.00.
*IV–V.   The Know-Nothing Party in Maryland.   By L. F. SCHMECKEBIER.
VI.   The Labadist Colony in Maryland.   By B. B. JAMES.   50 cents.
VII–VIII.   History of Slavery in North Carolina.   By J. S. BASSETT.   75 cents.
IX–X–XI.   Development of the Chesapeake & Ohio Canal.   By G. W. WARD.   75 cents.
XII.   Public Educational Work in Baltimore.   By HERBERT B. ADAMS.   25 cents.

EIGHTEENTH SERIES.—1900.—$4.00.

I–IV.   Studies in State Taxation.   Edited by J. H. HOLLANDER. $1.00; cloth, $1.25.
V–VI.   The Colonial Executive Prior to the Restoration.   By P. L. KAYE.   50 cents.
VII.   Constitution and Admission of Iowa into the Union.   By J. A. JAMES.   30 cents.
VIII–IX.   The Church and Popular Education.   By H. B. ADAMS.   50 cents.
X–XII.   Religious Freedom in Virginia: The Baptists.   By W. T. THOM.   75 cents.

NINETEENTH SERIES.—1901.—$4.00.

*I–III.   America in the Pacific and the Far East.   By J. M. CALLAHAN.
IV–V.   State Activities in Relation to Labor.   By W. F. WILLOUGHBY.   50 cents.
VI–VII.   History of Suffrage in Virginia.   By J. A. C. CHANDLER.   50 cents.
VIII–IX.   The Maryland Constitution of 1864.   By W. S. MYERS.   50 cents.
X.   Life of Commissary James Blair.   By D. E. MOTLEY.   25 cents.
*XI–XII.   Gov. Hicks of Maryland and the Civil War.   By G. L. RADCLIFFE.

TWENTIETH SERIES.—1902.
(Complete volume out of print.)

I.   Western Maryland in the Revolution.   By B. C. STEINER.   30 cents.
II–III.   State Banks since the National Bank Act.   By G. E. BARNETT.   50 cents.
IV.   Early History of Internal Improvement in Alabama.   By W. E. MARTIN.   80 cents.
*V–VI.   Trust Companies in the United States.   By GEORGE CATOR.
VII–VIII.   The Maryland Constitution of 1851.   By J. W. HARRY.   50 cents.
IX–X.   Political Activities of Philip Freneau.   By S. E. FORMAN.   50 cents.
XI–XII.   Continental Opinion on a Proposed Middle European Tariff Union.   By G. M.
FISK.   30 cents.

TWENTY-FIRST SERIES.—1903.
(Volume sold only with complete set.)

*I–II.   The Wabash Trade Route.   By E. J. BENTON.
III–IV.   Internal Improvements in North Carolina.   By C. C. WEAVER.   50 cents.
V.   History of Japanese Paper Currency.   By M. TAKAKI.   30 cents.
VI–VII.   Economics and Politics in Maryland, 1720-1750, and the Public Services of Daniel
Dulany the Elder.   By ST. G. L. SIOUSSAT.   50 cents.
*VIII–IX–X.   Beginnings of Maryland, 1631-1639.   By B. C. STEINER.
*XI–XII.   The English Statutes in Maryland.   By ST. G. L. SIOUSSAT.

TWENTY-SECOND SERIES.—1904.—$4.00.

I–II.   A Trial Bibliography of American Trade-Union Publications.   1st edition.   50 cents.
*III–IV.   White Servitude in Maryland, 1634-1820.   By E. I. MCCORMAC.
V.   Switzerland at the Beginning of the Sixteenth Century.   By J. M. VINCENT.   30 cents.
*VI–VII–VIII.   The History of Reconstruction in Virginia.   By H. J. ECKENRODE.
IX–X.   The Foreign Commerce of Japan since the Restoration.   By Y. HATTORI.   50 cents.
XI–XII.   Descriptions of Maryland.   By B. C. STEINER.   50 cents.

TWENTY-THIRD SERIES.—1905.—$4.00.

I–II.   Reconstruction in South Carolina.   By J. P. HOLLIS.   50 cents.
III–IV.   State Government in Maryland, 1777-1781.   By B. W. BOND, JR.   50 cents.

V–VI. Colonial Administration under Lord Clarendon, 1660-1667. By P. L. KAYE. 50 cents.
VII–VIII. Justice in Colonial Virginia. By O. P. CHITWOOD. 50 cents.
*IX–X. The Napoleonic Exiles in America, 1815-1819. By J. S. REEVES.
XI–XII. Municipal Problems in Mediaeval Switzerland. By J. M. VINCENT. 50 cents.

TWENTY-FOURTH SERIES.—1906.—$4.00.

I–II. Spanish-American Diplomatic Relations before 1898. By H. E. FLACK. 50 cents.
III–IV. The Finances of American Trade Unions. By A. M. SAKOLSKI. 75 cents.
V–VI. Diplomatic Negotiations of the United States with Russia. By J. C. HILDT. 50 cents.
VII–VIII. State Rights and Parties in N. C., 1776-1831. By H. M. WAGSTAFF. 50 cents.
IX–X. National Labor Federations in the United States. By WILLIAM KIRK. 75 cents.
XI–XII. Maryland During the English Civil Wars, I. By B. C. STEINER. 50 cents.

TWENTY-FIFTH SERIES.—1907.—$4.00.

I. Internal Taxation in the Philippines. By JOHN S. HORD. 30 cents.
II–III. The Monroe Mission to France, 1794-1796. By B. W. BOND, JR. 50 cents.
IV–V. Maryland During the English Civil Wars, II. By BERNARD C. STEINER. 50 cents.
*VI–VII. The State in Constitutional and International Law. By R. T. CRANE.
VIII–IX–X. Financial History of Maryland, 1789-1848. By HUGH S. HANNA. 75 cents.
XI–XII. Apprenticeship in American Trade Unions. By J. M. MOTLEY. 50 cents.

TWENTY-SIXTH SERIES.—1908.—$4.00.

I–III. British Committees, Commissions, and Councils of Trade and Plantations, 1622-1675.
By C. M. ANDREWS. 75 cents.
IV–VI. Neutral Rights and Obligations in the Anglo-Boer War. By R. G. CAMPBELL. 75
cents.
VII–VIII. The Elizabethan Parish in its Ecclesiastical and Financial Aspects. By S. L.
WARE. 50 cents.
IX–X. A Study of the Topography and Municipal History of Praeneste. By R. V. D.
MAGOFFIN. 50 cents.
*XI–XII. Beneficiary Features of American Trade Unions. By J. B. KENNEDY.

TWENTY-SEVENTH SERIES.—1909.—$4.00.

I–II. The Self-Reconstruction of Maryland, 1864-1867. By W. S. MYERS. 50 cents.
III–IV–V. The Development of the English Law of Conspiracy. By J. W. BRYAN. 75 cents.
VI–VII. Legislative and Judicial History of the Fifteenth Amendment. By J. M.
MATHEWS. 75 cents.
VIII–XII. England and the French Revolution, 1789-1797. By W. T. LAPRADE. $1.00.

TWENTY-EIGHTH SERIES.—1910.—$4.00.

I. History of Reconstruction in Louisiana (through 1868). By J. R. FICKLEN. $1.00.
II. The Trade Union Label. By E. R. SPEDDEN. 50 cents.
III. The Doctrine of Non-Suability of the State in the United States. By K. SINGEWALD.
50 cents; cloth, 75 cents.
*IV. David Ricardo: A Centenary Estimate. By J. H. HOLLANDER.

TWENTY-NINTH SERIES.—1911.—$4.00.

I. Maryland Under the Commonwealth: A Chronicle of the Years 1649-1658. By B. C.
STEINER. $1.00; cloth, $1.25.
II. The Dutch Republic and the American Revolution. By FRIEDRICH EDLER. $1.50.
*III. The Closed Shop in American Trade Unions. By F. T. STOCKTON.

THIRTIETH SERIES.—1912.—$4.00.

I. Recent Administration in Virginia. By F. A. MAGRUDER. $1.25.
II. The Standard Rate in American Trade Unions. By D. A. McCABE. $1.25; cloth, $1.50.
III. Admission to American Trade Unions. By F. E. WOLFE. $1.00.

THIRTY-FIRST SERIES.—1913.—$4.00.

I. The Land System in Maryland, 1720-1765. By CLARENCE P. GOULD. 75 cents; cloth,
$1.00.
II. The Government of American Trade Unions. By T. W. GLOCKER. $1.00; cloth, $1.25.
III. The Free Negro in Virginia, 1619-1865. By J. H. RUSSELL. $1.00; cloth, $1.25.
IV. The Quinquennales: An Historical Study. By R. V. D. MAGOFFIN. 50 cents; cloth,
75 cents.

THIRTY-SECOND SERIES.—1914.—$4.00.

I. Jurisdiction in American Building-Trades Unions. By N. R. WHITNEY. $1.00.
II. Slavery in Missouri, 1804-1865. By H. A. TREXLER. $1.25.
III. Colonial Trade of Maryland. By M. S. MORRISS. $1.00; cloth, $1.25.

THIRTY-THIRD SERIES.—1915.—$4.00.

I. Money and Transportation in Maryland, 1720-1765. By CLARENCE P. GOULD. 75
cents; cloth, $1.00.
II. The Financial Administration of the Colony of Virginia. By PERCY FLIPPEN. 50
cents; cloth, 75 cents.
III. The Helper and American Trade Unions. By JOHN H. ASHWORTH. 75 cents.
IV. The Constitutional Doctrines of Justice Harlan. By FLOYD BARZILIA CLARK. $1.00;
cloth, $1.25.

THIRTY-FOURTH SERIES.—1916.—$4.00.

I. The Boycott in American Trade Unions. By LEO WOLMAN. $1.00.
II. The Postal Power of Congress. By LINDSAY ROGERS. $1.00.

xi

The set of fifty-six series of Studies is offered (except volumes one two, seven, eight and twenty) uniformly bound in cloth for library use, $242.00 net.
The separate volumes may be had bound in cloth at the prices stated.

EXTRA VOLUMES OF STUDIES IN HISTORICAL AND POLITICAL SCIENCE

* Out of print

THE JOHNS HOPKINS PRESS · BALTIMORE

EXTRA VOLUMES OF STUDIES IN HISTORICAL AND POLITICAL SCIENCE

NEW SERIES

* Out of print

THE JOHNS HOPKINS PRESS · BALTIMORE

THE WALTER HINES PAGE SCHOOL OF INTERNATIONAL RELATIONS

THE PROTECTION OF NATIONALS: A Study in the Application of International Law. By FREDERICK SHERWOOD DUNN. *238 pages, $2.25*
" I can comment only in superlatives. It is splendid, perfectly splendid! "
—EDWIN D. DICKINSON, *University of Michigan Law School*

THE RUSSO-JAPANESE TREATIES OF 1907-1916 CONCERNING MANCHURIA AND MONGOLIA. By ERNEST B. PRICE. *176 pages, $1.75*
" Invaluable to scholars seeking a clearer understanding of the present conflict of interests between the Soviet Union and Japan." —*The Nation*

A STUDY OF CHINESE BOYCOTTS with Special Reference to Their Economic Effectiveness. By C. F. REMER with the assistance of WILLIAM B. PALMER.
318 pages, $2.75
This volume " will be of interest not merely to the student of the commerce and politics of the Far East, but also to political scientists generally."
—TYLER DENNETT, *American Political Science Review*

A VIEW OF EUROPE, 1932: An Interpretative Essay on Some Workings of Economic Nationalism. By PAUL VAN ZEELAND. *162 pages, $1.75*
" The book will commend itself to many general readers and not a few specialists."—JOHN DONALDSON.
Annals of the American Academy of Political and Social Science

MANIFEST DESTINY: A Study of Nationalist Expansionism in American History. By ALBERT K. WEINBERG. *572 pages, $4.50*
" If it is true that the world is on the verge of a new epoch in imperialism, initiated by the Japanese invasion of China and the Italian crusade against Ethiopia, then the publication of this book is both timely and embarrassing . . . because it reveals that the United States, now definitely hostile to expansionism on the part of other nations, has justified the taking of territory in the past by arguments even more shoddy than those today advanced by Italy or Japan." . . .
—RAYMOND LESLIE BUELL, *New York Herald Tribune Books*

INTERVENTION, CIVIL WAR, AND COMMUNISM IN RUSSIA, APRIL-DECEMBER 1918: DOCUMENTS AND MATERIALS. By JAMES BUNYAN.
610 pages, $4.50
" The volume covers the critical months of 1918, when everything seemed to indicate that the Soviet government, established in Moscow, had no chance to survive." —LEONID I. STRAKHOVSKY, *The Journal of Modern History*

THE ORIGINS OF THE FOREIGN POLICY OF WOODROW WILSON. By HARLEY NOTTER. *702 pages, $4.50*
To examine the foreign policy of President Wilson is to examine one of the most decisive factors in the contemporary history of the United States and of the world. The time seems opportune to analyze what the various policies were, how Wilson came to formulate them, and what he intended by them. Such an analysis has been the purpose of the author, who in this book has carried his study up to the entrance of the United States into the World War on April 6, 1917.

THE UNITED STATES AND SANTO DOMINGO 1798-1873. A CHAPTER IN CARIBBEAN DIPLOMACY. By CHARLES CALLAN TANSILL.
497 pages, $3.50
This work is the first attempt by any historian to write the history of American relations with Santo Domingo upon the basis of multiple archival research. Dr. Tansill has made effective use of the records in the Foreign Offices of France, Germany, and Great Britain, together with materials taken from the manuscripts in the Department of State and other American sources.

THE JOHNS HOPKINS PRESS · BALTIMORE

THE JOHNS HOPKINS HISTORICAL PUBLICATIONS

ECONOMICS AND LIBERALISM IN THE RISORGIMENTO: A STUDY OF NATIONALISM IN LOMBARDY, 1814-1848. By KENT ROBERTS GREENFIELD. *375 pages, $3.00.*

Every student of the Italian Risorgimento will recognize Professor Greenfield's volume as a pioneer work of prime importance and a model for what ought to be done for other Italian provinces. . . . Professor Greenfield has shown great historical imagination in interpreting the symbols of a movement that was primarily a movement of opinion.

—STRINGFELLOW BARR in *American Historical Review*

TREATIES DEFEATED BY THE SENATE: A STUDY OF THE STRUGGLE BETWEEN PRESIDENT AND SENATE OVER THE CONDUCT OF FOREIGN RELATIONS. By W. STULL HOLT. *335 pages, $3.00.*

This is an admirable study of what is perhaps the central problem in the conduct of international relations of the United States. . . . No one who would wish to hold a firm grip on the international issues before the American people can afford to be without this book.

—MANLEY O. HUDSON in *American Journal of International Law*

VENETIAN SHIPS AND SHIPBUILDERS OF THE RENAISSANCE By FREDERIC CHAPIN LANE. *294 pages, illustrated, $3.50.*

This book, written after long patient researches among largely unused materials in the archives of Venice, will be of interest not only to readers with a predilection for ships and shipping, but also to students of warfare, commerce, and industrial enterprise at the commencement of the modern era.

—EUGENE H. BYRNE in *The Journal of Modern History*

THE SCOURGE OF THE CLERGY: PETER OF DREUX, DUKE OF BRITTANY. By SIDNEY PAINTER. *163 pages, 1 map, $2.25.*

Peter of Dreux was a highly interesting individual who was the real founder of the Breton duchy of the later Middle Ages. His biography gives an excellent picture of a great French baron of the first half of the thirteenth century. Moreover the period covered by his life has received very little attention from modern scholars.

WILLIAM MARSHAL: KNIGHT-ERRANT, BARON, AND REGENT OF ENGLAND. By SIDNEY PAINTER. *316 pages, $3.00.*

Dr. Painter has had to work with sources which were often obscure and whose real meaning was frequently hidden by administrative and legal formalism. To have produced a clear and very readable account from such materials is a real achievement. . . . —JOSEPH R. STRAYER in *Speculum*

COSTUME AND CONDUCT IN THE LAWS OF BASEL, BERN, AND ZURICH, 1370-1800. By JOHN MARTIN VINCENT. *184 pages, 53 illustrations, $2.50.*

Historical works often refer to European laws concerning dress and expenditure but little has been said about the extent of their enforcement. To throw light on this matter Dr. Vincent has examined the court records of Basel, Bern, and Zurich. Not only clothing, but Sabbath observance, profanity, christenings, weddings, and funerals, as well as minor police offenses, came under the jurisdiction of the *Reformations-Kammer*.

THE JOHNS HOPKINS PRESS · BALTIMORE